PRAISE FOR *OUTLASTING THE GAY REVOLUTION*

In this remarkable book, Dr. Michael Brown reports on the "culture wars" with lucid, graphic clarity. He rigorously documents the complex issues driving the conflict. And more importantly, he calls Christians to hope and perseverance, and persuasively argues against caving in to pessimism. As Dr. Brown reminds us, the tired and tiresome appeal to "the right side of history" proves nothing. Rather, the question to ask is whether one is on the right side of God's truth. In sum, this is an invaluable resource to understand these critical issues, and shows how God intervenes, and prevails, in the affairs of men.

—GARY MCCALEB, CHIEF SOLICITOR, EXECUTIVE VICE PRESIDENT OF STRATEGY IMPLEMENTATION, ALLIANCE DEFENDING FREEDOM

Dr. Brown provides one of the most powerful, persuasive, and prophetic Christian voices worldwide. In *Outlasting the Gay Revolution*, Dr. Brown offers the perfect balance of Christ's truth with His unending love. Dr. Brown fearlessly confronts, head on, the most pressing cultural issues of today with a fearless approach that leaves those in rebellion against God no wiggle room to rationalize. We are left understanding evil as evil and good as good.

—MATT BARBER, ASSOC. DEAN AND LAW PROFESSOR, LIBERTY UNIVERSITY SCHOOL OF LAW

Outlasting the Gay Revolution is a clarion call for positive change in order to understand the radical left's efforts to remake society which, like other false dogmas that have fallen into the waste baskets of history, are ultimately doomed because those who truly believe in G-d's commandments and work to achieve His plan on earth shall succeed.

Michael Brown is one of the few brave warriors willing to stand up and tell the Truth that no one is born gay and growing out of unwanted same-sex attraction is very possible for many who believe in G-d's prohibition against homosexual acts. We at JONAH are honored to march alongside Dr. Brown in this momentous battle for Truth and Justice.

—ARTHUR GOLDBERG AND ELAINE SILODOR BERK, CO-DIRECTORS OF JONAH

Few are as eloquent or as knowledgeable or as gracious as Michael Brown when it comes to the subject of homosexuality. I pray that God uses this publication to equip the Church to be peacemakers, and bring light to those who sit in the shadow of death.

—RAY COMFORT, AUTHOR, EVANGELIST, AND FOUNDER OF LIVING WATERS MINISTRY

The Apostle Paul said we are to speak the truth in love. When it comes to the divisive issue of the homosexual agenda, Dr. Michael Brown exemplifies Paul's exhortation. He points out that we should deal with the individuals with compassion while opposing the agenda with courage. *Outlasting the Gay Revolution* candidly addresses this burning issue of our time and gives positive steps on how to deal with it.

—JERRY NEWCOMBE, D.MIN., COHOST, SENIOR PRODUCER, KENNEDY CLASSICS, AUTHOR/CO-AUTHOR OF TWENTY-FIVE BOOKS

In his new book *Outlasting the Gay Revolution*, Dr. Brown demonstrates how to lovingly oppose the homosexual agenda with reason and timeless truth. He thoughtfully exposes the folly of extending special status and special rights to the LGBT movement at the expense of the rest of our legitimate constitutional rights to religious liberty and true justice for all. It is a must read for everyone who wants to stand on the right side of Eternity with respect to one of the most defining issues of our time.

—PATRICK MANGAN, CITIZENS FOR COMMUNITY VALUES OF INDIANA

What if much of the gay revolution has been built on misinformation and misperception? What if children, families and America are being harmed by the gay revolution? What if those unintended harms could be reversed with grace and truth? Dr. Michael Brown will stun you with insight in this revealing and inspiring book. He not only gives you a practical plan to make a difference for good, but reminds us that being on "the wrong side of history" is actually being on the right side of HIStory.

—DR. FRANK TUREK, AUTHOR OF *I DON'T HAVE ENOUGH FAITH TO BE AN ATHEIST* AND *CORRECT, NOT POLITICALLY CORRECT*

While so many in the church are struggling and paralyzed when it comes to dealing with the gay agenda and same-sex marriage, Dr. Michael Brown offers a powerful strategy and agenda for victory. Instead of being timid and retreating on this issue, Brown presses forward with intellectual clarity and prophetic insight. *Outlasting the Gay Revolution* is an inspiring and timely reminder that throughout history God has always fulfilled his purposes regardless of the current political or cultural landscape.

—REV. PATRICK MAHONEY, DIRECTOR OF THE CHRISTIAN DEFENSE COALITION AND PASTOR OF CHURCH ON THE HILL, WASHINGTON, DC

Dr. Michael Brown's upcoming book *Outlasting The Gay Revolution: Where Homosexual Activism Is Really Going and How to Turn the Tide* is a well-researched, much-needed, and timely book that exposes the real intentions of today's homosexual movement—to take away the religious freedoms of Christians. There must be total acceptance of their agenda and just one negative word or your name on a petition will mean the laser beam of "tolerance" will be leveled at you to force you into compliance! As we see the constant attacks by homosexual activists against the religious beliefs of Christians here in the United States—many examples are included in Dr. Brown's book—we need to be reminded that we must not give in to this bullying by homosexuals. He reminds us that as Christians we must continually stand for truth in love—no matter what the costs to us. We must each step forward and never, never give up or bow to the homosexual agenda. Silence from Bible-believing Christians is what they want and that is something we must not be willing to give them. God expects more from us!

—DIANE GRAMLEY, PRESIDENT OF THE AMERICAN FAMILY ASSOCIATION
OF PENNSYLVANIA

With compassion and courage, Dr. Michael Brown's words sound a warning bell to the intrusion of gay activism on our religious liberties and first amendment rights. As a former homosexual and licensed mental health practitioner, the wisdom of Brown's principles should be heeded by the church and treasured in the faith-based community. Truly, Brown is *the* culture warrior of our time when it comes to issues surrounding sexual orientation.

—CHRISTOPHER DOYLE, MA, LCPC, LICENSED CLINICAL PROFESSIONAL COUNSELOR,
FORMER HOMOSEXUAL, AND FOUNDER OF VOICE OF THE VOICELESS

OUTLASTING THE
GAY REVOLUTION

WHERE HOMOSEXUAL ACTIVISM IS REALLY

GOING AND HOW TO TURN THE TIDE

MICHAEL L. BROWN, PH.D.

 WND Books

OUTLASTING THE GAY REVOLUTION

Unless otherwise indicated, Scripture quotations are taken from the Holy Bible, New King James Version', NKJV. Copyright © 1982 by Thomas Nelson. Used by permission. All rights reserved.
Scripture quotations marked ESV are from THE ENGLISH STANDARD VERSION. © 2001 by Crossway Bibles, a division of Good News Publishers.
Scripture quotations marked HCSB are from the HOLMAN CHRISTIAN STANDARD BIBLE. © 1999, 2000, 2002, 2003 by Broadman and Holman Publishers. All rights reserved.
Scripture quotations marked NJV are from the New Jewish Publication Society Version, © 1985 by The Jewish Publication Society.
Scripture quotations marked NET are from the NET Bible' copyright ©1996–2006 by Biblical Studies Press, L.L.C. http://netbible.com. All rights reserved.
Scripture quotations marked NLT are from the *Holy Bible*, New Living Translation. © 1996, 2004, 2007. Used by permission of Tyndale House Publishers, Inc., Carol Stream, Illinois 60188. All rights reserved.

Published by WND Books, Washington, D.C. WND Books is a registered trademark of WorldNetDaily.com, Inc. ("WND")

Book designed by Mark Karis

WND Books are available at special discounts for bulk purchases. WND Books also publishes books in electronic formats. For more information call (541) 474-1776 or visit www.wndbooks.com.

Hardcover ISBN: 978-1-938067-66-2
eBook ISBN: 978-1-938067-67-9

Library of Congress Cataloging-in-Publication Data
Brown, Michael L., 1955-
  Outlasting the gay revolution : where homosexual activism is really going and how to turn the tide / Dr. Michael L. Brown.
     pages cm
  Includes bibliographical references and index.
  ISBN 978-1-938067-66-2 (hardcover)
  1. Gay rights. 2. Social change. I. Title.
  HQ76.5.B76 2015
  323.3'264--dc23
                                    2015009515

Printed in the United States of America
15 16 17 18 19 20 MPV 9 8 7 6 5 4 3 2 1

CONTENTS

FOREWORD

We are at a time in our nation's history when true Biblical leaders are needed most—Jesus revolutionaries who stand at the midpoint of Biblical tension between personal brokenness and spiritual boldness. Leaders, like the Men of Issachar, who understand the times and know what God's people should do. Leaders who cry out for revival, ready to see a mighty move of God in our nation.

Dr. Michael Brown is a man just like this. As one of our spiritual mentors and dear friends, Dr. Brown has been a beacon of light and pillar of truth in our lives for over a decade. When we were fired by HGTV, we sought his council on a daily basis as we waded into the deep waters of media, and his wisdom guided us through a very difficult time in our lives.

Dr. Brown has done far more than simply equip us with the tools we need to stand strong for Jesus, he has inspired us to go further up and further in to God's Kingdom in our personal lives, to be men of humility and character, and to honor and love our wives and children. His personal life matches his message, so it's easy to receive instruction from him.

We met Dr. Brown in 2003 when he moved his ministry, Fellowship of International Revival and Evangelism (F.I.R.E.), to our hometown in Charlotte, North Carolina. After hearing him speak for the first time, our hearts burned inside of us. His messages penetrated our souls and called out the men inside of us. Both of us have spent quite a bit of time kneeling at the altar after Dr. Brown's sermons. Each time was another stepping stone in our journey toward becoming bold men of God.

Today, we're honored to stand beside him in this great battle over the souls of people and our nation. We'll follow him into battle any day, anywhere, and at any time! Dr. Michael Brown is a leader that the Church in America needs for such a time as this. We're thankful he's running his lap at this moment in history.

—DAVID AND JASON BENHAM, AUTHORS, *WHATEVER THE COST*

PREFACE

And reckon ye that it is for your sakes we have been saying these things; for it is in our power, when we are examined, to deny that we are Christians; but we would not live by telling a lie. —JUSTIN MARTYR, *THE FIRST APOLOGY*, CA. 155 AD

These words were spoken by Justin Martyr more than 1,850 years ago as he addressed the Roman Emperor Antoninus Pius in defense of his Christian faith. He knew quite well that this defense could cost him his life—he was ultimately martyred for his faith—but he was constrained by his conscience and could not deny the Lord. It is true, of course, that there was an easy way out, but, as he said, "we would not live by telling a lie."

It is the same with us today, even if people are not trying to kill us for our faith here in America. Instead, there is constant pressure on us to compromise our convictions and water down our words in order to seem acceptable to the culture, which has launched a very real attack on our values and freedoms.

But we too "would not live by telling a lie," and that is why this book has been written. We have an obligation to speak the truth, not just for our own souls' sake, but for the sake of our society as well. And make no mistake about it: it is not too late to speak the truth, and it not too late for America to experience a powerful, life-giving, moral and cultural revolution.

Writing in early February 2014, Dennis Prager noted that, "On the matter of same-sex marriage, mass passions and coercive judges are winning. Above all, hubris is winning. That is why proponents always assert that they are 'on the right side of history.'"

Indeed, between the time this preface is written (March 2015) and the publication of this book (September 2015), the Supreme Court will have made a major ruling on same-sex "marriage" and only God knows what other momentous events will have transpired during these months. Perhaps my optimism is completely misplaced? Perhaps there will *not* be a positive moral and cultural revolution after all? Perhaps America has turned away from biblical values and conservative morality forever?

Prager, however, had more to say on this issue, wisely remarking, "But history is very long. Our grandchildren, or their grandchildren, will judge whether this is true. The Left since Marx, has asserted that every one of their radical positions—such as the demise of capitalism—is on the right side of history. Virtually none turned out to be."[1]

Yes, history has taken some strange and dramatic turns along the way, and it could well be that history is about to unfold in some unexpected ways in the years ahead.

I have written this book to encourage, strengthen, inspire, and inform, laying out eight practical principles that will help us outlast the gay revolution, also explaining why, in many ways, the gay revolution has already failed and why it has within itself the seeds of its own destruction.

Although the first nineteen books I had written (from 1985 to 2010) said almost nothing about homosexual activism, in 2004 I started to pay closer attention to the effects of gay activism on society. At that time I began making a determination to understand the LGBT community better, reading the stories of the pioneers and leaders with great interest (and pain, because of their suffering), and doing my best to listen carefully to the stories of gays and lesbians I met. They are not my enemies, despite the many differences I may have with their goals.

Since early 2005, I have followed the philosophy of "reach out and resist," meaning reach out to the LGBT community with compassion;

resist the gay activist agenda with courage. And, in 2011, after years of research and writing, *A Queer Thing Happened to America* was published, laying out the impact of gay activism on every sector of American life, from our children's schools to the universities; from Hollywood to the Church; from the courts to the very words we speak.

Now, four years later, I have written this book, building on the research of *A Queer Thing Happened to America* but giving a clear plan for action, one that I pray will infuse you with courage and hope and clarity. This is our time to stand, not in hate but in love, not in frustration but in determination. Put another way, rather than capitulate, give up, throw in the towel, it's time for us to be energized and mobilized for action. It's time for heroes to arise, and those heroes can be ordinary people who make an extraordinary difference in the decisions they make and the values they embrace. You can be one of those heroes.

Melissa Moschella, assistant professor of philosophy at the Catholic University of America, said:

> Perhaps there are times and places in the history of the world in which it is possible to go through life as just an ordinary, good person—a faithful spouse, a loving parent, a concerned citizen, a regular church-goer, an honest and industrious professional—leading a normal, quiet life, not making waves or standing out in any way. Perhaps. But the United States of America in the year 2014 is *not* one of those times and places. Rather, in our contemporary society, the only way to be good is to be *heroic.* Failing to act with heroism inevitably makes us complicit in grave evils. . . .
>
> We must be prepared to live not just good, but heroic lives. We must be prepared to risk popularity, reputation, professional success, economic well-being, and—it may yet come to this—perhaps even our lives, in order to defend the dignity of human life in all its stages, the value of sexual integrity, the truth about marriage and family, and the right to live in accordance with one's beliefs in all spheres of life. . . . May we all heroically rise to this great challenge of our time.[2]

In a similar vein, Episcopal seminarian William Frey said, "One of the most attractive features of the early Christian communities was their radical sexual ethic and their deep commitment to family values. These things drew many people to them who were disillusioned by the promiscuous excesses of what proved to be a declining culture. Wouldn't it be wonderful for our church to find such counter cultural courage today?"[3]

Yes, that would be wonderful, and certainly, now is the time for us to recapture the power and beauty of sexual purity, to take hold of God's amazing purposes for marriage and family, and to determine afresh to swim against the tide of moral and cultural malaise, realizing that we are in the midst of a multigenerational battle (unless Jesus returns in this generation). Will you join me in this sacred task of cultural transformation? If you live by the eight principles articulated in the pages that follow, you will make a difference both for today and for the generations to come.

This book could not have been written without the support and input of Nancy, my bride of thirty-nine years, the most incredible friend and companion I have in this world, and a woman of uncompromising moral conviction. As I think about our children and grandchildren, I am all the more determined to do what is right for their sake as well.

I'm also indebted to my wonderful ministry team and staff, along with those who pray for me on a regular basis. Only God knows how deep my debt is to each of them.

And my appreciation is due to Joseph Farah of WND for approaching me with interest in publishing a project like this (one which many publishers would be afraid to touch) and to Geoffrey Stone and the skilled editorial team, along with WND's first-rate marketing and publicity team.

May God use this book to help ignite a Jesus-glorifying moral and cultural revolution!

INTRODUCTION

THE DAY THE LINE WAS CROSSED

Never in our history has religious freedom been so brazenly defied. A bold red line has been crossed. —ERIC METAXAS

I t came out of the blue, quite unexpectedly, but suddenly, people around the country began to take notice. The great city of Houston, Texas, had launched what some attorneys branded a "witch hunt" and "inquisition" against five local pastors, demanding that they turn over any sermons, speeches, presentations, and even e-mails to their congregants that addressed the issues of homosexuality and gender identity, among other subjects.[1] Sen. Ted Cruz immediately called the actions "both shocking and shameful."[2] Others quickly echoed his comments.

Who was behind this overt attack on religious freedom? None other than Annise Parker, the lesbian activist mayor of Houston, and city attorney David Feldman, who stood side by side with her in pushing this agenda.

The attorney general of Texas, Greg Abbott, rebuked Feldman, writing, "Whether you intend it to be so or not, your action is a direct assault on the religious liberty guaranteed by the First Amendment. The people of Houston and their religious leaders must be absolutely secure in the knowledge that their religious affairs are beyond the reach of the government."[3]

The former city attorney of Houston, Benjamin L. Hall, weighed in reluctantly, knowing the challenges of the job. But the actions of Mayor Parker, along with Attorney Feldman, had gone too far, forcing Hall to write. "Pastors," he said, "have the right to preach their convictions without second thought about city attorneys intruding upon their thought-processes or religious convictions. The very request by the city attorneys is reckless!"[4] Even the commissioner of the US Commission on Civil Rights, Peter Kirsanow, wrote an open letter to Mayor Parker, accusing her of an "abuse of government power . . . thus chilling future religiously informed speech."[5]

The situation was so extreme that Eric Metaxas, author of the *New York Times* bestseller *Bonhoeffer*, wrote, "If the church doesn't wake up now and stand and fight there IS no church in America. This is the red line. It has been crossed. When I read about this I immediately thought 'THIS IS RIGHT OUT OF MY BONHOEFFER BOOK.'"[6]

Two weeks later, on October 29, 2014, Mayor Parker dropped the subpoenas (after defending them initially), but not because "the request[s] were in any way illegal or intended to intrude on religious liberties." Rather, she said, it was because they were not "serving" the city of Houston.[7] Have you ever heard of too little, too late?

In this case, by the time Mayor Parker came to her senses about the subpoenas, a national movement had been launched, marked by a live rally in Houston on November 2, featuring guest speakers such as former governor Mike Huckabee and *Duck Dynasty*'s Phil Robertson. The rally, called "I Stand Sunday," which was webcast to the nation, called on Christians across the country to stand with these local pastors. Americans were waking up. Gay activism—not gay people in general— had indeed become the principal threat to our freedoms of conscience, speech, and religion.

IT'S THE AGENDA, NOT THE PEOPLE

Before I share the background to the Houston story, I want to make one thing perfectly clear. I do not believe that homosexual practice is the worst sin in the world, or that LGBT people are the wickedest people in the world. Some of the nicest, kindest, most considerate and honorable people you will meet identify as LGBT, and some of them are devoted parents, faithful employees, hardworking bosses, caring friends, and good neighbors.

Speaking from personal experience, my first organ teacher, when I was just six years old, was an openly gay man. He and his partner often would come to our home and have dinner with our family, and so from my earliest years, "homophobia" was foreign to me. To this day (really, now more than ever), I care deeply for those who identify as LGBT, and I have often wrestled with their personal stories, challenging my own views and trying to put myself in their shoes when reading books such as Linda Hirshman's *Victory: The Triumphant Gay Revolution*.[8]

In 2006 I reached out to a gay editor in Charlotte, North Carolina, where I have lived since 2003. He was in his forties and had been in a committed relationship with his partner for a number of years. I asked him if we could get together to discuss how we could both be out and proud about our beliefs and values and yet live side by side as neighbors in the same city. We ended up meeting together a couple of times and interacting by e-mail and phone.

A few days after our initial lunch meeting, I was taking a walk with my wife, Nancy. (We've been married since 1976.) As I told her how much I loved her, my heart was suddenly saddened as I thought about this gay editor and his partner, with their own relationship not recognized by the state and with the need at times to hide that relationship. These are not emotions experienced by a homophobic bigot.

On another occasion, I attended a meeting at the local LGBT center where a gay pastor gave a talk about the Bible and homosexuality, with perhaps twenty people in attendance. As I looked around the room, I didn't see angry, hostile faces (although some were, understandably, not happy with my presence). Instead, I saw some broken, hurting people who were looking for acceptance and love, especially from God. I wanted to stand with them and help them rather than be perceived as their enemy.

And I remember how I felt when I heard that Andrew Sullivan, the well-educated, highly influential, seemingly tough-skinned gay journalist, wept when President Obama announced that he was now in favor of redefining marriage. Sullivan even said that he found himself relating to the president as a father figure.[9] (Mr. Obama is only two years older than Sullivan.) Rather than mocking him, I asked myself why this was so meaningful to him and what insights I could gain into his own experience as a homosexual man. Again, these are not emotions experienced by a homophobic bigot.

Why, then, have I devoted so much time and energy to the issue of homosexuality? It is because this issue came knocking at my door, impacting the education of our children in their schools, shouting at us through the airwaves, marching down our city streets (literally), affecting our courts, threatening our liberties, and challenging our churches and synagogues. My issue is with gay activism, and I believe there are serious consequences for a society once you normalize homosexuality and redefine marriage. And so, while I want every person in our country to receive equal protection under the law, and while I deplore any hatred and mistreatment of LGBT people, I stand against many of the goals of gay activism.

Because of this I have been branded a Nazi, a monster, and much more, but I hold no animosity toward my accusers, and I understand why some people view me with such hostility, since many gays and lesbians will say, "If you stand against gay activism, you stand against us." Again, I appreciate their sentiments, but I will still do what is right in the sight of God and in the best interest of our country, and it is with the long-term goal of outlasting the gay revolution that I have written this book. I ask you, the reader, to evaluate only one thing: Have I spoken truthfully? If so, you must stand with the truth.

THE BACKDROP TO THE HOUSTON STORY

Getting back to Houston, Mayor Parker had aggressively promoted an LGBT bill known as HERO, the Houston Equal Rights Ordinance, calling it something "intensely personal." As she said, "The debate is about me. . . . It's not academic. It is my life that is being discussed."[10]

The mayor's words, of course, raised the concerns of other Houston citizens, as Rev. Max Miller of the Baptist Ministers Association of Houston and Vicinity stated in response to her public comments, "One thing we did hear: It's personal. You cannot represent the people of this city on a personal matter." Or, as expressed by conservative city councilman Michael Kubosh, also responding directly to Parker in the same public meeting, "I know you say it's about you, but, mayor, this is really about all of us. It's not really about you; it's about everybody here."[11]

At the heart of the opposition to the bill was concern expressed over the transgender bathroom ordinance. This would allow anyone who identified as transgender to use the bathroom of his or her choice, regardless of biological sex, thereby ignoring the rights of a multitude of women and men who would find this a real intrusion. As noted by Steve Riggle, senior pastor of Grace Community Church and an executive committee member of the Houston Area Pastor Council (HAPC), "Forcing women in particular using city facilities to be subjected to cross-dressing men invading their privacy is beyond the pale and offensive to every standard of decency."[12] The bill would also open the door to potential heterosexual predators who would use the ordinance as a guise for their perversion.

Unfortunately, Mayor Parker was able to push the bill through, despite very strong opposition, after which Pastor Riggle and other leaders launched a petition campaign asking that the people of Houston be allowed to vote on the new ordinance. They needed a little over seventeen thousand signatures to get this on the ballot, so when they had more than fifty thousand, they submitted the petition, only to have it invalidated—many would say without a shred of legal authority—by city attorney Feldman.

In response to this outrage, a number of individuals (not including any clergy) filed a lawsuit against the city, in response to which the city issued the subpoenas that caused such national uproar. For good reason, the Alliance Defending Freedom (ADF) stated that the mayor's actions were "overbroad, unduly burdensome, harassing, and vexatious," and therefore should be flatly rejected. As the ADF explained, "The city is illegitimately demanding that the pastors . . . turn over their constitutionally protected sermons and other communications simply so the city can see if the pastors have ever opposed or criticized the city."[13]

GAY ACTIVISTS ARE NOT RETREATING

You might say, "But why beat a dead horse? The subpoenas were dropped, weren't they?"

Yes, they were, but only under duress. More importantly, gay activists have not dropped their assault on our freedoms, nor did they urge Mayor Parker to back down. To the contrary, they mocked the pastors and the I Stand Sunday rally, an event that was not an attack on gays and lesbians but rather a call for Christians to be true to their convictions.[14]

Before the subpoenas were dropped, one headline declared, "Right-Wing Freaks Out over Houston's Subpoena of Pastors' Role in City's Equal Rights Ordinance Case." The article stated, "As you can imagine, right-wing commentators pounced on the story as the latest example of religious liberties being crushed under the supposed tyranny of LGBT equality. Check out their crazed, knee-jerk reaction. . . ."[15] So, conservatives were just "freaking out" with a "crazed, knee-jerk reaction." What's wrong with pastors having their sermons and e-mails subpoenaed?

When the I Stand Sunday rally was announced, one gay website wrote:

> The right-wing freak out over subpoenas sent to Houston area pastors for "all speeches, presentations, or sermons related to HERO, the Petition, Mayor Annise Parker, homosexuality, or gender identity prepared by, delivered by, revised by, or approved by you or in your possession" is set to continue via live telecast next Sunday as anti-gay leaders and organizations from across the country join together to "stand with these pastors and stand against the radical agenda sweeping our nation."

Significantly, this website knew exactly what the subpoenas were about and still the site mocked the Christian reaction as a "right-wing freak out," labeling the rally an "anti-gay extravaganza."[16]

Similarly, a Texas gay website labeled the event an "anti-gay hatefest," defending the subpoenas and speaking against the pastors.[17] Another site ran the headline "Anti-gay Forces Unite to Oppose Houston Mayor Annise Parker and the 'Radical Agenda' of LGBT Equality." It was clear where their sentiments lay. In fact, a man named Ethan added this comment on the website: "Like the racist who rallied against ending slavery and ending racial segregation and then later against blacks and whites being allowed to marry so too shall the homophobes and bigots unite against gay equality but slant of history always bends towards justice in the end and so in the end they shall fail and they along with their hatred will inevitably be washed away by sands of time."[18] Other opinions posted on the site echoed this sentiment.

During and after the rally, gay activists took to Twitter and other social media to mock the pastors, to put false words in participants' mouths, and to paint things in the most deceptive light possible. This confirms what I have said for the last ten years: those who came out of the closet now want to put us in the closet. It is becoming increasingly difficult to deny.

THE MAYOR OF ATLANTA DECLARES WAR ON RELIGIOUS FREEDOM

Further confirmation that gay activists want to silence their opponents came from Atlanta, where Mayor Kasim Reed dismissed fire chief Kelvin Cochran for his views on homosexuality.

In 2013 Cochran, a committed Christian active in his local church who had served the city of Atlanta for thirty years, wrote and self-published a Bible-based, 160-page book that contained a few lines speaking against homosexual practice (along with other sexual sins) in very strong terms. According to Cochran, he got verbal clearance to publish the book by the proper city authority and also gave a copy to the mayor personally, claiming that the mayor promised to read it. But when word got out about the book's contents, gay activists demanded that Mayor Reed dismiss Cochran. Instead, he suspended Cochran from his job for thirty days without pay—this alone boggles the mind—and required him to go to sensitivity training. (Apparently it is forbidden even to believe what the Bible says about sexuality. You must be reprogrammed if you are to be a public servant.) Then, after the suspension was over, Mayor Reed fired Cochran. His motives for doing so defy reason.

Speaking at a press conference on January 6, 2014, he explained, "The city's position is a very clear one. The city's nondiscrimination policy, endorsed by my office and by the Atlanta City Council, unequivocally states that we will not negotiate. We will not discriminate on the basis of race or gender or religion or creed or sexual orientation or physical ability or gender identity."[19]

What? This *was* discrimination on the basis of religion and creed. Yet Mayor Reed had the gall to say, "The city and my administration stand firmly in support of the right of religious freedom, freedom of speech, and the right to freely observe their faith. . . . This is not about religious freedom, this is not about free speech. Judgment is the basis of the problem."[20] Is this anything less than blatant double-talk?

And then the most outlandish statement of all: "If we had made the decision to retain Chief Cochran . . . folks in the first rescue department who may have been discriminated against in some future occasion would have had a valid case in my mind. But after the fire chief so clearly stated his position on a number of issues, I thought that it created a potential liability for the city."[21] In other words, although there have been no instances of discrimination under Chief Cochran's leadership, we'll fire him now in case he might discriminate against someone in the future! That's like arresting someone because one day that person might commit a crime.

And how did gay activists respond to Cochran's dismissal? City council member Alex Wan, who is openly gay, not only applauded the mayor but also repeated his doublespeak: "I support the administration's decision to terminate Kelvin Cochran's employment with the

City of Atlanta. This sends a strong message to employees about how much we value diversity and how we adhere to a non-discriminatory environment."[22]

Diversity? A "non-discriminatory environment"? Seriously?

Make no mistake about it: if you hold to conservative Christian beliefs and values, you could be targeted next by gay activists and their allies. You can also be assured that the *New York Times* agrees with this targeting, claiming that the "religious freedom" bills that various states are passing "do little more than provide legal cover for anti-gay discrimination," affirming that if Kelvin Cochran "wants to work as a public official . . . he may not foist his religious views on other city employees [which he did not do] who have the right to a boss who does not speak of them as second-class citizens [which he also did not do]."[23]

For his part, Cochran is standing firm, praising God, and refusing to wallow in self-pity. And one week after his firing, hundreds of Christians, including top national leaders, rallied together in Atlanta to protest his dismissal and to declare their faith.[24] The line was crossed yet again, and the backlash is building. As Bishop Wellington Boone said in his address at the rally in Atlanta, the mayor awakened a sleeping giant.

I HATE TO SAY I TOLD YOU SO

On April 7, 2014, I wrote an article for Townhall.com titled "I Hate to Say I Told You So." It began:

> For years I've been sounding the alarm about an impending social, cultural, and spiritual crisis, and for years critics have compared me to Chicken Little, discounting my warnings as the ravings of a hysterical, religious fundamentalist. Well, it's a little late for that now.
>
> Ten years ago, I charted this progression and made this prediction:
>
> • First, gay activists came out of the closet
>
> • Second, they demanded their "rights"
>
> • Third, they demanded that everyone recognize those "rights"

- Fourth, they want to strip away the rights of those who oppose them

- Fifth, they want to put those who oppose their "rights" into the closet

Initially, I was met with scorn and derision: "No one wants to put you in the closet!"

The last few years, the tone has changed to: "Bigots like you belong in the closet!"

I hate to say it, but I told you so.

I then related the following statements I had written several years earlier:

In my 2011 book *A Queer Thing Happened to America*, I noted that, "It would appear, then, that 'civil rights' for some means 'limited rights' for others, and that by specific design. As stated explicitly in a teacher's lesson aid published by the Gay and Lesbian Educators [GALE] of British Columbia: 'We must dishonour the prevailing belief that heterosexuality is the only acceptable orientation even though that would mean dishonouring the religious beliefs of Christians, Jews, Muslims, etc.'"[25]

In that same book, I explained what was already here and what was on the immediate horizon, including the following:

- From here on, embracing *diversity* refers to embracing all kinds of sexual orientation, (homo)sexual expression, and gender identification but rejects every kind of religious or moral conviction that does not embrace these orientations, expressions, and identifications.

- From here on, *tolerance* refers to the complete acceptance of GLBT lifestyles and ideology—in the family, in the work place, in education, in media, in religion—while at the same time refusing to tolerate any view that is contrary.

- From here on, *inclusion* refers to working with, supporting, sponsoring, and encouraging gay events, gay goals while at the same time systematically refusing to work with and excluding anyone who is not in harmony with these events and goals.

- From here on, *hate* refers to any attitude, thought, or word that differs with the gay agenda, while gays are virtually exempt from the charge of hate speech—no matter how vile and incendiary the rhetoric—since they are always the (perceived) victims and never the victimizers.

What exactly would this look like?

- Children in elementary schools will be exposed to the rightness and complete normality of homosexuality, bisexuality, and transgender expression . . . and opposing views will be branded as dangerous and homophobic, to be silenced and excluded from the classroom.

- Middle schools, high schools, and colleges will go out of their way to encourage both the celebration of homosexuality and deep solidarity with gay activism. . . .

- The federal and state governments will legalize same-sex marriages . . . meaning that all heterosexuals must accept the legality of these marriages and that anyone refusing to do so could be prosecuted for discriminatory behavior.

- Corporate America will embrace every aspect of non-heterosexuality (including bisexuality, transgender, and beyond)—calling for the dismissal of those who refuse to follow suit—and religious groups will no longer be allowed to view homosexual practice as immoral, branding such opposition as "hate speech."[26]

In the Townhall.com article, I listed a litany of shocking gay activist advances that had taken place since my 2011 book release. After stating again, "I hate to say it, but I told you so," I then asked, "Do you believe me now? And would you like to know what is coming next and what we can do about it?"[27]

It is in that spirit that I have written this book, realizing that, in many ways, the bad news is the good news. By this I mean, as painful as it is to see many of these negative societal changes, at least people are now waking up to reality. They can no longer deny the accuracy of these predictions and descriptions. The only question is, how will we respond?

A MATTER OF FREEDOM AND FAMILY, NOT HATRED

On Wednesday, November 12, 2014, a concerned mother from Massachusetts called my radio show. Her son, a freshman in high school, came home from school and informed her that all the students had been required to attend an assembly, one that had not been announced in advance. The assembly was sponsored by the Gay-Straight Alliance, and it had one goal only, namely, promoting homosexuality as perfectly normal and acceptable, even for Christians and other people of faith. The mother, who had always taught her son to be kind to others and not to bully, was shocked at the news and asked me what to do.

The next day, while I was speaking at a pastors' gathering in Queens, New York, a pastor told the group that his son, also in high school, came out from his sex-ed class with some upsetting news. His teacher had responded to the question, "How do you know if you're gay?" by saying, "You should try it out for one month and see." Yes, a *teacher* had encouraged these impressionable students to experiment with homosexual practice to determine if they were gay.

None of this, of course, should surprise us, since gay activists have focused on our children's schools for years now, not just with anti-bullying campaigns but also by indoctrinating young people with pro-homosexual presentations. Family activist Linda Harvey points to events such as "Prideworks," a "one-day conference held in White Plains, NY every year [since 1998], sponsored by [gay activist organizations like] PFLAG and GLSEN . . . where even kids as young as middle school take the school day off and arrive in school busses to this off-site conference. Some of the topics are explicit, it's total indoctrination, and there are even 'spirituality' components that endorse 'gay' Christianity."[28] Included in the 2010 Prideworks event were seminars on topics such as "Gender Queer. Transgender. What's It All About"; "Taking a Stand—Advocating in Your School"; and "Queer Kingdom: Diversity in the LGBT Community"—and remember: this was for kids as young as twelve.[29]

Getting back to the Queens pastors' event, a young woman, perhaps in her twenties, tearfully shared her own experience. As a girl, she was given up for adoption, after which she was adopted by a lesbian who then raised the child with her partner. The lesbian couple ultimately raised three daughters, all of whom—including the woman who shared her story with us—came out as lesbians. It was only in 2010, when this young woman came to faith in Jesus, that her life was transformed (she'd also had a serious drug problem in the past) and she left lesbianism behind. Does it strike you as odd that all three daughters raised by this lesbian couple became lesbians?

I asked her what her adoptive parents thought about men, and she responded, "We didn't talk about men in the home." In other words, like many other lesbians, these women had a very negative outlook on males, virtually guaranteeing that that bad attitude would be passed on to the daughters, who would never see how a husband and wife should interact in the home or how a man was supposed to treat a woman. And so, while it is commendable that these women wanted to adopt needy children, it is tragic that they also deprived these girls of the mother-father nurture and example that they so desperately needed. Is this right?

As for those who think they can just sit out the "culture wars," think again. A gay couple recently sued the United Methodist Church for refusing to perform their "wedding," despite the fact that official church policy forbids gay "marriages." (See principle #4—Refuse to Redefine Marriage—to understand why I put "marriage" in quotes when speaking of same-sex couples.) As one of the gay men in question explained to the media, "Change seldom happens unless an agitation happens first."[30] That "agitation" could well be coming to your congregation or denomination in the very near future, and, in all likelihood, it's already been in your neighborhood schools for years.

BUT ISN'T IT TOO LATE?

There are many, of course, who believe that the culture wars are over and that America, from here on, will embrace homosexuality just as it embraces heterosexuality, without a second thought. And certainly, as I write these words, almost everything in today's society says that the complete success of the gay revolution is inevitable. We are told that soon enough, people like me will be extinct, remembered as oddities of a bygone age, when Americans actually believed that homosexual practice was sinful and that there was something wrong with same-sex "marriage." As stated by a journalist and researcher in May 2013, "Simply put, gays have won the culture war."[31]

Wise political pundits tell us that the die has been cast and there is no turning back, unless people like me are foolish enough to believe that homosexual couples will simply dissolve their unions, go back into hiding, and close the closet doors behind them. Does anyone really believe that?

In November 2014, "a student at Marquette University, a Roman Catholic institution in Wisconsin run by the Jesuits, [said] his philosophy professor [stated] that he was not allowed to express his view against same-sex 'marriage' in her classroom [remember that this is a Catholic school].

"The student, speaking to The College Fix, said that MU philosophy instructor Cheryl Abbate told her 'Theory of Ethics' class that 'gay rights' was a settled issue because, unlike issues such as immigration, civil rights and the death penalty, *everybody agrees on this, and there is no need to discuss it.*"[32] The student was ultimately banned from the class after protesting the professor's actions.

The fact is that "everybody" does *not* agree on this, and regardless of what the courts might say (including the Supreme Court) and despite what the popular media tells us, the cultural battle is far from over. In fact, the startling success of the gay revolution, coupled with the rising attack on our freedoms, has only awakened a sleeping giant, in which case the battle has barely begun. As theologian Douglas Wilson said, "I am against surrendering in any case, but I am really against surrendering before the battle is really joined."[33]

I invite you to join me, then, in standing for what is right and best for America (and the nations) by living by the eight principles I lay out in the chapters that follow. They are not principles meant to bash the LGBT community—in fact, one whole chapter is devoted entirely to taking quite the opposite stance—but they explain, by encouragement and example, why it is imperative that we take a stand, mingling compassion together with courage. And so, the call here is not so much to defeat the gay agenda as it is to promote a better agenda, one that by design will outlast the gay revolution.

Are you ready to join me in confronting the greatest moral, cultural, and spiritual issue of our generation? Are you ready to be an agent of positive change? Then turn the page, and let's begin.

PRINCIPLE #1

NEVER COMPROMISE YOUR CONVICTIONS

Courage is contagious. When a brave man takes a stand, the spines of others are often stiffened. —BILLY GRAHAM

It was October 29, 1941. Winston Churchill had returned to his old school, Harrow, just ten months after his previous visit, when things looked very bleak for England in the midst of World War II. It was against this background that he delivered his "Never Give In" speech, not to soldiers but to students.

"You cannot tell from appearances how things will go," he explained, noting that "for everyone, surely, what we have gone through in this period—I am addressing myself to the School—surely from this period of ten months this is the lesson: never give in, never give in, never, never, never, never—in nothing, great or small, large or petty—never give in except to convictions of honour and good sense."

He continued, "Never yield to force; never yield to the apparently overwhelming might of the enemy. We stood all alone a year ago, and to many countries it seemed that our account was closed, we were finished. All this tradition of ours, our songs, our School history, this part of the history of this country, were gone and finished and liquidated."

But in just ten months, there had been a dramatic shift—although the war was still in its early stages—and Churchill explained, "Very different is the mood today. Britain, other nations thought, had drawn a sponge across her slate. But instead our country stood in the gap. There was no flinching and no thought of giving in; and by what seemed almost a miracle to those outside these Islands, though we ourselves never doubted it, we now find ourselves in a position where I say that we can be sure that we have only to persevere to conquer."[1]

Nine times he uttered the word *never*. Three times he exclaimed, "Never give in." Twice he said, "Never yield." And I repeat: he delivered this speech to students in a school, not to soldiers on the battlefield.

How does this apply to us today? We are not in a physical war but an ideological war, and our opponents are not Nazis—God forbid—but rather family members, friends, coworkers, and neighbors who identify as LGBT and who simply want to normalize homosexuality. "We just want the same rights that all of you have," they tell us repeatedly.

With tremendous motivation, massive funding, brilliant strategy, and the help of their straight allies, they have brought about one of the most far-reaching and rapid cultural revolutions in history. And there is only one thing standing in the way of their complete success: the Church, or, more broadly, people of faith and conservative moral values. Gay activists understand this fully.

IT'S TIME TO STRENGTHEN OUR RESOLVE

In the early days of their movement, gay leaders had to overcome two main obstacles: the psychological profession, which considered homosexuality a mental disorder, and the religious world, which considered homosexual practice a sin.[2] And so they began to deconstruct and systematically attack the idea that homosexuality was a disordered condition, using bullying tactics as well as scientific arguments (many of which remain disputed), and within a few short years, the major psychological and psychiatric organizations changed their views (under duress, to be candid), and they have since become major allies of the homosexual community.[3]

That was back in 1973. Since then, the focus has been on the Church—a battle of more than forty years now—and the only way the gay revolution can fulfill its goals is by silencing people of faith or by changing their minds on the issue. In light of this onslaught, I say to every religious leader and to every individual believer, "Never give in, never give in, never, never, never, never—in nothing, great or small, large or petty—never give in except to convictions of honour and good sense."

No matter what pressure is put on you—the loss of status; being kicked out of your denomination; losing a pension or a position or a raise or a scholarship; being disowned by family or friends; loss of income—do not compromise your biblically based convictions. The moment you do, something in you dies. You are no longer free, but you are a slave to public opinion and public sway, and you have sacrificed your integrity on the altar of expediency. What could possibly be worth a loss like that?

I'm not talking about being stubborn and unreasonable, or about believing falsehoods about gays and lesbians. I'm talking about being true to your convictions, especially those that are based on the clear teachings of the Bible, about doing what is right rather than what is convenient or politically correct. We owe it to God, to our society, and to future generations.

After all, if we cave in and compromise, who will be left to stand? That's why the attack on people of faith has intensified greatly in the last few years, and you can be sure that gay activists are in this for the long haul. Wouldn't you be if you were in their shoes? After all, this is about their very lives, and I fully understand why they do what they do. That's why this issue is completely unavoidable.

As Dr. Albert Mohler wrote of same-sex "marriage":

> For some time now, it has been increasingly clear that every congregation in this nation will be forced to declare itself openly on this issue. That moment of decision and public declaration will come to every Christian believer, individually. There will be no place to hide, and no place safe from eventual interrogation. The question will be asked,

an invitation will be extended, a matter of policy must be decided, and there will be no refuge.[4]

What will your answer be?

HOW THINGS HAVE CHANGED

It wasn't that long ago that gay activists assured us that they had no desire to interfere with religious liberties. They simply wanted their own liberties. Now, however, the tide has turned, and increasingly, gay rights are trumping religious rights. Of course, a more militant tone was already sounding as early as 1969, following the Stonewall riots, when drag queens and other gay men fought back violently against police who had raided the Stonewall Inn bar in New York City, leading to a series of riots and mass protests But even after Stonewall, gay activists and their allies continued to tell conservatives, "We're not trying to take away your rights or infringe on your beliefs. We just want our rights."

Yet no sooner did gay activists begin to achieve their goals than they said, "It's not enough. If we allow you to have your rights and hold to your views, then we are giving place to bigotry. We will not tolerate homophobia!"

And so, children's schools that once encouraged the "tolerance and acceptance" of homosexuality now brand those values "homophobic," calling instead for appreciation, support, nurture, and admiration of homosexuality. And in New York State, shortly after the same-sex "marriage" bill was passed with religious exemptions (which was the only way the bill would pass), some gay leaders began to protest, saying the bill now gave legal sanction to religious bigotry. On January 10, 2015, *New York Times* op-ed columnist Frank Bruni wrote an editorial complaining that "religious people [are] getting a pass that isn't warranted," and claiming that we use our beliefs "as a fig leaf for intolerance."[5] Churches must conform too! Similarly, in Denmark, several years after Danes won the right to have homosexual "marriages" in the Lutheran State Church (of which the vast majority of Danes are nonpracticing members), a ruling was passed requiring clergy to perform these ceremonies.[6]

Back here in the States, the ACLU and a number of leading gay activist organizations have opposed religious exemptions for ENDA (the Employment Non-Discrimination Act, which now includes the categories of sexual orientation and gender identity), meaning that a Christian book-store would not be able to fire a male employee who began to come to work wearing a dress. Conversely, a Christian college that forbade homo-sexual practice for students, staff, and faculty would be required to hire a sexually active, out-and-proud gay man who was otherwise qualified.[7]

In keeping with this, the ACLU has opposed the rights of Christian businesses to exercise their religious freedoms when they come in con-flict with LGBT freedoms. In the words of James Esseks, director of the ACLU's Lesbian Gay Bisexual and AIDS Project, "Courts have said time and again that firmly held religious beliefs don't justify discrimination based on race and sex. The legislation should apply the same rule for sexual orientation and gender identity."[8]

And what happens if you run a private business, like a bakery, and a customer asks you to do something that fundamentally contradicts your religious beliefs? Esseks has the answer: "Look you're in busi-ness and you got to open your business to everyone. . . . [Y]ou're not running a religious establishment, you are operating a cake shop."[9] Presumably, then, if a Christian baker could be required by law to bake a cake for a same-sex "wedding" and a Christian photographer could be required to photograph the ceremony and reception—which would include posing the same-sex couple in romantic embraces and sharing a kiss—then a Muslim or Orthodox Jewish caterer could be required to provide pork for the event.

While the last scenario seems utterly absurd, the first two (and many more) have already taken place, with Christian businesses being found guilty of discrimination. That's why Esseks and the ACLU are so dead set against any religious exemptions. As he explained, "These religious freedom arguments, these religious exemption arguments are so powerful . . . it's going to completely undermine the equality principles that we need."[10]

In other words, this is not simply a matter of "live and let live." It is now a matter of, "You shall not have your religious freedoms when they conflict with the goals of gay activism, and you are not entitled to your convictions, no matter what the Bible or your faith or history or your conscience have to say. You must conform to the goals of gay activism or else."

I ask you again: What will you do when this comes knocking at your door? Will you uphold biblical morality and marriage as God intended it, or will you wave the white flag of surrender?

THERE'S A PRICE TO PAY FOR DOING RIGHT

I'm fully aware that this spiritual and cultural battle can be very draining, and these days in particular, it can be downright discouraging. But you are responsible only to do what you can do, and what you can and must do is stand tall and strong and proud for what you believe is right and best.

So what if you're branded a homophobe and a bigot? Jesus was called far worse. So what if your business gets boycotted or your church gets disfellowshipped or your name gets blacklisted? Christians who fought against slavery in America faced far greater opposition than this, and they didn't cave in and collapse. In fact, gay activists themselves had to overcome far more than this to fight for their cause, and they didn't back down. How can we?

As I write these words, Christians in radical Muslim countries are literally losing their heads for their faith, yet we here in the West are concerned about losing our Facebook popularity. How can we be so cowardly? How can we be so easily moved? How can we capitulate when, deep down in our hearts, many of us know that God's standards haven't changed in the least?

The words of Dr. Martin Luther King Jr. have never been more relevant: "Cowardice asks the question, is it safe? Expediency asks the question, is it politic? Vanity asks the question, is it popular? But conscience asks the question, is it right? And there comes a time when one must take a position that is neither safe, nor politic, nor popular; but one must take it because it is right."[11] That time is now.

The gay rights movement often resorts to bullying, and it will try to silence you or defame you if it can't win you over. This, of course, is deeply ironic, since many gays have themselves been bullied, and they have made constant appeal to this in gaining public sympathy. After all, people tend to side with the victim and *against* the bully, and to the extent that we who stand for biblical morality can be portrayed as the bullies, the public will turn against us.

But today it is we who are being bullied, to the point that the unspoken mantra of gay activism is: "We will intimidate and we will manipulate until you capitulate." I'm here to announce that we will not capitulate, regardless of cost or consequence. We cannot deny our conscience, and we will not compromise our deeply held moral and spiritual convictions.

WHAT GAY ACTIVISTS REALLY THINK ABOUT YOU

Don't deceive yourself into thinking that the storm will pass or that your school or your business or your church or congregation will be exempt from conflict. Not a chance. Many gay leaders truly believe that you and I are no different from the KKK or the Nazis, and they adamantly oppose their more moderate colleagues who respect and tolerate opposing views. As expressed by homosexual activist John Becker:

> Our culture doesn't treat other forms of bigotry with "respect" and "tolerance." To the contrary, prejudices like sexism, racism, and anti-Semitism are overwhelmingly regarded with revulsion and scorn—because society has rightfully decided that these toxic social evils deserve to be shamed and stigmatized, and that sexists, racists, and anti-Semites no longer deserve a seat at the table of civil discourse. The lesson of the Brendan Eich controversy [the Internet CEO who was forced to step down because he contributed to a pro-marriage bill in 2008] is that the public is increasingly ready to add homophobes to that list.[12]

In the words of Josh Barro, who writes for the *New York Times*, "Anti-LGBT attitudes [by which he meant opposition to same-sex 'marriage' and the like] are terrible for people in all sorts of communities. They linger and oppress, and we need to stamp them out, ruthlessly."[13]

These men mean what they write, which makes their rhetoric all the more chilling: If we affirm biblical morality, we are guilty of "bigotry"; we hold to "prejudices like sexism, racism, and anti-Semitism"; we embrace "toxic social evils"; our views "linger and oppress." Therefore, they believe our views should be "shamed and stigmatized" and "regarded with revulsion and scorn" and we should be excluded from "the table of civil discourse" because we are homophobes. Indeed, they say, our attitudes must be stamped out "ruthlessly."

And you really think that just by being nice and smiling a lot you'll be treated any differently? Not on your life. In the gay activists' eyes, there's not much difference between a nice homophobe and a nice racist. As Becker asked gay and straight leaders who signed a "Freedom to Dissent" document in the aftermath of Eich's ouster:

> If Brendan Eich had donated to a white supremacist or neo-Nazi group, would you make similar pleas for "serious consideration" of and "vigorous public debate" about the merits of those "dissenting" views? Would you work so hard to uphold the fiction that two morally equivalent sides exist on issues like racism and sexism and anti-Semitism?
>
> Or is it just homophobic bigotry that deserves this special form of "tolerance?"[14]

THE VICTIMS HAVE BECOME THE BULLIES

To give you an idea of the degree to which gay activism has become a bullying movement, after Brendan Eich was forced to resign, Andrew Sullivan, a prominent gay journalist, wrote, "The whole episode disgusts me—as it should disgust anyone interested in a tolerant and diverse society. If this is the gay rights movement today—hounding our opponents with a fanaticism more like the religious right than anyone else—then count me out."[15] The ultraliberal Bill Maher also weighed in on his *Real Time* program: "I think there is a gay mafia. I think if you cross them, you do get whacked."[16]

This echoes comments made years earlier by lesbian journalist and author Camille Paglia in her book *Vamps and Tramps*. She wrote, "One reason I so dislike recent gay activism is that my self-identification as a lesbian preceded Stonewall: I was the only openly gay person at the Yale Graduate School (1968–72), a candor that was professionally costly. That anyone with my aggressive and scandalous history could be called 'homophobic,' as has repeatedly been done, shows just how insanely Stalinist gay activism has become."[17]

Stalinist? Gay mafia? Hounding their opponents with fanaticism, just like the religious right that they so fiercely criticized?

In *A Queer Thing Happened to America*, I devoted more than 50 pages and 138 endnotes to the topic of "Big Brother Is Watching and He Really Is Gay," noting that "the really frightening thing is that it would be easy to write an entire book focusing on the subject matter of this chapter alone, and the book could be much longer than this present book—and this is one long book!" (*A Queer Thing Happened to America* is a 700-page book.) In fact, Bill Muehlenberg, an incisive and prolific cultural commentator based in Australia, documented "165 examples of this growing war on faith, freedom and family" over a period of just thirty-four months (January 2011–October 2013), still noting that "these are just some of the cases that took place during this period, but not all."[18]

A tiny sampling of the headlines Muehlenberg cited includes the following:

- "Quebec Human Rights Tribunal Fines Man $12,000 for 'Homophobic' Remarks"

- "Death Threats Against UK Columnist for Opposing Homosexualist Agenda"

- "Army: Court-Martial [USA] Chaplains for 'Religious, Conscience' Objection to Homosexuality"

- "Gay Columnist: Let's Face It, We Want to Indoctrinate Children"

- "Top Sports Anchor Fired over Beliefs on Marriage"

- "Florida High School Removes Christian Teacher for Criticizing Gay 'Marriage' on Facebook"

- "Macy's Fires Woman for Refusing 'Transgender' Man Access to Women's Fitting Room"

- "Amsterdam Chief Rabbi Suspended for Gay Stance"

- "Criticize Homosexuality in Sweden and Go to Jail: No Problem for European Rights Court"

- "14-Year-Old Homeschooled Girl Receives Death Threats for Defending Marriage"

- "Christian Marriage Conference in UK Banned for Opposition to Gay Marriage"

- "'Dad' Deleted from [Scottish] NHS Baby Guide—for Sake of Gay Couples"

- "Denmark Forces Churches to Perform Same-Sex 'Marriages'"

- "Christian B&B Owners Ordered to Pay Gay Couple $4,500 in Damages"

- "Democrat Admits, 'Attack on Parental Rights' Is 'the Whole Point' of Banning Sex Orientation Therapy"

- "University Suspends Chick-fil-A from Campus"

- "Christian Arrested for Calling Homosexuality a 'Sin' Warns of 'Real-Life Thought Police'"

Remember: this is just a sampling of a sampling, illustrated by the fact that Robert Oscar Lopez, an English professor at California State

University–Northridge, wrote an article titled "300 Examples You Have to Read to Understand the Term 'Homofascism.'" Included in those "300 examples" are these:

- 14-year-old receives death threats for defending traditional/ natural marriage;

- Supporters of Proposition 8 in California were subjected to harassment, intimidation, vandalism, racial scapegoating, blacklisting, loss of employment, economic hardships, angry protests, violence, at least one death threat, letters mailed with white powder in it;

- Human Resources surveys at banks and other major corporations expand the gay police state.[19]

Professor Lopez provides links for every example cited, and even that lengthy list of incidents was selective rather than comprehensive, and that by necessity. Is the picture becoming clearer? We will need courage and determination to stand for what is right, but stand we must. Otherwise, what we will say to our kids and grandkids in years to come when they ask us how we allowed such sweeping societal changes to happen on our watch, often with barely a whimper of ideological resistance?

Here are some recent examples of the extreme intolerance that people of faith and moral convictions are experiencing. This is why we must determine today that we will not compromise, cower, or cave in.

YOU SHALL NOT RECEIVE PROFESSIONAL COUNSELING

In California and New Jersey, it is now illegal for a minor with same-sex attraction to receive professional counseling if he or she wants to get to the root of that attraction and experience change. Illegal. That means that a seventeen-year-old girl, with the full support of her family, cannot sit with a trained counselor to discuss her struggles, even if she had been sexually abused and feels that her sexual confusion can be traced back to that abuse. And she cannot receive counseling for her unwanted same-sex attraction, even if homosexuality violates her religious convictions or her personal morals or simply her desire to be married with children of her own. Illegal![20]

To add insult to this outrage, Sen. Ted Lieu, who sponsored the California legislation and who is a married heterosexual man, explained that "the attack on parental rights is exactly the whole point of the bill because we don't want to let parents harm their children."[21] What outlandish reasoning. First, his bill prevents children from having the right to get counseling. Second, there are countless testimonies of young people being helped by such counseling. Third, no counseling or therapy is 100 percent helpful all the time, so if he wants to ban counseling that could potentially harm children, he would have to ban almost all forms of counseling.

Really now, who gave the state the authority to forbid a teenager to receive professional counseling when it is that teen's own choice and he or she has parental backing? This is absolutely outrageous, regardless of the justification offered. This is all the more true when one realizes that many people can trace unwanted attractions and desires to previous sexual abuse, as demonstrated (intentionally or not) by a study released at a bisexual summit in 2009, which claimed that 74 percent of bisexuals experienced childhood sexual abuse.[22]

Mental health professional David Clarke Pruden exclaimed, "Imagine a world where a mental health professional's opposition to limiting by law their client's freedom to explore all their potential healthy life options and their advocating for every citizen's right to sexual self-determination—shaping our sexual behavior, identity and feelings according to our own personal goals or values—could be branded as hateful or homophobic. Welcome to America in the year 2015."[23]

But it gets even worse. About one year before the California bill became law, two lesbians in the same state made headlines when it was learned that they had put their young adopted son on hormone blockers to prevent the onset of puberty:

> The lesbian parents of an 11-year-old boy who is undergoing the
> process of becoming a girl . . . defended the decision, claiming it was

better for a child to have a sex change when young. Thomas Lobel, who now calls himself Tammy, is undergoing controversial hormone blocking treatment in Berkeley, California to stop him going through puberty as a boy. . . . At age seven, after threatening genital mutilation on himself, psychiatrists diagnosed Thomas with gender identity disorder. By the age of eight, he began transitioning.[24]

So, it is *legal* in California for the adoptive parents of a small boy to subject him to hormone-blocking therapy (which has not been tested in the long run in terms of the child's future health), and to dress him and relate to him as if he were a girl, to get him ready for permanent, irreversible, sex change surgery at the earliest possible age.[25] Yet it is illegal for a minor with unwanted same-sex attractions to sit down and talk with a psychologist, psychiatrist, or any other professional counselor or therapist.

Some states have already pushed back and said no to similar bills.[26] I urge every legislator to stand against this attack on client-counselor rights and to expose it for the overreach that it is, and I urge church leaders to let their legislators know where they stand on this critical issue.

An online group called Homosexuals Anonymous, "dedicated to serving the recovery needs of men and women who struggle with unwanted same sex attraction," has published its SOCE Bill of Rights (SOCE stands for Sexual Orientation Change Efforts), declaring that:

I. Every individual has an ethical, medical and legal right to sexual self-determination.

II. Every individual has an ethical, medical and legal right to explore and research their options in order to make informed decisions.

III. Every individual has a right to be fully informed of the true science regarding human sexual fluidity by relevant agency or practitioner.

IV. Every individual has a right to be informed of the known medical and psychological risks associated with their choice by relevant agency or practitioner.

V. Any professional sworn by oath to make no attempt to coerce, suppress or confound the individual cultural, ethical or religious convictions of any client be held to honor their oath.

VI. Any professional or agency attempting to coerce, suppress or confound the individual right to sexual self-determination be held in violation of their oath, in contempt of legal precedence and hostile to the welfare of their client.[27]

For them, this is a matter of fundamental liberty—really now, who can deprive them of the right to self-determination?—and they conclude their document by stating, "We, whose lives these decisions affect, and our supporters demand our right to liberty and a life of our choosing that is in accordance with creation as intended, good health and a virtuous spirit."[28]

How can we not stand with them and for them?

YOU SHALL NOT HAVE AN OPINION

Tony Dungy is a highly respected former NFL coach who now serves as a TV analyst for the league. When asked by a reporter if he would have drafted Michael Sam, the league's first openly gay player, he answered, "I wouldn't have taken him. Not because I don't believe Michael Sam should have a chance to play, but I wouldn't want to deal with all of it." He further explained, "It's not going to be totally smooth . . . things will happen."[29] And from these remarks, in which he simply answered a question honestly in terms of his own football philosophy, a firestorm of criticism erupted.

Dungy, for his part, went out of his way to clarify his response, noting that for several months prior to his much-criticized comments, he had been asked (1) whether or not Sam deserved an opportunity to play in the NFL; Dungy said he absolutely did; (2) whether Sam's "sexual orientation should play a part in the evaluation process"; Dungy said it should not; and (3) whether Dungy would personally have a problem having him on his team; he said he would not. Dungy also emphasized that "playing in the NFL is, and should be, about merit," and he wished Sam great success in the league, stating, "My sincere hope is that we will be able to focus on his play and not on his sexual orientation." The question to which he responded was whether he would have drafted Sam *himself,* and given the media attention Sam had drawn to himself and all the potential distractions he would bring, Dungy said no.

Let's not forget that Oprah was going to do a reality show about how Sam performed for the team in training camp before the idea was dropped, probably under the NFL's influence. It was against this larger backdrop that Dungy explained, "What I was asked about was my philosophy of drafting, a philosophy that was developed over the years, which was to minimize distractions for my teams."

His response was logical and surely one that other teams also considered: "I do not believe Michael's sexual orientation will be a distraction to his teammates or his organization. I do, however, believe that the media attention that comes with it will be a distraction. Unfortunately we are all seeing this play out now, and I feel badly that my remarks played a role in the distraction."[30] To paraphrase:

Interviewer: Coach, what's your honest opinion on this situation?

Coach: That's a great question. Here's my opinion.

Interviewer: How dare you give that opinion! It is in violation of our gay activist talking points!

As ridiculous as it seems, it is now dangerous for a sports analyst and former coach to respond honestly to a question unless it is in harmony with a politically correct, gay-themed point of view. How in the world did we get to this place so quickly? One day there is controversy about an NFL player declaring that he is gay. The next day, there is controversy for saying there is controversy.

And this is not an isolated incident. About the same time Tony Dungy was getting blasted, the New York Giants football organization came under criticism for hiring David Tyree as its director of player development. Tyree is legendary in Giants' circles for the "miraculous" catch he made in his team's Super Bowl victory over the New England Patriots. Tyree is also a committed Christian, and in the past he has made clear that he opposes redefining marriage (to the point that he would donate his famous football helmet to raise funds to defend marriage), that "there is no scientific evidence to support the claim of being born gay," and that he has met "former homosexuals."

His passion to stand for marriage is highly commendable, and his statements about people being born gay and about former homosexuals are quite accurate, despite hysterical claims to the contrary. (For more on this, see below, "Principle #6: Keep Propagating the Truth Until the Lies Are Dispelled.") But in keeping with gay bullying tactics, which seek to suppress and vilify all opposing views, the poorly named Human Rights Campaign laid into the Giants for their decision. They stated that Tyree's claim "has been debunked and condemned by every major medical and mental health organization in the country, including the American Medical Association, the American Psychiatric Association, American Psychological Association, and many others." HRC president Chad Griffin asked, "When did Tyree decide to be straight? The idea that someone can change their sexual orientation or gender identity is ludicrous, and the New York Giants are risking their credibility by hiring someone who publicly advocates this junk science. His opposition to basic legal equality aside, David Tyree's proselytizing of such dangerous practices goes against the positive work the Giants organization has done in recent years."[31]

In other words, we'll repeat the standard gay talking points and bash anyone who dares raise an opposing viewpoint. And if anyone dare question the gay bullies, there will be serious professional consequences.

In lockstep with this oppressive mentality, New York sports journalist Dan Graziano opined, "Tyree might well be qualified to hold the job of director of player development. Heck, he might be great at it. And maybe his medieval views on this issue won't affect his ability to do the job or relate to players in any way. But given what's going on in the NFL and the world right now, I have to think the Giants could have made a less tone-deaf hire."[32]

Did you get that? Believing that marriage is the union of a man and a woman is "medieval"? Recognizing that there is still no reputable scientific evidence that anyone is born gay is "medieval"? And knowing people, as I do too, who are former homosexuals is "medieval"? Perhaps this assault on diversity and truth in the name of gay political correctness is "medieval."[33]

The Giants, for their part, simply stated that these were Tyree's views and not their own. Tyree, for his part, had no response to the HRC and simply stated that he was glad to work for the organization. As for Tony Dungy, he continues to broadcast without interruption. This means that one of the best ways to overcome gay activist overreach is simply by holding your ground: Sorry, but we're not firing David Tyree and we're not disciplining Tony Dungy. End of story.

YOU SHALL NOT SIGN A PETITION

In January 2011 Dr. Angela McCaskill was appointed as the first chief diversity officer at Gallaudet University in Washington, DC, hailed as the nation's foremost university for the deaf. She seemed ideally suited for her job, being female, African American, and deaf. In fact, she was the first deaf African American woman to earn a PhD from Gallaudet, had served at the school for more than two decades at the time of her new appointment, and was very popular with the student body.

Then she committed a cardinal sin. She exercised her freedom as an American and signed a petition calling on Maryland legislators to allow the people of her home state to vote on the issue of redefining marriage. That was it. She did not denounce same-sex "marriage"; she did not take a public stand against it; she did not engage in any kind of hate speech; she did not demonstrate "homophobia." Instead, she, along with her husband, signed a fair-minded petition after hearing a sermon on marriage by her pastor, and she joined more than two hundred thousand others who signed this petition.

How then did this personal act become a matter of public concern? In typical gay-intimidation fashion, the names of the signers were released in a gay publication, after which a lesbian professor reported Dr. McCaskill to school authorities. In turn, the school promptly suspended her from her job, with the support of the university president, causing Dr. McCaskill such personal distress that she had to be placed under doctor's care.

What kind of strong-arming is this? But this is a perfect example of the "diversity police" in action, and this is how they respond.

The claim against Dr. McCaskill had been that there was no way she could function as the chief diversity officer while believing that marriage was the union of one man and one woman. In reality, her job was not specifically related to LGBT issues (at the time of her suspension, the school's website description of the Office for Diversity and Inclusion did not mention gay or lesbian concerns). More important, even Planet DeafQueer, a "community website devoted to empowering the DeafQueer community," noted that "Dr. McCaskill is well liked by students. 'She's been a great ally to the LGBT community and supported many of the LGBTQA Resource Center's programs,' said one student, who asked to remain anonymous. 'I'm heart broken about this.'"[34] So, regardless of her Christian convictions, she was supportive of all students, a tribute to her genuine care for the student body.

Would anyone claim that only a person who was simultaneously Christian and Buddhist and Muslim and Hindu and Jewish and atheist could function as the school's chief diversity officer because of the religious mix of the student body? Or that the officer would have to be an ethnic mixture of all races of the current student body in order to function properly? Why then would anyone argue that by personally holding to biblical Christian values, she could not serve the school's multireligious, multiethnic, coed student body? Whatever happened to "diversity" and "inclusion"?

To use the language of the school's website, is it possible for the chief diversity officer "to promote an academically enriching and supportive climate that allows all the diverse members of its community to thrive and succeed" without believing that a man should be able to marry a man and a woman marry a woman? The answer is obviously yes, since you can be a friend of the LGBT community without believing that marriage should be redefined.

Fortunately, within a week of Dr. McCaskill's suspension, the *Washington Times* reported that "leaders on both sides of the Maryland fight over same-sex marriage are urging Gallaudet University to reinstate an employee who was suspended because she signed a petition in favor of traditional marriage."[35] The thought of bullying this woman who communicated at a press conference via sign language was a bit too much to bear.

The good news is that she was reinstated. The bad news is that it took three, long, traumatizing months, not to mention it was outrageous that she had to go through this at all. As Rev. Derek McCoy, executive director of the Maryland Marriage Alliance, rightly asked, "If her employer is able to restrict her right to engage in the petition-gathering phase of democracy, are they also allowed to enter the voting booth and dictate how she votes?"[36]

Is this the kind of America you want to live in? Do you want your kids and grandkids to grow up in a country that restricts and intimidates like this?

Unfortunately, there was one more indignity that Dr. McCaskill was to experience: a federal judge dismissed her lawsuit in which she accused the school of harassment and discrimination because of her Christian beliefs (with specific reference to the lesbian professor who initially reported her). According to Judge James Boasberg, the treatment she suffered was not illegal: "Any Mistreatment McCaskill suffered . . . was not based upon her sexual orientation, her marital status, or her race. If the mistreatment occurred, it was based on her decision to sign a political petition."[37]

Seriously? This was the ruling of a federal judge? Can you imagine him ruling the same way against a lesbian professor who, for argument's sake, had suffered what Dr. McCaskill did after signing a petition in favor of homosexual "marriage"? Is he actually saying that the school's employees had a right to belittle Dr. McCaskill and cause her personal and professional trauma because she joined two hundred thousand fellow citizens in calling for the right to vote on redefining marriage in her state?

Still, as ugly as this particular case is, there is light in the midst of the tunnel. Gay bullying was exposed and defeated, even though the victory was not complete and unnecessary suffering was endured. Things can go only so far before having a boomerang effect.

YOU SHALL NOT DONATE TO A FAMILY CAUSE

In the aftermath of the passage of Proposition 8 in California in 2008, gay activists released the names of those who donated to the bill's passage, resulting in both vandalism to churches and threats to individuals and businesses.[38] And so, when word got out that Marjorie Christofferson, co-owner of a legendary Mexican restaurant in Hollywood, had donated $100 to Proposition 8, gay websites began to call for a boycott of the restaurant, resulting in Christofferson making a public apology to an LGBT gathering: "I'm sick of heart that I've offended anyone in the gay community," she said. "I have had, and do have family, friends, and people I work with of course who are gay . . . and you are treasured people to me."[39] And in fact, a patron reported, "When one of the guys died from AIDS, Marjorie paid for his mother to fly out for his funeral."[40]

The tall, frail Christofferson stood in the center of the group. She appeared to be shaking during her prepared remarks, which lasted about three minutes. Her daughters flanked her to prevent her from fainting, according to a restaurant employee. At several points during her speech, Christofferson simply became too emotional to continue. Yes, this was her necessary penance for daring to support a bill that defined marriage as the union of a man and a woman, a bill the people of California passed not once but twice, and one that, at that time, defined marriage just as candidate Barack Obama defined it.

Shaking and tearful, Christofferson, who is a Mormon, said, "I cannot change a lifetime of faith in which I believe in very deeply. I cannot and will not, no matter what, change my love and respect for you and your views." Not long after her talk, with negative sentiments still running high, she resigned from her job.

Pro-family leader Maggie Gallagher noted:

> Marjorie's . . . resignation has only whetted the appetite of the anti-Prop 8 crowd. West Hollywood News is reporting, "In other boycott news, No On 8 activists are gathering lists of Yes On 8 donors to publish online in hopes of punishing those businesses for their support of the effort to strip fellow Californians of a civil right."
>
> This is a totally new tactic by the way. Boycotts against businesses who donate to a cause or mistreat their customers have long been an accepted part of the American democratic practice. But targeting an entire business because one person associated with it made (in their personal capacity) a donation to a cause is brand new. It's essentially McCarthyite in spirit. Gay-marriage activists hope to make you unemployable if you publicly disagree with them.
>
> I'm sure many ordinary gay-marriage supporters deplore what happened to Marjorie. But this is now the face of their movement: agree with us, or we will hurt you.[41]

Gallagher did not overstate this in the least, but our response cannot be to run and hide. Instead, we should be all the more active and unashamed.

YOU SHALL NOT PRACTICE LAW

Trinity Western University, located in British Columbia, Canada, is a Christian school that requires its students and teachers to sign a "community covenant," which includes a commitment to abstain from sex outside of marriage, by which is meant the union of a man and a woman.[42] That, however, has caused the university to run afoul of Canada's law societies, and on April 24, 2014, "the law society of

Canada's largest province voted against admitting among their ranks graduates of Trinity Western University," followed shortly thereafter by the law society of Nova Scotia.[43]

Then, on June 10, 2014,

[l]awyers in British Columbia . . . rejected a Christian university's plans to open a law school—a result that, while not binding, represents a strong rebuke of the school's policies forbidding sex outside heterosexual marriage. The vote is the latest setback for Trinity Western University, a school with about 4,000 students in B.C.'s Fraser Valley, and is sure to amplify an ongoing debate over the rights of a private institution to impose its religious views about homosexuality on students.[44]

Bob Kuhn, the president of Trinity Western, had rightly argued that "a vote to disapprove TWU's law school communicates to TWU, its religious community and many other men and women of faith that they're not welcome to engage in the public square of Canadian pluralistic society."[45] The vote, however, went against the school decisively, 3,210 to 968.

The university challenged these rulings in the courts, but without success, as it was announced on December 12, 2014, that "Trinity Western University has lost the approval of the B.C. Advanced Education ministry for its proposed law school, which stirred up controversy for its stance on same-sex relationships."[46] And so, in the name of LGBT "equality," graduates of a Christian law school are being told, "You shall not practice law," regardless of their academic training. They are being discriminated against simply because, as Christians, they hold to Christians beliefs and therefore cannot affirm same-sex relationships.

Here in America, it was announced on August 18, 2014, that the four-hundred-thousand-member American Bar Association "adopted a new resolution calling for an end to 'discrimination' against lesbian, gay, bisexual and transgender people in the United States and around the world."[47] Will this have implications for Christian law schools? Some Christian colleges and seminaries are already experiencing accreditation challenges because of their biblical opposition to homosexual practice. Will they commit spiritual and ethical suicide in order to maintain their standing in the eyes of the world?[48]

To every educator and administrator reading this book, I urge you to not to sell your soul to accrediting agencies, bar associations, wealthy donors, or foundations. If you cave in to the pressure, what message are you sending to your students and alumni? And at what point will you draw the line and say, "This goes too far!"

If such a line exists, why not draw it now? It is far better to stand on principle and be people of honor and integrity than to submit to the demands of LGBT activism. And if you have any doubt, just ask yourself this question: which decision will God bless?

YOU SHALL NOT ADOPT

A Christian couple in England who had previously provided foster care or adoption for fifteen children was told by the British High Court that they could not provide care for any more children, simply because they could not affirm homosexuality. Eunice and Owen Johns, a couple in their sixties, were interviewed by a gay counselor before taking in their next child, and he pressed them on their views about homosexuality. They made it clear that they would provide equal love and care for a child who identified as gay, but they wouldn't affirm the child's homosexuality. As a result, a complaint was brought against them by a gay activist organization, and the High Court ruled against them.

Eunice Johns explained, "All we wanted to do was to offer a loving home to a child in need. We have a good track record as foster parents, but because we are Christians with mainstream views on sexual ethics, we are apparently unsuitable as foster parents."[49]

The ruling was so extreme that even gay atheist David Starkey was concerned: "I am gay, and I am atheist, but I have profound doubts about this case. It seems to me that what we are doing is producing a tyrannous new morality that is every bit as oppressive as the old. When I grew up being gay was very difficult, it was frowned upon . . . but I am very very concerned that a new sort of liberal morality is as intolerant, oppressive and intrusive into family life . . . I do not support thought crime."[50]

BBC News reported, "The court discriminated between kinds of Christianity, saying that Christians in general might well make good foster parents, while people with traditionalist Christian views like Mr and Mrs Johns might well not."[51]

But this case is not an isolated example of anti-Christian prejudice, as courts in England have consistently favored homosexual rights over Christian rights.[52] In fact, the Supreme Court deputy president, Baroness Brenda Hale, has admitted that she and the court may have been wrong about a previous, much-publicized ruling that found a Christian couple guilty for refusing to rent a room in their bed-and-breakfast to a gay couple. (According to the owners' written policy, they rented double rooms only to married couples, which for them obviously meant heterosexual.) A report in England's *Daily Mail* noted that "Lady Hale said in a speech that the law has done too little to protect the beliefs of Christians. And she cast doubts over her own judgment in the landmark case in which a gay couple sued Christian hoteliers Peter and Hazelmary Bull. . . . Lady Hale suggested that the law should develop a 'conscience clause' for Christians like the Bulls."[53]

More remarkably still, the British High Court ruled that the Bulls did not have to pay for legal costs, which included the costs of the attorneys for the gay couple who took them to court. As noted by Colin Hart from the Christian Institute, "The penny is beginning to drop among judges that the law is unfair. I hope the Supreme Court will find more room to protect Christian consciences."[54] Could the tide be turning in the UK, even ever so slightly?

We've already suffered significant setbacks here in America, such as Catholic Charities having to discontinue their adoption services because they would be forced to place children in homosexual homes. We don't need to sit around passively to see what's coming next. We need to do our best to turn the tide by pushing for our pro-family agenda as aggressively as our opponents have pushed for theirs.

YOU SHALL NOT DISSENT

In his forcefully worded article "Gays Gone Wild," Prof. Robert Oscar Lopez titled one section "For People Who Are Helpless Victims, Gosh These People Are Vicious." He wrote:

The list of people smeared and targeted, almost universally based on overblown reactions, and none of them having any real impact on the serious problems facing everyday gays, is long and chilling. Major gay rights organizations wage endless war against Barilla Pasta, Brendan Ambrosino, Brett Easton Ellis, Michelle Shocked, Rupert Everett, Kirk Cameron, Ben Carson, Michele Bachmann, Brendan Eich, *Duck Dynasty*, Chick Fil-A, Bob Newhart, the Catholic Church, bakers, photographers, florists, college professors, black professionals, and countless other messengers, in order to avoid having to deal with the truthful message: gay culture is screwed up. Gay leaders screwed up. Gay people are suffering because of gay people.[55]

The baker that Lopez referred to was Jack Phillips of Masterpiece Cakeshop in Denver, Colorado, who was found guilty of discrimination when he refused to bake a cake for the "wedding" ceremony of two homosexual men. (Other Christian bakers had experienced a similar fate.)[56] That, however, was only the beginning of the story. The court ordered Phillips to undergo sensitivity training, then to report quarterly to the court to demonstrate that he was in compliance with the law.[57] In other words, Phillips must not only violate his conscience and his faith, but he must attend reprogramming classes to correct his wrong thinking. Shades of communist reeducation camps, sans the physical torture and imprisonment.

The baker's attorney addressed the absurdity of the ruling:

Nicolle Martin, an attorney with Alliance Defending Freedom, called the ruling Orwellian and said they are considering an appeal.

"They are turning people of faith into religious refugees," Martin told [journalist Todd Starnes]. "Is this the society that we want to live in—where people of faith are driven out of business?"

Martin said it was "truly frightening" that Phillips will be forced to submit quarterly reports to the government disclosing whether he turned away any wedding cake business.

"There will be some reporting requirements so that Jack can demonstrate that he doesn't exercise his belief system anymore—that he has divested himself of his beliefs," she said.

He will also be required to create new policies and procedures for his staff.

"We consider this reporting to be aimed at rehabilitating Jack so that he has the right thoughts," Martin said. "That's offensive to everything America stands for."[58]

Martin was absolutely right, and I have no doubt that there are millions of Americans who will refuse to submit to the bullying of the thought police. No court has the power—or the right—to strip away our legitimate freedoms. Here too the courts, cheered on by gay activists, have overplayed their hand.

As for Phillips, he has no intention of bowing down to the pressure of the courts, stating, "If a couple were to come in and ask me to do an erotic cake for a wedding, I would refuse to do that as well. These are my personal standards taken from Jesus Christ and the Bible."[59]

Not surprisingly, corporate America is in lockstep with this oppressive overreach, as employees of J.P. Morgan Chase learned when the company's semiannual survey, which was normally fairly benign, contained some unexpected new questions in 2014, including this unlikely sequence:

Are you:

1. A person with disabilities;

2. A person with children with disabilities;

3. A person with a spouse/domestic partner with disabilities;

4. A member of the LGBT community;

5. An ally of the LGBT community, but not personally identifying as LGBT.[60]

Aside from the strangeness of the list (what is the connection between the first three questions and the last two?), what happens if you do not say, "Yes, I'm an ally!"? What is the price of nonconformity?

Influential Princeton professor Robert P. George provides the answer: "The message to all employees is perfectly clear: You are expected to fall into line with the approved and required thinking. Nothing short of assent is acceptable. Silent dissent will no longer be permitted."[61]

Catholic activist Austin Ruse also pointed out

the oddness of actually asking employees about their sexual orientation. Chase Bank actually feels comfortable asking such a question. Talk about your boss occupying your bedroom. Any self-respecting LGBT ought to respond, "none of your damn business."

And then the last question: Are you an ally of the LGBT community?

More than one Chase employee saw that and blanched. They were put into an immediate quandary. Everyone knows answering such a question incorrectly can place your job in jeopardy. Just ask Brendan Eich, short-time CEO of Mozilla, who was bounced because he, like President Obama several years ago, did not support gay marriage. . . .

The question arises: isn't this illegal? The answer is no, not at all. . . .

Can someone be fired for answering the JP Morgan Chase question incorrectly? Certainly, they can. There is very little protection for holding the wrong view on homosexuality unless, that is, your opposition is explicitly based on religious belief.[62] [Not surprisingly, the survey did not ask questions about the employees' religious beliefs.]

Christian legal associations, along with leaders like Professor George, are fighting back against this corporate thought-policing, and while it is extremely unlikely that a company as rich as J.P. Morgan Chase can be intimidated financially—the company "has sales of $105 billion, profits of $17 billion, assets of $2.4 trillion and a market value of $229 billion"—right will eventually triumph over might.[63]

Ruse is also correct in pointing out the difference between the black civil rights movement and the current call for "LGBT rights": "Have you figured out yet that the LGBTs are the most powerful aggrieved minority the world has ever known? Black Americans really were aggrieved: enslaved, not allowed to vote, discriminated against in housing, banking, and much else, hunted down and lynched."[64]

As the LGBT community quickly moves from the bullied to the bullies, let's remember the example of black Americans, who triumphed against all odds by standing up for what was right rather than what was convenient, willing to make real sacrifices to advance the cause of liberty.

YOU SHALL NOT DEBATE

As soon as my book *A Queer Thing Happened to America* came out in March 2011, I offered to debate any of the subjects covered in the book with any qualified spokesperson representing the opposite side. My goal was twofold: first, to debate the relevant issues in a public setting for the sake of the issues themselves; second, to conduct the debates with civility and respect in order to set a tone for dialogue and interaction.

Colleagues of mine in different cities, including radio station managers, pastors, campus workers, and others, began to reach out to their networks, wanting to organize a debate in their region. With consistency, the response they received was the same, especially on the college campuses: "It's not going to happen!"

In one city, a respected black pastor who also served as a professor at a local campus agreed to debate me on the subject of the Bible and homosexuality, but the organizers could not find a single campus willing to host the debate. The schools refused to go near the topic, not because they were afraid to discuss homosexuality—to the contrary, some of them were openly and proudly pro-gay—but because they dared not allow a contrary opinion to be aired in a public setting. Dissent from the prevailing status quo was considered too divisive and disruptive, even in the context of an academic, civil debate between two professors.

In several states, Christian campus groups informed us that there was no way they would touch this issue: they were concerned it would negatively impact their relationship with LGBT students, and they were afraid that by addressing these topics publicly, their status on campus could be threatened. That was a risk they were not willing to take. Yet it is on college campuses where all kinds of ideological debates take place on a daily basis and where professors can hold to some of the wackiest views imaginable. It appears, then, that all manner of dissent and discussion is welcomed *except* dissent against homosexuality.

A Christian ministry in Orlando, Florida, was very interested in finding a campus venue for a debate, but they could not find a campus group willing to sponsor it either. Finally, after every group they contacted declined the invitation to host the debate—including political groups, LGBT groups, and Christian groups—the ministry found a professor at the University of Central Florida who booked a large room in her own name in order to have a venue for the debate. (I was told that for this action she was reprimanded by the university and almost lost her job.)

A professor from another local college, Eric Smaw, said he would be happy to debate me, and we asked him to choose the topic. He proposed "Same-Sex Marriage: Should It Be Legal?" and that's when things got interesting. According to the reports I received, first a gay campus leader tried to shut down the event; then someone in the "diversity" department tried to shut it down; then at least one university vice president recommended it be shut down.

Bear in mind that this is a campus of more than sixty thousand students, meaning that for vice presidents to get involved, the issue must be fairly significant. And recall that in 2008, Floridians voted 62 to 38 percent to pass a marriage amendment, defining marriage as the union of one and one woman. So in that respect, I was taking the legal, popular position. Not so on a college campus!

The day before the debate, there was a conference call involving eleven people—I was not invited to participate in the call—including as many as five vice presidents; the aforementioned gay campus leader and the official from the diversity department; Professor Smaw; the leader of the Christian ministry that had organized the event; and the chief of police for the campus. (Because of the size of the student body, there is actually a campus police department.) After much deliberation, they decided that it would be worse publicity to cancel the debate than to hold it, but they would only allow it to go forward if we paid for four armed officers to be present. (One of the police officers told me they were not concerned with protestors in sympathy with my viewpoint but with those hostile to my viewpoint.)[65]

This is the atmosphere that gay activists have helped create on our campuses, an atmosphere of censorship, suppression of contrary ideas, bullying of opposing viewpoints, and intimidation. Hence, there is a growing list of faculty, students, and staff who have been fired, expelled, or punished for failure to bow the knee to homosexual activism.[66] But we are more than ready for the battle. You can fire us, expel us, or punish us, but we will stand on principle and do what is right. In the long run, we'll be glad we did. *The bullying is backfiring.*

IT'S TIME TO FACE REALITY

Tish Harrison Warren learned the hard way that, in the eyes of a hostile world, you can be moderate and enlightened, but if you hold to the fundamentals of the Christian faith, you will be ostracized. As she wrote in *Christianity Today*, "I thought a winsome faith would win Christians a place at Vanderbilt's table. I was wrong."

"I thought I was an acceptable kind of evangelical," she explained, stating that she was not a fundamentalist and that "[m]y friends and I enjoy art, alcohol, and cultural engagement. We avoid spiritual clichés and buzzwords. We value authenticity, study, racial reconciliation, and social and environmental justice."[67]

Warren had been involved in Graduate Christian Fellowship—a chapter of InterVarsity Christian Fellowship at Tennessee's Vanderbilt University—and her husband was a PhD candidate in the school's religion department when she learned that the Christian Fellowship had been put on probation by the school. Why? Because they required the leaders of their group to be Christian—not the members, but the leaders—which makes perfect sense.

Could you imagine the campus's atheist club being led by a devout Muslim or the Jewish club being led by a devout Christian? Or could you imagine the school's Democrat club being led by a staunch Republican or its LGBT club being led by a conservative activist? (This is actually the decision Vanderbilt made. Anyone can lead anything, other than men leading sororities and women leading fraternities—at least for now.)

The InterVarsity branch had always opened its doors to everyone, but for obvious reasons, as a Christian campus ministry, it required its leaders to be Christians. But these days, simply holding to Christian values on campus can be costly, especially if a professing "gay Christian" challenges your biblically based bylaws.[68] One online petition even accused the widely respected Campus Crusade for Christ (now simply known as CRU) of being a "terrorist" group, calling for their removal from all California campuses. And the petition claims that "they have engaged in and practiced Religious Discrimination."[69]

At Vanderbilt, Warren was sure there had been some kind of misunderstanding and that, with a little dialogue, things would be resolved. She was informed that "during the previous school year, a Christian fraternity had expelled several students for violating their behavior policy. One student said he was ousted because he is gay. Vanderbilt responded by forbidding any belief standards for those wanting to join or lead any campus group." In other words, one student's sexual desires and romantic attractions overrode the ability of a Christian organization to function as a Christian organization.

Warren explained, "The new policy privileged certain belief groups and forbade all others. Religious organizations were welcome as long as they were malleable: as long as their leaders didn't need to profess anything in particular; as long as they could be governed by sheer democracy and adjust to popular mores or trends; as long as they didn't prioritize theological stability."

After an initial, positive meeting with the dean of students, when Warren met with "other administrators, the tone began to change."

The word *discrimination* began to be used—a lot—specifically in regard to creedal requirements. It was lobbed like a grenade to end all argument. Administrators compared Christian students to 1960s segregationists. I once mustered courage to ask them if they truly thought it was fair to equate racial prejudice with asking Bible study leaders to affirm the Resurrection. The vice chancellor replied, "Creedal discrimination is still discrimination."

Feeling battered by these exchanges, she talked with her InterVarsity supervisor. "He responded with a wry smile, 'But we're moderates!' We thought we were nuanced and reasonable. The university seemed to think of us as a threat."

And that's when the light came on for Warren:

For me, it was revolutionary, a reorientation of my place in the university and in culture.

I began to realize that inside the church, the territory between Augustine of Hippo and Jerry Falwell seems vast, and miles lie between Ron Sider [a left-wing evangelical] and Pat Robertson [a right-wing evangelical]. But in the eyes of the university (and much of the press), subscribers to broad Christian orthodoxy occupy the same square foot of cultural space.

The line between good and evil was drawn by two issues: creedal belief and sexual expression. If religious groups required set truths or limited sexual autonomy, they were bad—not just wrong but evil, narrow-minded, and too dangerous to be tolerated on campus.

It didn't matter to them if we were politically or racially diverse, if we cared about the environment or built Habitat homes. It didn't matter if our students were top in their fields and some of the kindest, most thoughtful, most compassionate leaders on campus. There was a line in the sand, and we fell on the wrong side of it.

Within the year, "14 campus religious communities—comprising about 1,400 Catholic, evangelical, and Mormon students—lost their organizational status."[70]

IF YOU'RE STILL SLEEPING, WAKE UP!

It's wake-up time, dear readers. You can fashion yourself a moderate. You can call yourself enlightened. You can join in with critics of "religion" and talk about the hypocrisy of the Church. You can even be an environmentalist and have a really cool blog. But for Vanderbilt University (and, increasingly, other campuses as well), if you hold to the most fundamental tenets of the Christian faith and affirm biblical morality, then you are "not just wrong but evil, narrow-minded, and too dangerous to be tolerated on campus." Do not be deceived![71]

The national climate has changed, and today those who say marriage is the union of one man and one woman are considered bigoted extremists, while those who believe homosexual practice is sin are likened to terrorists. Even Dr. Mel White, a pioneer in the "gay Christian" movement and the founder and leader of Soulforce, an organization that "works to end the political and religious oppression of lesbian, gay, bisexual, transgender, queer and intersex people through relentless nonviolent resistance,"[72] has engaged in similar rhetoric. His writings have moved from his biographical account, *Stranger at the Gate: To Be Gay and Christian in America,*[73] to the openly confrontational *Religion Gone Bad: The Hidden Dangers of the Christian Right.*[74] In fact, in the second, virtually unmodified edition of this book, the title was changed from *Religion Gone Bad* to *Holy Terror* (the subtitle was also changed to *Lies the Christian Right Tells Us to Deny Gay Equality).*[75]

Things have gotten to the point that when the Southern Baptist Convention reaffirmed that same-sex "marriage" was not a civil right (as they were fully expected to do), White wrote an article entitled "Resist Southern Baptist 'Terrorism.'" While not calling for physical violence, he did reiterate the call for another type of aggressive resistance: "I'm a tired old activist from the 20th century. You are 21st-century activists with Internet tools that could be used to launch a powerful new resistance movement. Just don't wait for someone else to do it. Please, for the sake of millions of our sisters and brothers who are victims of holy terrorism, *resist!*"[76]

Yes, this is how you are being viewed if you affirm God's design for marriage. You are a holy terrorist, and you will be *resisted.*

This does not mean that we fight hatred with hatred or that we mistreat those with whom we differ. Perish the thought. (We'll address that in the next chapter.) But it does mean that we wake up to the reality that we are in the midst of an all-out cultural war, and wars are not won through compromise and capitulation.

For Tish Harrison Warren, the difficult experience at Vanderbilt had both a sobering and positive effect. Not only did she recognize the truth about the world's opposition to the Gospel (as Jesus said in John 15:18, "If the world hates you, know that it has hated me before it hated you" [ESV]), but she also recognized that there was no need for panic. As she expressed so articulately, "We need not be afraid; the gospel is as unstoppable as it is unacceptable."[77]

And so, despite losing its campus status, InterVarsity has continued to be involved on the campus, with Christian students sharing their faith in countless ways in the daily life of the school. The good news simply cannot be stopped.

THE LESSON OF NERO AND PAUL

According to reliable tradition, the apostle Paul was beheaded by Nero sometime in the mid-60s AD, and the contrast between the two men could not have been greater. Paul, the lowly prisoner, brought in chains before the great emperor, who was one of the most powerful men in the world. Yet today the memory of Nero is despised while that of Paul is revered.

As Prof. Frank S. Thielman wrote:

> Twenty centuries ago an itinerant tentmaker was tossed into prison
> for creating a public disturbance. [He was speaking of Paul, who was

imprisoned for his preaching, which often drew violent public attack.] There he spent considerable time dictating a letter that might have taken up a dozen sheets of stiff, scratchy paper. Today few people would recognize the name of the Roman emperor at the time, and, although Nero was a prolific author, nothing of his literary output remains. Paul's name, on the other hand, is instantly recognized by millions [really, multiplied hundreds of millions], and existing copies of his [letters] . . . run easily into the millions. Indeed, the time has come, as T. R. Glover observed, when people call their dogs Nero and their sons Paul.[78]

We do well to heed Paul's words: "So then . . . be firm. Do not be moved! Always be outstanding in the work of the Lord, knowing that your labor is not in vain in the Lord" (1 Corinthians 15:58 NET). Or as he wrote in another letter, "let us not grow weary of doing good, for in due season we will reap, if we do not give up" (Galatians 6:9 ESV).

I encourage you to make a fresh determination today: "With God's help, I am not giving up, backing up, backing down, or throwing in the towel. I will do what is right no matter what, living to please God and not people."

If you live like this, you will never have a regret, and in the long run, history will vindicate you and society will thank you.

PRINCIPLE #2

TAKE THE HIGHEST MORAL GROUND

Do not be overcome by evil, but overcome evil with good. —THE APOSTLE PAUL, ROMANS 12:21

When people lie about you, mock you, and vilify you, it's only natural to respond in kind, but by doing so you become the very thing you detest. You also defeat yourself in the process since you have allowed others to drag you down rather than holding your high moral ground or, better still, lifting others up.

Dr. Martin Luther King Jr. once wrote, "Returning hate for hate multiplies hate, adding deeper darkness to a night already devoid of stars. Darkness cannot drive out darkness; only light can do that. Hate cannot drive out hate; only love can do that."

What do we gain by responding to hatred with more hatred? How can we practice love for God and love for our neighbor if there is no love in our hearts? How can we overcome evil if we become evil ourselves?

I know it's frustrating to get slandered and maligned and misrepresented and demonized. It happens to me all the time, with people posting choice comments like this on my social media sites on a regular basis:

- "You are quite possibly one of the stupidest men on the face of Earth, you are no less dangerous than Hitler, and you are a threat to society."

- "He is a [expletive] stupid man."

- "This 'Man' is an ignorant hateful and biased racist. A hypocrite of the highest caliber who should only appeal to those who blindly believe what they are told to and lack the intelligence to research facts and develop ideas and opinions of their own." [Note that I am described as a "man" in quotes.]

- "Brownie boy is one of the most biggest [*sic*] liars known to mankind."

- "Crackpot right wing neo Nazi using the Bible to spread hatred. Jesus was about love not hate."[1]

But every time I see posts like this, I don't feel hate for the haters. Instead, I pity those who make such comments, I ask myself what I can do to reach them more effectively, and I see a picture of what we cannot ever become.

We cannot become the name-callers or the nasty bigots. We cannot become what the critics falsely claim we are (while, ironically, doing the very things they accuse us of doing). We must overcome evil with good, and that means treating our ideological opponents with civility, regardless of how they treat us. But that does not mean we are spineless, indecisive, or hesitant. It simply means we don't use the same ugly tactics that have often been used against us, and under no circumstances do we surrender our integrity. In short, if we want to outlast the current social crisis, we must get to the highest (moral) ground and live there consistently. That's the only way we can rise above the tide.

We must also remember that love is anything but weak; rather, true love is unstoppable and indomitable. As Paul famously wrote, "Love bears all things, believes all things, hopes all things, endures all things" (1 Corinthians 13:7 ESV). If we truly love God and our neighbor, no one can stop us from doing good and standing up for what is right.

EXPOSING THE REAL HATE GROUPS

Several decades ago, the Southern Poverty Law Center became famous for exposing hate groups, especially white supremacist groups, to the point of helping shut down the KKK in the South. And because of their groundbreaking work, the SPLC became an important source of information for American law enforcement agencies, including the FBI, and even for our military intelligence. If the SPLC said an individual or organization was dangerous, that meant a lot, even in public perception. You did not want to get on one of the SPLC's lists.

At that time, their work was highly commendable. Today, however, it has become sadly contemptible, as the SPLC now categorizes as hate groups fine, pro-family, Christian organizations, such as the American Family Association (AFA) and the Family Research Council (FRC).[2] In fact, their work has been so effective that some of you may immediately say, "But they are hate groups."

The SPLC has targeted individuals as well: in 2012, I was placed on the SPLC's list of "30 New Activists Heading Up the Radical Right," along with men like Malik Zulu Shabbaz (then leader of the New Black Panthers), David Duke (a former grand wizard of the Knights of the Ku Klux Klan), Don Black (a Jew-bashing white supremacist), and Morris Gullet (a neo-Nazi).[3]

What did I do to earn a place on a list like this, and what did the AFA and FRC do to make it on the SPLC's hate group list along with some truly vile, genuinely hateful groups? According to the Southern Poverty Law Center, we were guilty of being anti-LGBT, specifically, of disseminating lies and misinformation about the LGBT community. We have been branded as dangerous!

On a personal level, I found their accusations laughable and even flattering. But given the power of the SPLC and the scope of its influence, being on their hit lists is no small thing, since they are equally adept at exposing the guilty as they are at demonizing the innocent. And by denigrating the solid, fair-minded research of conservative Christians whom they vilify, they provide a convenient excuse to others who don't want to evaluate that research or consider the facts presented. After all, why should anyone listen to you if you are on the SPLC's lists of hate groups?[4]

"YOU TELL LIES ABOUT GAY PEOPLE"

To give a typical example, on May 31, 2014, shortly after my book *Can You Be Gay and Christian?* was released, a man named Bryan tweeted out this message: "You tell lies about gay people. It's your business. You're not a messenger of truth."[5] I responded, "Sigh. Repeating gay-based propaganda doesn't change facts,"[6] to which he answered, "You don't have facts or truth, just a fundamentalist faith and antigay money making business," citing an SPLC page attacking me. If the SPLC says so, it must be true!

Interestingly, a Christian colleague named Lyndon went to the page and noticed that the SPLC admitted that "Michael Brown is not typical of most who push the idea that a cabal of liberal media elites have orchestrated a so-called 'homosexual agenda' to indoctrinate children into a lifestyle that makes a mockery of Christian values."[7] Yet I was still demonized and placed on their "dangerous leader" list along with neo-Nazis and anti-Semites. As Lyndon jokingly noted on my Twitter feed, "How ironic that Brown has a Brownophobia page [on SPLC] that says he is above board and generally fair." ("Brownophobia," he said, is "the irrational fear of Dr. Michael Brown, often manifest in irrational argumentation.")

Unfortunately, many others take the SPLC's accusations seriously, resulting in unintentionally hilarious media segments. A case in point is the July 2, 2014, episode of the *David Pakman Show*, where Pakman castigates Fox News for bringing on "a hate group extremist" to "clear up some of the controversy" regarding the Hobby Lobby case in the Supreme Court. And who was this "hate group extremist"? It was none other than Cathy Ruse, senior fellow, Legal Studies, with the Family Research Council, which Pakman categorized as "having incredibly bigoted and hateful views as designated by the Southern Poverty Law Center."[8]

David Pakman was clearly oblivious to the extreme irony of the moment, as he was the one engaging in hate speech when he referred to an upstanding Christian organization as a hate group, singling out Cathy Ruse as an extremist, no less. As for Ruse, according to her official bio, she was

> Chief Counsel to the Constitution Subcommittee in the House of Representatives where she had oversight of civil rights and human rights issues, as well as religious freedom and free speech matters which came before the House.
>
> Mrs. Ruse received her law degree from Georgetown University and a certificate from the National Institute for trial advocacy during her work as a litigator in the District of Columbia. She holds an honorary doctoral degree from Franciscan University of Steubenville.
>
> She has published scholarly legal articles on a variety of constitutional issues, has filed "Friend of the Court" briefs with the U.S. Supreme Court in cases involving abortion, euthanasia, and pornography, and has testified as an expert in congressional hearings in the U.S. House and Senate.[9]

This is just part of the outstanding bio of this alleged "hate group extremist," but we know she's an evil liar. After all, the SPLC says so!

As for the FRC, every year they hold a Values Voter Summit in Washington, DC, which is a major gathering place for conservative leaders. The 2014 event featured speakers such as Israel's prime minister, Benjamin Netanyahu; Dr. Ben Carson of Johns Hopkins fame; former or current governors Rick Perry, Mike Huckabee, and Bobby Jindal (and others); senators Rand Paul, Marco Rubio, and Tim Scott (and more), among many others. That is the respect in which top political leaders hold the FRC, an organization with a fine track record of integrity, yet the SPLC has the gall to call it a "hate group."

This, then, leads to a fascinating question. What if the FRC and AFA and people like me are not the ones guilty of disseminating lies and misinformation about gays and lesbians? What if it is the SPLC that is guilty of disseminating lies and misinformation about conservative

Christian groups and individuals, while conservative Christians (and Jews and others) are disseminating truth? Based on its own criteria, wouldn't that make the SPLC the real hate group?[10] What happens when the real truth gets out?

FOLLOW THE MONEY TRAIL

On March 10, 2014, Catholic leader Austin Ruse (the husband of Cathy Ruse) reported:

> An academic study has accused the Southern Poverty Law Center (SPLC) of having an anti-Christian bias in its reporting on hate groups in America.
>
> Once considered the "gold standard" in reporting on violent anti-government or racist groups in America, the Southern Poverty Law Center's reputation has begun to wither as it has started targeting conservative Christian groups including the Family Research Council (FRC) for what SPLC claims is anti-gay animus. . . .

Prof. George Yancey of the University of North Texas says he is not arguing one way or the other about FRC's inclusion on the list but merely demonstrating SPLC's outrage is subjective and selective, and never reckons progressive groups guilty of the same things of which it accuses conservative ones.[11]

Do the words *hypocritical* and *biased* come to mind?

Worse still, the SPLC is spending a lot of liberal money to mislead America, and Professor Yancey "concludes the reason SPLC cannot or will not change its criteria or at least begin including left-wing groups on its hate lists is that it cannot go against its progressive donors who are sending in such sizable sums—$38.5 million a year, with $256 million in assets feeding $300,000-plus salaries."[12] Does the word *corrupt* come to mind? And isn't it ironic that conservative organizations with minimal funding are accused of spreading lies about gays to make money—this is actually a double lie, since we disseminate truth and don't get rich doing it—and yet the SPLC, along with ultraliberal groups like the ACLU and gay activist groups like the HRC, are bringing in money hand over fist.

Yet it's more serious than that. By defaming groups like the FRC and putting them in the same category as neo-Nazis and white supremacists, the SPLC now has blood on its hands—literally. On August 15, 2012, Floyd Lee Corkins entered the FRC building in Washington, DC, pulled a gun, and wounded a guard, who heroically subdued Corkins before he could carry out his plans, which were to "kill as many employees as possible." The report stated, "He was targeting FRC because of its views, including its opposition to gay marriage." In addition, "Corkins was carrying 15 Chick-fil-A sandwiches that he intended to smear on employees' faces in a political statement, he told the FBI."[13] (We will discuss hateful attacks against Chick-fil-A shortly.)

What does this have to do with the SPLC? Corkins confessed that he learned about the FRC through the SPLC's website, believing that they were, in fact, a dangerous hate group and locating their offices with the help of the SPLC's hate group map. As Corkins explained to his interrogators in an FBI video, "Southern Poverty Law lists anti-gay groups. I found them online, did a little research, went to the website, stuff like that."[14]

Please hear me: the SPLC is not telling you the truth about these conservative Christian organizations and individuals. Instead, they are provoking hatred and fear to the point that they were almost complicit in a mass murder.[15] The reality is that compassionate, family-based Christian organizations are not hate groups. Rather, it is those who demonize them who are hateful, and we cannot respond to their hatred with our own hatred, nor can we defame those who defame us.

YOU CAN'T BE A "HATER" IF YOU DON'T HATE

One of the most pervasive gay activist claims is that anyone who opposes their goals is a hater. As noted by Jeff Jacoby, a conservative columnist with the *Boston Globe*, "Dare to suggest that homosexuality may not be something to celebrate and you instantly are a Nazi. . . . Offer to share your teachings of Christianity or Judaism with students 'struggling with homosexuality' and you become as vile as a Ku Kluxer."[16]

This was the result of a carefully planned gay strategy, as outlined in the late 1980s:

> Our goal is here is twofold. First, we seek to replace the mainstream's self-righteous pride about its homophobia with shame and guilt. [How things have changed since then!] Second, we intend to make the antigays look so nasty that average Americans will want to dissociate themselves from such types.
>
> The public should be shown images of ranting homophobes whose secondary traits and beliefs disgust middle America. These images might include: the Ku Klux Klan demanding that gays be burned alive or castrated; bigoted southern ministers drooling with hysterical hatred to a degree that looks both comical and deranged; menacing punks, thugs, and convicts speaking coolly about the "fags" they have killed or would like to kill; a tour of Nazi concentration camps where homosexuals were tortured and gassed.
>
> A campaign to vilify the victimizers is going to enrage our most fervid enemies, of course. But what else can we say? The shoe fits, and we should make them try it on for size, with all of America watching.[17]

The problem, of course, is that the shoe does not fit, since there are millions of kind, compassionate, reasonable, gentle people who simply feel it is best not to redefine marriage. They believe biological design indicates that men and women were made for each other and that a child should not be willingly deprived of either a mother or father. They are uncomfortable with a man in the ladies' bathroom, and their religious beliefs do not allow them to sanction homosexual relationships.

The truth is that these people are neither haters nor homophobes, neither Nazis nor Klansmen, neither violent nor vile, and at a certain point in time, the lies being told against them will be exposed. Truth will triumph and, ironically, just as many LGBT people did not live up to their exaggerated, negative stereotypes, the same will prove true of those who have been branded as haters by gays and lesbians, but even more so.

DESCRIBING FRIENDLY FAMILIES AS "DESPICABLE BULLIES"

In 2011, after several hundred Christians in Charlotte, North Carolina, engaged in a loving outreach at the city's annual gay pride event, gay activist Wayne Besen wrote an article entitled "Michael Brown Is an Anti-Gay Monster." He claimed that my "game is to try inciting followers to possible violence against LGBT people, while innocently maintaining that he loves homosexuals and simply wants them to meet his militant and perverted version of God." He called me "a slick dude," a "sick and cynical" person with "a messiah complex," and a "diabolical individual who aims to manipulate impressionable followers to launch some sort of holy war," noting, however, that I'm "too much of a coward to start the war" myself. "I . . . strongly believe to my core that Brown's ultimate goal is to create the conditions for a nasty physical clash," he said. "The madman fully understands that he only has to create a hostile climate to inflame the most unstable of his thugs and they will eventually provoke the type of confrontation that this pathological monster deeply desires."[18] These are literal, in-context quotes; I kid you not.[19]

But Wayne wasn't done yet. In a subsequent article he claimed that we "confronted and harassed festival attendees with [our] arrogant slogan 'God Has A Better Way,'" and he referred to us as "despicable bullies" who exhibited "fanatical behavior."[20]

In reality, our group of roughly four hundred participants consisted of grandparents, moms, dads, kids, and college-age singles who, over the course of about one hour, handed out almost twenty-five hundred free bottles of water (labeled "Jesus Loves You") and engaged in civil and respectful conversation with any who cared to talk with us. And to identify ourselves, we wore T-shirts with the words "God Has a Better Way." Since when did this positive message, worn by smiling families handing out water for free, become a symbol of fanatical bullying?

The gay pride event was sponsored by the biggest companies in the city; the mayor himself made an appearance and expressed solidarity with the participants. The local power company lit up its building in lavender to celebrate gay pride. Our group was vastly outnumbered, and there was not a single confrontation or ugly conversation in our time there. In fact, a local gay activist told me privately that our presence there set the "gold standard" for a "Christian protest." And those who actually met any of our friends who participated in the outreach know that Besen was not telling the truth when he called them "thugs" and "despicable bullies."

THE GAY PROTEST THAT ENCOUNTERED "PERFECT LOVE"

In 2012 local police informed us that there was going to be a gay pride protest outside our church building that coming Sunday morning, and the leader of the protest announced on Facebook, "We will meet just before Service begins, and protest as they gather, we will have a silent protest as service is going and let them have it as they leave for the day. Remember we will be peaceful and respectful, something they don't understand. We are going to STAND TOGETHER AS A COMMUNITY to show that our love is stronger than their hate."

In response, I wrote on my blog:

> On behalf of FIRE Church, I want to extend to you the warmest welcome and let you know that we are thrilled that you are here with us on Sunday. We have been praying for you for a long time!
>
> As always, you will only meet with love, kindness, and respect from the FIRE leadership and congregants, and we proclaim to you once again the amazing grace of God. Jesus died to save us from our sins, heterosexual and homosexual alike, and only in Him can we find forgiveness, redemption, and transformation. Jesus alone is the Healer, Savior, Deliverer, and Transformer.

On my radio show, I also encouraged them to come in good numbers so we could greet them, and Scott Volk, then the lead pastor of our congregation, posted a note on a local gay website that had announced the protest, saying:

> As the pastor of FIRE Church, I just want you to know that you'll be greeted with the same love and compassion as we always endeavor to

show anyone—you are more-than-welcome! You make mention of the "hate" that we show. Yet, in all our years here we've only desired to reach out with love to everyone in the local community here whether they are labeled as gay or straight. Hopefully, you'll see that love demonstrated on Sunday as you protest.[21]

On Sunday morning, about ten protesters showed up (we were disappointed there were so few), and some of our congregants met with them, offered them water and snacks, shared God's love and truth, and then invited them to join us in the service. After a few minutes they left, explaining that we were too nice and too loving to deserve a protest!

Bear in mind that these protesters know the stands we have taken for biblical values and some of them have listened to my radio broadcasts or read some of my writings, so they recognize how strongly we differ with them on many key issues. Yet they also recognized our genuine love for them and saw that we were full of kindness, not hate.

The next day the leader of the protest called my radio show to apologize publicly for the protest, explaining that their "anger . . . was aimed [in] the wrong direction." And then he said this: "Once we got there Sunday morning we were greeted with absolutely perfect love. I mean, it was fantastic."

Subsequently, Scott Volk and I invited him and his partner to join us for dinner, the four of us discussing how we could live amicably as neighbors and coworkers in the same city given the depth of our differences. The dinner was as candid as it was cordial, without the slightest hint of anything that remotely resembled hate from any of us at the table, which reinforces the problem created by gay activist rhetoric. The vast, vast majority of us are not bigoted backwoods preachers, let alone Islamic terrorists (more on this charge in a moment).

We simply don't fit the description, and that will be one of the keys to our success, since the more we are demonized, the more the real demonizers will be exposed. Light will always expose darkness, so it's incumbent that we continue to be people of the light, filled with integrity and truth and love.

WHEN CHRISTIANS ARE LIKENED TO ISLAMIC TERRORISTS

Now, you might be wondering where the reference to "Islamic terror-ists" came from just a few lines ago. I experienced this firsthand as well when the local gay newspaper ran a story about me in 2008, replete with a picture of my head photoshopped onto the body of a Muslim terrorist carrying an AK-47.[22] It really was quite hysterical, aside from the fact that some people actually believe this stuff to be true, thinking that conserva-tive followers of Jesus are the Christian equivalent of Islamic jihadists.[23]

An absolutely shocking example of this comes from a city council in Canada, where Chick-fil-A was likened to Boko Haram, the brutal, murderous, Islamic terrorist group in Nigeria that has committed some of the most barbarous atrocities in our times. Not content with butchering innocent victims with knives or with the mass kidnapping of Christian schoolgirls, they have burned schoolchildren alive.

To compare these butchers with any civilized human being is obscene, let alone to compare them to a terrific company known for its consistent Christian values (they are even closed on Sundays), its high customer service ratings, and the pleasant demeanor of its employees. Chick-fil-A is also known for helping communities in times of need, and without any history of employment or customer discrimination based on sexual orien-tation. Their one "transgression" was to donate small amounts of money from their foundation to conservative Christian groups, including one ministry that helped people deal with unwanted same-sex attractions.[24] And for that they were vilified and singled out for attack.

Still, as ugly and unmerited as those attacks have been, including political leaders saying that Chick-fil-A was not welcome in their city and students trying to get Chick-fil-A kicked off their campuses,[25] this city council in Canada went off the deep end entirely. As reported on LifeSite News, "City councilors from Nanaimo, B.C. voted last month to ban a Christian leadership conference scheduled to be podcast at the city's convention centre because one of the sponsors of the conference was U.S. restaurant chain Chick-fil-A. According to one councilor, the chain spreads 'divisiveness, homophobia . . . [and] expressions of hate' because of its CEO's pro-marriage views."[26]

The council's actions were so egregious that a local website was created called TheRealBigots.com, designed to call attention to the council's anti-Christian rhetoric. (Videos of the relevant speeches can be seen there.) As the website explained, "City councillors condemned the event as 'hateful', compared it to the Nigerian terrorist group Boko Haram, and said the decision to ban the event from public property was no different than if they had voted to ban an organized crime ring, too."[27] And the vote was eight-to-one in favor of the ban.

In the same spirit, British gay activist Peter Tatchell issued a "call on people everywhere to stand with us to establish an international front against the religious-Right and for secularism." And what exactly does Tatchell mean by "the religious-Right"? He means "the Islamic State (formerly ISIS), the Saudi regime, Hindutva (Rashtriya Swayamsevak Sangh) in India, the Christian-Right in the U.S. and Europe, Bodu Bala Sena in Sri Lanka, Haredim in Israel, AQMI and MUJAO in Mali, Boko Haram in Nigeria, the Taliban in Afghanistan and Pakistan to the Islamic Republic of Iran and the Islamic Salvation Front in Algeria."

So, conservative Christians in America and Europe are not just like Boko Haram; they are like ISIS too! In response, Christian Institute spokesman Simon Calvert rightly observed that "they're hijacking genuine concern about murderous terrorists to slander evangelicals."[28] Is anyone surprised?

Getting back to the event in Canada, not only was there nothing hateful or homophobic about the event, but some of the speakers included Laura Bush and Desmond Tutu, the former a mild supporter of same-sex "marriage," the latter a strong proponent. Yet this misinformed and misguided city council voted against allowing one of their buildings to be used for a simulcast of the event because Chick-fil-A was one of the sponsors. Talk about anti-Christian bigotry on steroids.

But the strategy backfired, as the backlash against the event and the embarrassment caused by the city council's statements and decision forced the council to reverse their decision. Anti-Christian hatred, based on lies and misinformation, can exist only so long before it collapses on itself.

Yet we must be on guard. When mud is thrown at you, it's easy to throw mud back. When someone calls you a jerk, you're tempted to reply in kind.

"A LITTLE LEAVENS THE WHOLE LUMP"

To underscore how important this issue is, consider what happens when people claiming to be devout believers act in genuinely hateful ways. It makes everyone else look bad. And given the antireligious sentiments of many media leaders, the voices of a few bigots will be amplified and multiplied until they virtually drown out the voices of the large number of truly caring and gracious people who do not affirm homosexual activism.

Think of the late, notorious Fred Phelps and his Westboro Church, infamous for their "God hates fags" protests. If any group is a genuine hate group, it is that one. Here's a sampling of some of their past protests and announcements:

God hates America!

Thank God for IEDs killing American soldiers in strange lands every day. WBC [Westboro Baptist Church] rejoices every time the Lord God in His vengeance kills or maims an American soldier with an Improvised Explosive Device (IED). . . . WBC will picket the funerals of these Godless, fag army American soldiers when their pieces return home. WBC will also picket their landing spot, in Dover, Delaware early and often. . . . Face it, America! You have become a fag-filled nation of flag worshipers and necromancers. Your only terrorist is the Lord your God! He fights against you personally. . . . Bloody butcher Bush thinks he can distract from these facts by taking over Babylon with his fag army. As a result of his foolishness, body bags are coming home by the truckload.[29]

God hates Sweden!

THANK GOD FOR ALL DEAD SWEDES!!! Unconfirmed numbers of Swedes are dead as a result of the tsunamis which ravaged Thailand and the other lush resorts of that region, and thousands more are unaccounted for, either still rotting in the tropical conditions or buried, as they deserve, as asses in mass graves. . . . Scarcely a family in Sweden has been untouched by the devastation. Bible preachers say, THANK GOD for it all![30]

Without qualification or hesitation, I can say that these Westboro protesters are religious bigots of the worst kind (outside of those who actually kill and rape in God's name), and I and every true Christian I know in the world absolutely repudiate these comments and sentiments. Yet because of their venomous hate and the cooperation of the media, this very small group of people has become the face of "Christian" opposition to gay activism.[31] As the old saying goes, "a little leaven leavens the whole lump" (1 Corinthians 5:6 ESV), and so these few bad apples—they are very bad but very few—make millions of good apples look bad.

All the more, then, do we need to dispel these false characterizations by our godly words and conduct, and the more we get called "Fred Phelps"—it happens to me all the time—the more people will see that the description doesn't fit, thereby exposing the real hatred and bigotry.

BACK TO MARTIN LUTHER KING

At the beginning of this chapter, I quoted Dr. King's comment, "Darkness cannot drive out darkness; only light can do that. Hate cannot drive out hate; only love can do that." His quote continued:

Hate multiplies hate, violence multiplies violence, and toughness multiplies toughness in a descending spiral of destruction. So when Jesus says "Love your enemies," he is setting forth a profound and ultimately inescapable admonition. Have we not come to such an impasse in the modern world that we must love our enemies—or else? The chain reaction of evil—hate begetting hate, wars producing wars—must be broken, or we shall be plunged into the dark abyss of annihilation.[32]

The issue is not our right to self-defense, nor was King denying that there was such a thing as a just war. The issue is perpetuating a cycle of hatred, which brings everyone into "a descending spiral of destruction." Yet it is all too easy to deceive ourselves, as if our hatred were different from the hatred of those who vilify us, and to thereby become self-righteous hypocrites, looking down our long, religious noses and heaping scorn on those with whom we differ. When we do this, how are we any better than the haters?

Dr. King quoted the words of Jesus ("Love your enemies"), but the context of Jesus' teaching in what's called the Sermon on the Mount is more radical than just those three words. He said, "You have heard that it was said, 'You shall love your neighbor and hate your enemy.' But I say to you, Love your enemies and pray for those who persecute you, so that you may be sons of your Father who is in heaven. For he makes his sun rise on the evil and on the good, and sends rain on the just and on the unjust" (Matthew 5:43–45 ESV).

Paul offered similar, radical advice to the believers in Rome:

> Repay no one evil for evil, but give thought to do what is honorable in the sight of all. If possible, so far as it depends on you, live peaceably with all. Beloved, never avenge yourselves, but leave it to the wrath of God, for it is written, "Vengeance is mine, I will repay, says the Lord."[33] To the contrary, "if your enemy is hungry, feed him; if he is thirsty, give him something to drink; for by so doing you will heap burning coals on his head."[34] Do not be overcome by evil, but overcome evil with good. (Romans 12:17–21 ESV)

This is quite a tall order, since it completely goes against human nature, but with God, it is possible.

"REACH OUT AND RESIST"

When I first began to address the issue of homosexuality, I was primarily concerned with the agenda of aggressive gay activists. But as I began to read their own stories and better understand their perspectives, taking advantage of face-to-face conversations whenever possible, I became equally concerned for the well-being of the people themselves. This led to the approach of "Reach Out and Resist," meaning, "Reach out to the people with compassion. Resist the agenda with courage." Both compassion and courage are equally needed.

Now, to be honest, I never in my life hated homosexuals (the thought of hating them never once occurred to me), but I certainly had a few misconceptions, and the more I read and I listened, the more I understood and the more my heart broke. That's why there's no hatred toward them on my lips, because there's no hatred for them in my heart. That's why I can't be provoked into hate-filled, degrading comments.[35] There's nothing hateful inside me to provoke.

Unfortunately, by not affirming same-sex "marriage" we're considered hateful. (Looking at things through the eyes of gays and lesbians, I understand why.) And when we say that God didn't make men to be with men and women to be with women, we're vilified as homophobic bigots. So be it. What I will not do, and what we cannot do, is descend into the gutter of name-calling and lying, nor can we soften our stance because we don't want to offend. To repeat: Both compassion and courage are needed, and if we are absolutely sure we are doing what is right and standing for what is right, then compassion and courage fit together like a hand and a glove.

I was reminded of this when reading a best-selling book on healthy eating written by a medical doctor who listed all the health complications caused by obesity, and it was quite a devastating list. Did he write these things because he hates fat people? Perish the thought. He has devoted decades of practice and research to helping obese people reach a healthy weight, and so he can be direct and clear and forthright because he cares. In the same way (without comparing obesity to homosexuality[36]), we can combine love and truth, care and confrontation, compassion and courage.

Let us, then, have hearts of compassion and backbones of steel. We will need both if we are to outlast the gay revolution and be agents of positive change.

PRINCIPLE #3

SEXUAL PURITY TRUMPS
SEXUAL ANARCHY

Purity is the feminine, truth the masculine of honor. —DAVID HARE

here is a biblical principle that everything reproduces after its own kind: fruit trees reproduce fruit trees; cats reproduce cats; dogs reproduce dogs; human beings reproduce human beings.[1] It is the same with our character and way of life: we reproduce what we do and who we are, which is why the children of alcoholics have a much higher chance of becoming alcoholics while those who are abused often end up being abusers.

But there's an interesting variation in this equation. Love, multiplied endlessly, reproduces more love, and truth, multiplied endlessly, reproduces more truth. But hatred, multiplied endlessly, doesn't just reproduce more hatred. It reproduces rage and violence and murder. And lying, multiplied endlessly, doesn't just reproduce more lying. It leads to a lifestyle of deceit, often opening the door for all kinds of criminal acts. In the same way, sexual purity, multiplied endlessly, reproduces more sexual purity, while sexual impurity doesn't just reproduce more sexual impurity. It leads to every kind of imaginable (and even unimaginable) perversion.

That's why sexual purity will outlast and ultimately trump sexual anarchy. The former leads to long-term, stable relationships, to fidelity and loyalty, to physical health and mental wholeness, to thriving families. The latter leads to shattered relationships, to infidelity and mistrust, to STDs and substance abuse, to broken families and broken lives. As Stephen Covey said, "Sow a thought, reap an action; sow an action, reap a habit; sow a habit, reap a character; sow a character, reap a destiny."

"But what does this have to do with homosexuality?" you ask. "After all, there are plenty of committed gay couples and plenty of messed-up heterosexual couples. Plus, the reason our society affirms homosexuality today is because we're more enlightened than past generations."

Hold that thought, and we'll come back to it shortly. Right now I want to take you on a journey through recent history that will help us put today's embrace of homosexuality in context.

1956 WASN'T THAT LONG AGO

The year was 1956, and Russian-born Harvard sociology professor Pitirim Sorokin was concerned. Writing in his book *The American Sex Revolution*, he noted that "divorce, desertion and scandal have ceased to be punished by public ostracism." Worse still, he continued, "many a divorced professor is teaching in our colleges; some of them are even regarded as authorities in the fields of marriage, sexual adjustment and family."[2]

Let those words sink in. Professor Sorokin was concerned that not only were divorce and desertion no longer grounds for exclusion, but colleges were employing divorced professors. And *that* was considered scandalous. What's more, some of those divorced faculty members were even regarded as marriage and family experts. How things have changed!

Nineteen fifty-six was not that long ago (I was born in 1955), but it was obviously long before the path to stardom was having your sex tape released; reality TV shows featured stories about teenage moms and their babies born out of wedlock; middle schoolers engaged in "sexting," ubiquitous porn cams flooded the Internet, and universities hosted plays like *The Vagina Monologues* and held drag queen competitions.

IT'S AMAZING WHAT CAN HAPPEN IN ONE LIFETIME

Ann Coulter discussed some of these changes in an article about the disgraced NBA owner Donald Sterling, noting, "I had listened to roughly eight hours of commentary on Donald Sterling and the ugly remarks he made in conversations secretly tape-recorded by his girlfriend, before I heard anyone mention a wife."[3]

Yes, Sterling was still married to his wife of fifty years, yet his mistress would openly attend his team's basketball games. And the fact that it was his mistress who secretly recorded their phone conversations was virtually a nontopic in the scandal. (The scandal was over remarks he made that were derogatory to black Americans.)

Coulter wrote:

> Cultural mores certainly do change. In 1947, it was a scandal when Brooklyn Dodgers manager Leo Durocher was alleged to have been having an affair with a married actress, Laraine Day.
>
> Durocher himself was not married, but Day, a Mormon who never smoked or drank, divorced her husband and married Durocher the day after being granted a provisional divorce decree. The divorce wasn't final, so the judge who signed the decree ordered Day and Durocher to live separately in California. (Yes, this was so long ago, the institution of marriage was still respected in California.)
>
> And they did. She lived with her mother in Santa Monica and Durocher moved into a nearby hotel.

Can you imagine a scenario like that today, where a judge orders a couple to live in separate locations until a divorce is finalized? On every level, it is unthinkable, and yet not only did it happen; it happened *in California*, home today of the explicit TV show *Californication*.

Coulter continued:

> Yet and still, the Catholic Youth Organization withdrew its support for the Brooklyn Dodgers and advised its members to boycott the team as long as Durocher remained manager.

As CYO director Rev. Vincent J. Powell explained in a letter, Durocher was not the sort of person "we want our youth to idealize and imitate," adding that the CYO could not be "officially associated with a man who presents an example in contradiction to our moral teachings."

Durocher was suspended from the Dodgers for a year, purportedly over some long-standing gambling charges.

And that was in New York City! The reaction might have been a bit rougher in Kansas City, Mo., or Grosse Pointe, Mich.

BUT AREN'T WE MORE SEXUALLY ENLIGHTENED TODAY?

At this point you might still be thinking, "Sure, our country's sexual mores have changed. But in the case of homosexuality, we are more accepting today because we are a more enlightened society." Not so. We are more accepting of homosexuality today because our sexual morals are lower. Put another way, the gay revolution is not the successor of the civil rights movement of the 1960s; it is the successor of the sexual revolution of the 1960s. Getting a grasp on this, we understand where our culture is really headed, helping us recognize that our embrace of homosexuality (even the more committed, less promiscuous kind) is part of our larger descent into sexual anarchy.

The popular explanation is that we are more accepting of homosexuality today because almost all of us know someone who is gay, whereas in the past, with so many gays in the closet, we believed that most (or all) gays were perverted sexual predators, debased deviants of the worst kind. Now that we actually know them—they are our friends, family members, and coworkers—we see that they are no different from anyone else, other than being attracted to the same sex rather than the opposite sex.

And there is some truth to this. Many of us *did* hold to exaggerated and even false views of homosexual men and women, and those views changed when one of our own children came out as gay, or when we found out that Aunt Sally was gay, or when a gay couple moved in next door and proved to be the nicest neighbors we ever had.

But the same thing can be said for other relationships and sexual expressions as well. We all know couples living together out of wedlock, even having kids together out of wedlock, and plenty of them seem like nice, run-of-the-mill people. So fornication and cohabitation seem like no big deal. And extramarital sex is just a way of life in the movies and on TV, further shaping our opinions. Recent polls have even revealed that, little by little, the stigma associated with polygamy is decreasing in America, primarily due to media influence. (For more on the polling data, see page 60–61.) Hey, those folks on *Sister Wives* seem to make a really neat family!

We simply cannot separate our society's acceptance of men having sexual and romantic relationships with other men (and women doing the same with each other) from our acceptance of other forms of sexual immorality. The fact that homosexuality is actually *celebrated* in today's culture is a further indication of our moral decline.

Really now, why celebrate homosexuality and other LGBT expressions? Why are gay teenage boys being nominated as high school prom queens by their classmates? What is there to celebrate with news announcements like this one from Florida: "A Lake County High School student is making a statement, looking to become his school's first *male Homecoming Queen*"?[4] Why is it that a male athlete becomes a national hero and even receives a phone call from the president because he says, "I'm attracted to other men"?[5] The celebration of homosexuality is something that even the most prescient gay activists didn't predict.

In 1987, two influential gay strategists wrote:

> At least in the beginning, we are seeking public desensitization and nothing more. We do not need and cannot expect a full "appreciation" or "understanding" of homosexuality from the average American. You can forget about trying to persuade the masses that homosexuality is a good thing. But if only you can get them to think that it is just another thing, with a shrug of their shoulders, then your battle for legal and social rights is virtually won. And to get to shoulder-shrug stage, gays as a class must cease to appear mysterious, alien, loathsome

and contrary. A large-scale media campaign will be required in order to change the image of gays in America.[6]

These strategists were quite aware of the "gay is good" mantra coined by pioneer activist Frank Kameny in 1968, and the goals they outlined for "the overhauling of straight America" were quite ambitious. But with all their vision and ambition, they still warned, "You can forget about trying to persuade the masses that homosexuality is a good thing." It was just too far-fetched to imagine.

That's why it is so important to understand that homosexuality is not celebrated in today's culture due to an increase in moral tolerance. Rather, it is celebrated due to a decrease in sexual morality. Expressed conversely, it is celebrated due to an increase in immorality. There is no other way to explain this radical societal shift.

THE POLLS PROVE MY POINT

Let me illustrate this with some recent polling data. You will see at once where homosexuality fits in.

On May 30, 2014, Gallup announced, "On a list of 19 major moral issues of the day, Americans express levels of moral acceptance that are as high or higher than in the past on 12 of them, a group that also encompasses social mores such as polygamy, having a child out of wedlock, and divorce." They produced this chart to summarize their findings:

MORAL ACCEPTABILITY Do you believe that, in general, the following are morally acceptable?		
Highly Acceptable	Birth control*	90%
Largely Acceptable	Divorce*	69%
	Sex between an unmarried man and woman*	66%

Largely Acceptable	Medical research using stem cells obtained from human embryos	65%
	Gambling	62%
	The death penalty	61%
	Buying and wearing clothing made of animal fur	58%
	Having a baby outside of marriage*	58%
	Gay or lesbian relations	58%
	Medical testing on animals	57%
Contentious	Doctor-assisted suicide*	52%
	Abortion*	52%
Largely unacceptable	Cloning animals*	34%
	Pornography	33%
	Sex between teenagers	30%
Highly unacceptable	Suicide*	19%
	Polygamy, when a married person has more than one spouse at the same time	14%
	Cloning humans*	13%
	Married men and women having an affair	7%

% Yes, morally acceptable
* Denotes moral acceptability at or near record high

Note that the acceptance of gay and lesbian relationships is actually lower than the acceptance of fornication, described here as sex between an unmarried man and woman.

Another chart, released by Gallup in May 2013, helps us put this into recent, historical context:

CHANGE OVER TIME IN MORAL ACCEPTABILITY
% Morally acceptable

	2001	2013	
	%	%	Change in %
Gay or lesbian relations	40	59	19
Having a baby outside of marriage	45	60	15
Sex between an unmarried man and woman	53	63	10
Divorce	59	68	9
Medical research using stem cells from human embryos	52	60	8
Polygamy	7	14	7

Do you see the significance of this? The same public that now views homosexuality more favorably also views sex outside of marriage more favorably, along with having children outside of marriage and even polygamy. As the 2013 Gallup study explained, "Americans have generally become more tolerant of a series of moral behaviors over the past 10–12 years. This trend is particularly evident in views of gay and lesbian relations and having a baby outside of wedlock."[7]

As reported more fully by Gallup in 2014:

Americans' views on the morality of many of these issues have undergone significant changes over time. For example, acceptance of gay and lesbian relations has swelled from 38% in 2002 to majority support since 2010. Fifty-three percent of Americans in 2001 and 2002 said sex between an unmarried man and woman was morally acceptable, but this year it is among the most widely accepted issues, at 66%. Similarly, fewer than half of Americans in 2002 considered having a baby outside of wedlock morally acceptable, but in the past two years, acceptance has been at or near 60%.

Additionally, a few widely condemned actions, such as polygamy, have become slightly less taboo. Five percent of Americans viewed polygamy as morally acceptable in 2006, but that is now at 14%. The rise could be attributed to polygamist families being the subject of television shows—with the HBO TV show "Big Love" one example—thus removing some of the stigma.[8]

Do you see the point I am making? Our embrace of homosexuality is part and parcel of our larger decline in sexual morality.

THE SURVEY SAYS . . .

Let's dig a little deeper into the 2014 survey and things will be even clearer. According to the poll, Democrats approved of these activities in the following percentages:

- Divorce (78%)

- Sex between an unmarried man and woman (77%)

- Having a baby outside of marriage (72%)

- Gay or lesbian relations (71%)

- Sex between teenagers (33%)

- Polygamy (19%)

- Married men and women having an affair (13%)

In contrast, Republicans approved of these same activities at much lower rates:

- Divorce (60%)

- Sex between an unmarried man and woman (54%)

- Having a baby outside of marriage (40%)

- Gay or lesbian relations (39%)

- Sex between teenagers (23%)

- Polygamy (6%).

- Married men and women having an affair (1%)

Prof. Mark Regnerus found this same trend when surveying professing Christians who supported same-sex "marriage." He wrote, "Churchgoing Christians who support same-sex marriage are more likely to think pornography, cohabitation, hook-ups, adultery, polyamory, and abortion are acceptable."[9] This graph summarizes his findings:

Percentage who "agree" that:	Churchgoing Christians who oppose same-sex marriage	Churchgoing Christians who support same-sex marriage	Population average	Gay and lesbian Christians	Gay and lesbian non-Christians
Viewing porn is ok	4.6%	33.4%	31.4%	57.0%	78.1%
Premarital cohabitation is good	10.9%	37.2%	43.0%	49.7%	74.1%
No-strings sex is ok	5.1%	33.0%	35.0%	49.0%	80.5%
Couples with kids should stay married except if abused	52.5%	33.5%	26.9%	22.9%	18.5%
Marital infidelity is sometimes ok	1.3%	7.5%	7.5%	14.2%	26.9%
It is ok for 3+ adults to live in a sexual relationship	1.2%	15.5%	16.3%	31.9%	57.8%
Abortion rights are good	6.5%	39.1%	37.8%	57.5%	71.7%
Sample size:	2,659	990	15,738	191	233

No matter how you slice the cake, the results are the same: those who are more accepting of sexual immorality are more accepting of homosexuality; those who are less accepting of sexual immorality are less accepting of homosexuality. It doesn't take a rocket scientist to figure this out, and it is hardly a coincidence that the same decade that witnessed the rise of the sexual revolution, culminating in Woodstock in 1969, witnessed the rise of the gay liberation movement, marked by the Stonewall riots of 1969.

With these perspectives in mind, let's look at the state of America in the second decade of the twenty-first century. It is best described as sexual anarchy.

WELCOME TO THE WORLD OF SEXUAL ANARCHY

In April 2010 word that got out that Kendra Wilkinson had a sex tape recorded when she was a teenager. Who is Kendra Wilkinson? She became famous for her nude *Playboy* pictorials and for being part of Hugh Hefner's harem, featured on a reality TV show with some other Hefner playmates. By 2010 she was married to an NFL football player and they had their first child together, so you can see why it was a considerable source of embarrassment for this old sex tape to be released at this time in her life.

Well, not quite. As the Internet tabloids bemoaned the news of the sex tape, it was also revealed that she was doing another nude pictorial shoot—and this after the birth of her first child and as a married woman.

Do you see the moral insanity of this? It's fine for her to become famous as a nude starlet and a member of an old man's harem. And it's fine for her to do a nude photo shoot as a married woman and mother. But how embarrassing for her that an old sex tape had been uncovered and might be released.

As for sex tapes, it appears that as long as you're not married when they're first released, you're in good shape. In fact, they just might make you into a celebrity. Just ask Paris Hilton and Kim Kardashian, among others. As Barbara Walters once said to the Kardashian family (but clearly focusing on Kim), "You don't really act, you don't sing, you don't dance. You don't have any—forgive me—any talent!"

True enough, but she did have a sex tape, after which she had a reality TV show. And, as Kim said to Barbara, "I think it's more of a challenge for you to go on a reality show and get people to fall in love with you for being you. There's more pressure to be famous for being yourself than if you're being a character."[10] Now that is talent.

Sarcasm aside, what kind of society rewards people for releasing videos of themselves having sex with one or more people? In generations past, the shame would have been so great that a person filmed in the act would never show his or her face again in public. Today this is what gets people's faces (and more) in public and makes them into celebrities.

On June 6, 2014, Fox News reported that Playmate of the Year Kennedy Summers was using the $100,000 she received for her nude photo shoot to help pay her way through medical school. (She is reportedly "fluent in three languages and already has a Master's degree in Health Administration.") She wants to become a plastic surgeon to help treat burn victims. But will the *Playboy* spread ultimately hurt her medical career? Not according to SiriusXM host Rich Davis.

First, he says, because she's planning to do plastic surgery rather than pediatrics, her patients will probably not judge her for the nude photos. Instead, they'll use them as a point of reference. More important, "Davis said Summers' *Playboy* spread may be even seen by her future patients as a quaint reminder of a more innocent time." (Yes, *today* is that "more innocent time.")

> "It was months ago we were debating whether it was ok for a girl to be a porn star to pay her way through college. No one is going to care at all," he said. "If you fast-forward ten or 20 years, kids that are growing up now that are teenagers and are in college, they lived in a world where butt-shots on Instagram and Snap chatting nudie photos to their boyfriend or girlfriend is normal. Posing for Playboy is going to be a non-factor."[11]

That really says it all.

FROM DEBASED HETEROSEXUAL ACTS TO POMOSEXUALITY AND POLYAMORY

In these days of sexual anarchy, you can go from being a children's favorite named Hannah Montana to a troubled teenager named Miley Cyrus, posing naked on a wrecking ball for a music video and performing on TV with a giant phallus, and you go from star to superstar overnight. Or you can make tens of millions of dollars as a rap artist, grabbing your crotch as you sing and describing women's body parts in the foulest of terms, with little children mimicking your every word and move.[12]

Actress Lily Tomlin, herself a lesbian, voiced concerns about the music of Beyoncé, claiming, "She's selling a lot of sex to teeny-boppers. If I was a 10-year-old, I would try to emulate her like most 10-year-olds do." Tomlin explained:

> I'm familiar with her image and how incredibly vivacious and sexual she is to watch, so I just chalk it up to the culture. I don't pay any attention to it anymore. . . . The culture is so sexualized with girls and women. I was in a recording studio and a little girl who was about 4 years old was watching TV, and somebody's dancing on the TV in very elaborate sexually overt dance steps and the little girl goes, "Oh, she's hot." I'm thinking, this is a 4-year-old![13]

Yet the same society that celebrates these hypersexual expressions also celebrates homosexuality. In fact, the same article that raised Tomlin's concerns about the selling of sex to young children casually noted that she "married longtime girlfriend Jane Wagner on New Year's Eve [of 2014]." How ironic.

Significantly, the society that embraces homosexuality is the same society that is beginning to embrace pomosexuality (aka pansexuality), meaning having sexual attraction to both sexes, regardless of whether the person identifies as male or female. In other words, anything goes! As videographer and apologist Eric Holmberg notes, pomosexuality "is the real face of the sexual revolution."[14]

In July 2009 *Newsweek* ran a feature article on "relationships with multiple, mutually consenting partners" entitled "Polyamory: The Next

Sexual Revolution?"[15] As noted in the *Newsweek* article, it's "enough to make any monogamist's head spin." Then, in 2012, Showtime launched its *Polyamory: Married & Dating.* (Perhaps if the title hadn't already been used, the show could have been called *One Happy Family*—but with quite a twist on the meaning of "family." This should be carefully distinguished from being "swingers," yet another mark of societal decadence.) And all this, of course, is being touted as a great thing, a celebration of love and freedom, a deliverance from the monotony and constraints of monogamy.

The Showtime promo pulled no punches and made no excuses:

Narrator: The polyamorous lifestyle may shock some. But with American divorce rates hovering around 50 percent, these families are on the front line of a growing revolution in the traditional monogamous relationship.

Michael: I want people to know it's okay to live a life this way, it can be good. Because it is. It's beautiful. We love it.

Jennifer: I want people to know that monogamy isn't the only way.

Vanessa: If it were socially acceptable, I think there would be way more poly people.

Tahl: It feels like how we really should all be living.

Natalia Garcia, director: I really believe that a lot of people are going to watch this show and their jaws are going to drop. And they're also probably going to wonder, Am I poly?

Narrator: Follow two not-so-typical families—

Kamala: Mommy and Daddy are going to ask Jen and Tahl to come and live with us. How would you like that?

Kid: Yeah. I like 'em.

Narrator:—that are changing the way America thinks about love.[16]

Is it any wonder that polyamorists march in gay pride parades and consider themselves the successors to their LGBT predecessors? Is anyone really willing to argue that we are becoming more open to polyamory and pomosexuality for different reasons than we are becoming more open to homosexuality? Can't all of these changes be summed up by the narrator's comment that these different sexual and romantic expressions are "changing the way America thinks about love"? As expressed by polyamory advocate Anita Wagner Illig, "We polyamorists are grateful to our [LGBT] brothers and sisters for blazing the marriage equality trail." She added, "A favorable outcome [in the Supreme Court] for marriage equality is a favorable outcome for multi-partner marriage, because the opposition cannot argue lack of precedent for legalizing marriage for other forms of non-traditional relationships."[17]

Christian news editor Jennifer LeClaire noted:

NBC rolled out a report called *True Believers*, that gets up close and a little too personal with a polyamorous "family" about what it's like to "live with multiple partners without sacrificing the comforts of home." This so-called "family" includes five adults and a 9-year-old girl who believe their lifestyle is completely normal.

Even the NBC reporter who was an instrument of an immoral agenda asked questions like, "How is that not awkward?" . . .

Yes, polyamory is the new darling of an immoral media. I mentioned *The Atlantic* article earlier this year that profiled Diana Adams, who runs a Brooklyn-based legal firm that fights to offer traditional marriage rights to untraditional lovers—and is in a polyamorous relationship. Valentine's Day saw article after article on polyamory and sites like Live Science are working to debunk the myths around polyamory.

But it grows worse. I just learned there's even an app for that! A mobile application called 3nder advertises polyamory in a way I won't repeat.[18]

Yes, there's now an app for "making threesomes easy." And on and on it goes, with a headline on FoxNews.com declaring, "'Naked Dating,' 'Naked and Afraid' and More Showcase Nude TV Trend." The article itself noted that Ryan McCormick, a former TV producer and now media relations specialist at Goldman McCormick PR, "said he suspects the acceptance of these shows relates to Americans' tendency to seek out sexually explicit content. 'We are the most porn-viewing nation in the entire world,' he said."[19]

SEXUAL BURNOUT, PORN, AND STDS

One of my colleagues who has conducted extensive marital and sexual counseling sessions stated that he frequently deals with married couples in their twenties who have sexless relationships, the reason being that they got so burned-out on sexual promiscuity in high school and college that they lost interest in sex altogether. Another experienced sexual addiction counselor told me that young men today often need Viagra to perform sexually because they have become so absorbed with pornography that they are not aroused by real sexual and romantic relationships. And it is these same young people who embrace and even celebrate homosexuality.

Simply stated, a fundamental distinction between heterosexual immorality and all forms of homosexual practice (including more committed gay relationships) just doesn't exist. It's all part of society's immoral (and sometimes amoral) descent.

Here's another report from 2014:

One in four adolescents is likely to acquire a sexually transmitted disease, according to the first ever Youth Sexual Health Plan released by New York State.

. . . The state Department of Health said some 60 percent of high school students in New York state reported they'd had sex by their senior year of high school, and more than 25 percent by their freshman year of high school.

. . . The statistics surrounding STDs in youth from 2012 were scary. Those between the ages of 15 and 24 accounted for 63 percent of reported STDs.

For newly diagnosed cases of HIV, one in five cases affected individuals under 25.[20]

Not surprisingly (but certainly tragically), a 2014 report from the US Centers for Disease Control (CDC) stated, "Gay, bisexual, and other men who have sex with men (MSM) are more severely affected by HIV than any other group in the United States." Worse still, "among all gay and bisexual men, black/African American gay and bisexual men accounted for 10,600 (36%) estimated new HIV infections in 2010. The largest number of new infections among black/African American gay and bisexual men (4,800; 45%) occurred in those aged 13 to 24. From 2008 to 2010 new infections increased 20% among young black/African American gay and bisexual men aged 13 to 24."[21]

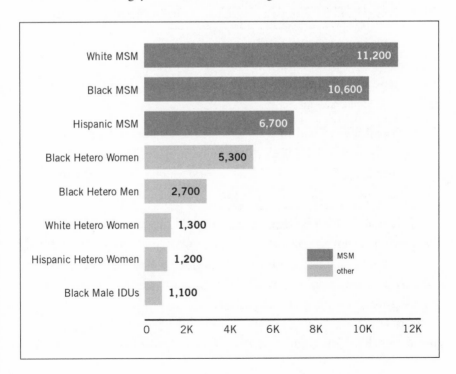

Put whatever spin on this you like, but the conclusions remain the same: young people are accounting for a disproportionately high number of all reported STDs, and of those, young men who have sex with other men account for an even more disproportionately high number of the cases, especially given the fact that male homosexuals account for less than 2 percent of the population. This is some of the lasting fruit of the sexual revolution: a deadly increase in promiscuity, homosexual practice, and sexually transmitted diseases among our youth.[22]

CONDOMS FOR ELEMENTARY SCHOOL CHILDREN?

How have our school systems responded? With sex educations programs like these, as reported by the *New York Post*:

- High-school students go to stores and jot down condom brands, prices and features such as lubrication.

- Teens research a route from school to a clinic that provides birth control and STD tests, and write down its confidentiality policy.

- Kids ages 11 and 12 sort "risk cards" to rate the safety of various activities, including "intercourse using a condom and an oil-based lubricant," mutual masturbation, French kissing, oral sex and anal sex.

- Teens are referred to resources such as Columbia University's Web site Go Ask Alice, which explores topics like "doggie-style" and other positions, "sadomasochistic sex play," phone sex, oral sex with braces, fetishes, porn stars, vibrators and bestiality.[23]

Quite naturally, this same curriculum will present homosexuality as just another sexual option, and to voice any disapproval of homosexual practice would make one guilty of promoting heteronormativity—a grave sin in today's enlightened world. In reality, however, the issue is not enlightenment; it is moral decline.

Is it anything less than sexual anarchy when a sex-ed program announces that "5th grade students—ages 10 and 11—[will] be taught how to use female condoms and lube for both vaginal and anal sex, with an emphasis on longer-lasting intercourse and enhanced sexual pleasure," and that "a photo of a child on a 'Slip N Slide' water toy" accompanies "instructions on how to use lube to facilitate anal penetration"?[24] Or when, in "a very jarring transition," *It's the Great Pumpkin, Charlie Brown* segues directly into a "steamy sex scene" on an adult program?[25] How about when 78 percent of men have viewed pornography by age sixteen, nearly nine in ten of them first viewed it *before* age sixteen, and 17 percent of them first viewed pornography before turning *nine*?[26]

Is it anything less than sexual anarchy when the school board of an *elementary school* in Provincetown, Massachusetts, votes unanimously to begin distributing condoms to the school's kids? This happened in 2010.[27] The condoms were to be distributed upon the student's request, *beginning in the first grade* and without parental knowledge or consent. What possible use could a *six-year-old* have for a condom?

After a public outcry, the school district agreed to consider restricting condom distribution to grades five and up, meaning to kids as young as ten. According to the official policy, "the school nurse is to give counseling and abstinence information to a student prior to handing out the condom," although, again, without parental knowledge or consent.[28] What kind of madness is this?

In Portland, Oregon, a "school district plans to offer condoms to students starting in sixth grade as part of an updated sex education policy aimed at decreasing teen pregnancy, sparking debate over whether 11-year-olds are too young for such a program."

The news article explains:

> The board decided to include middle school students because the middle and high schools are close in proximity and run by the same administration—and because middle school girls are getting pregnant too.
>
> "Every few years, a middle school student either becomes pregnant or is associated with a pregnancy," he said. "The board felt that the curriculum should reach the students of the middle school."

But some question whether sixth graders, who are typically 11 or 12 years old, need condoms.[29]

Can you imagine this subject being discussed in the generations that lived before the sexual revolution of the '60s? Sadly, in the year 2014, the board voted unanimously for the new policy.

In California a June 9, 2014, article announced, "Parents are infuriated after their children were shown 'X-rated' photos as part of a sexual education slideshow at Pine Valley Middle School in California." One of the pictures showed a man with his mouth and face covered in menstrual blood, with the caption, "A real man loves his woman every day of the month." This was shown to middle schoolers.

Dr. Kathy Granger, the superintendent of schools, seemed nonplussed, stating that the curriculum is "factually and medically accurate." She also stated, "We will continue to review materials and collaborate with Mountain Health to ensure that the instruction that is delivered is age appropriate with an emphasis on abstinence as the best way to prevent pregnancy and HIV/Aids infection."[30]

In our culture of sexual anarchy, is it now "age appropriate" to instruct eighth graders on the best ways to prevent pregnancy and STDs? And how, pray tell, does the picture of a grown man with his faced covered in menstrual blood help thirteen- and fourteen-year-old students put an emphasis on abstinence?

Also in California, the Fremont Unified School District "has adopted as part of the ninth-grade curriculum a 'health education' book titled *Your Health Today* that teaches children about sadomasochism, sex toys, masturbation, and orgasms. It doesn't even do so in a tactful manner, showing pictures of sex organs in various states of arousal and describing in detail how to buy and use condoms."[31] This is nothing less than pornography, yet it is part of the *required school curriculum* for ninth graders.

Late in 2012 a high school teacher from New York City called my radio show, wanting me to know that things were far worse in the schools than I could imagine, from the way the kids dress and act to the fact that many of them spend far more time playing terribly violent (and often sexually charged) video games than reading books. He also told me that in his school, there is a table in the hallway with condoms and lubricants. The students can take them freely, as desired. (Other teachers and youth workers have informed me that this is common in many cities throughout America.)

This New York City schoolteacher explained that just a few days earlier, a student put a stack of Gideon Bibles on the table, also for the students to take freely. As a result, there was outrage in the school—outrage over the presence of the Bibles, not the presence of the condoms. The Bibles were promptly removed. This is the environment in which the gay revolution has gained traction, and without such widespread, culturally accepted promiscuity and immorality, homosexual practice would not be accepted, endorsed, or celebrated.

REALITY TV SMUT AND HOLLYWOOD PERVERSION

Consider some of the other reality TV shows for more vivid (too vivid!) examples. One show featured a young woman who identified as bisexual. She and a group of men and women lived together in one big house, and each week she would spend a night with a different man or woman—presumably to have sex—until she decided which one she liked best.[32]

The same audience that smiled on her serial immorality also smiled on her bisexuality, and it is this same audience that is being entertained by all kinds of sexual trash. As noted by cultural commentator Larry Tomczak:

> Growing up with wholesome Westerns you probably enjoyed John Wayne and Gary Cooper or shows like The Lone Ranger, Bonanza, Roy Rogers and others. Hollywood grabs hold of the western genre and gives us a "humorous" spoof. One in theaters now is "A Million Ways to Die in the West."
>
> This movie has 50plus F-words and blasphemes God's name 24 times with obscenities and sexual crudities throughout. There's masturbation, anal and oral sex, bestiality, nudity, defecation, copulation, prostitution, drugs and nonstop profane dialogue.

Serious actor and star of the film, Liam Neeson appeared on the *Today Show* recently and said, "They can't shoot this. They won't be allowed to get away with this! But they did!" Har. Har. Har.[33]

And this is the same Hollywood that so openly and shamelessly celebrates homosexuality. Need I say more?

MILLENNIALS AND MARRIAGE

Looking at this from another angle, it is interesting to note that the millennials, the younger generation that is so much more accepting of homosexuality than the previous generation, is also much less interested in the institution of marriage.[34] According to a 2012 report published by the National Center for Family and Marriage Research at Bowling Green State University, "U.S. marriage rates have reached historic lows in recent years. Since 1970—when about 74 marriages happened annually for every 1,000 unmarried women—the marriage rate declined by nearly 60%, dropping to 31 marriages per 1,000 unmarried women by 2012." Not surprisingly, "the descent is even more pronounced for millennials. In 1960 a little over two-thirds (68 percent) of all 20-somethings were married. In 2008, just 26 percent were hitched, according to the Pew Research Center."[35]

As reported by *Time* magazine on June 17, 2014, "most American women aged 26 to 31 who have children are not married. And the number of these millennial single mothers is increasing. In fact, in a study just released by researchers at Johns Hopkins University, only about a third of all mothers in their late twenties were married."[36]

Chew on those striking statistics for a moment—two-thirds of all babies born to women in their twenties are born out of wedlock—and then remember that this is the same age group that is so supporting of same-sex "marriage." The pattern is clear and undeniable. This younger generation is much more embracing of sex outside of marriage, of having children outside of marriage, and of homosexuality and homosexual "marriage," and much less interested in marriage itself.

What are some of the reasons for this lessening interest in marriage?

According to *Business Insider*, one of them is "Shifting Public Attitudes." The article explains: "Aside from economic factors, people simply feel differently about marriage as an institution today. A notable decline in religiousness could hold the blame for this attitude shift." Fascinating!

Another reason, the article says, for the declining interest is "Contraception Use," a factor that has "made waiting to marry easier for both genders because they could have sex outside of wedlock without worrying as much about getting pregnant."[37] Once again, this should come as no surprise. When sex is trivialized, committed relationships become less and less common while alternative relationships and sexual expressions become more and more common.

The polling data confirm this as well:

- 44 percent of those aged 18–29 "agree marriage is becoming obsolete."

- 46 percent of that same age group believe that "new family arrangements are a good thing."

- 44 percent of those aged 18–29 agree that "children don't need a mother and father to grow up happily."

- 20 percent of those aged 18–29 believe that "more gay/lesbian couples raising children is a good thing."

- When asked, about four in 10 Americans, regardless of age, agreed that "marriage is becoming obsolete," according to a 2010 Pew survey. In a similar poll of voters conducted by *Time* in 1978, only 28 percent felt that way. The divorce rate was also at a near all-time high then too.[38]

WHAT IS BEST FOR SOCIETY?

The obvious questions are: Are these changes in the best interest of a society? What happens when sex and childbirth outside of wedlock become the norm? What happens when sexual immorality is celebrated and committed, lifelong marriages become nearly extinct? (In the next chapter we'll discuss what happens when marriage becomes meaningless.) Commenting on the aforementioned Johns Hopkins study on young women having children out of wedlock, Janice Shaw Crouse, senior fellow at Concerned Women for America's Beverly LaHaye Institute, noted:

> The bottom line of the Johns Hopkins study is that those unmarried parents who live together tend to break up during the very stressful first years of parenting; the enormous growth in this choice by today's young adults gives sad validity to what the sociologists call the "multi-partner fertility" and the popular culture calls multiple "baby mamas." It is long past time for America's opinion leaders to face up to a harsh reality: the liberals' myth that all types of families are equally viable (if only we pour enough money into government programs to support them) has produced a toxic brew of family instability, complex family dynamics, and constant changing household structure leading "to the calcification of social inequality."
>
> That's a fancy way of saying that unwed parenting is disastrous for women and children, and even worse for American society.[39]

As summarized by conservative policy analyst Rachel Sheffield, "Restoring a culture of marriage is crucial to today's generation and to the generations they will raise. The goal for all individuals, families, churches, communities and policymakers should be to give every child—regardless of economic background—the greatest opportunity to be reared by their mother and father in a stable married relationship."[40]

Benjamin Franklin, even without modern-day statistical data-bases, recognized the importance of stable marriages and families. He wrote, "The happy State of Matrimony is, undoubtedly, the surest and most lasting Foundation of Comfort and Love; the Source of all that endearing Tenderness and Affection which arises from Relation and Affinity; . . . the Cause of all good Order in the World, and what alone preserves it from the utmost Confusion; and, to sum up all, the Appointment of infinite Wisdom for these great and good Purposes."[41]

The moral and social chaos we are witnessing in our society today is a vivid illustration of what happens when this "Cause of all good Order in the World" and "what alone preserves it from the utmost Confusion" is assaulted from every side. This means that there is a very real price to pay for sexual anarchy, and as Christian author Philip Yancey noted in 1994, "If we make a god of sexuality, that god will fail in ways that affect the whole person and perhaps the whole society."[42] Yancey based his statement on an important but long-forgotten study by British social anthropologist and ethnologist J. D. Unwin titled *Sex and Culture*, published in 1934.[43]

THE FASCINATING STUDY OF J. D. UNWIN

Yancey gives the background to Unwin's research.

Seeking to test the Freudian notion that civilization is a byproduct of repressed sexuality, the scholar J. D. Unwin studied 86 different societies. His findings startled many scholars—above all, Unwin himself—because all 86 demonstrated a direct tie between monogamy and the "expansive energy" of civilization.

Unwin had no Christian convictions and applied no moral judgment: "I offer no opinion about rightness or wrongness." Nevertheless, he had to conclude, "In human records there is no instance of a society retaining its energy after a complete new generation has inherited a tradition which does not insist on pre-nuptial and post-nuptial continence."[44]

As Unwin explained in 1927, "The whole of human history does not contain a single instance of a group becoming civilized unless it has been absolutely monogamous, nor is there any example of a group retaining its culture after it has adopted less rigorous customs."[45] What an extraordinary observation, especially coming from a scholar who was surprised by his findings. Unwin was anything but a "Bible thumper."

Yancey pointed out that Unwin was not just looking at tribal societies in isolated parts of the world. He was looking at major civilizations that had endured for many centuries: "For Roman, Greek, Sumerian, Moorish, Babylonian, and Anglo-Saxon civilizations, Unwin had several hundred years of history to draw on. He found with no exceptions that these societies flourished during eras that valued sexual fidelity. Inevitably, sexual mores would loosen and the societies would subsequently decline, only to rise again when they returned to more rigid sexual standards."[46]

Right now America is in the midst of a severe decline in sexual mores, hence the celebration of homosexuality, bisexuality, and beyond, which in turn leads to further moral decline. At some point we will experience either cultural collapse or cultural revitalization.[47] If it is the latter—which is where my efforts are being invested—that revitalization will include changed perspectives on homosexuality. At present, the embrace of homosexuality is helping speed our cultural collapse.

WILL THE GAY "MARRIAGE" MODEL CHANGE HETEROSEXUAL MARRIAGE?
Interestingly, a leading gay Jewish intellectual has articulated the connection between homosexuality and marital infidelity, although for him this is actually a positive. I'm speaking of Jay Michaelson, who holds a PhD in Jewish thought from Hebrew University and is presently a visiting scholar at Brown University. He writes that

> the future of marriage, in fact, may turn out to be a lot like the Christian Right's nightmare: a sex-positive, body-affirming compact between two adults that allows for a wide range of intimate and emotional experience. Maybe no one will be the "husband" (as in, animal husbandry) and no one the chattel. Maybe instead of jealousy, non-monogamous couples will cultivate "compersion" to take pleasure in their partners' sexual delight. And most dangerously, maybe marriage will be only one of many forms of such a compact; maybe people will choose their own intimate futures without coercion from the state. The horror![48]

While Michaelson is being sarcastic, for many of us the nightmare he predicts is hardly a laughing matter. He continues:

I do like the notion of same-sex marriage as a liberation gateway drug. Inclusion of LGBT people within institutions like marriage will eventually transform those institutions, just as including women, non-whites, non-Anglos, and non-Christians has done. The experiences and perspectives of LGBT people are different from those of straight people, and different in a good way.

So, if I had to predict, I'd go with a gradual realization of the conservative nightmare—only it won't be a nightmare, and plenty of straight people will thank us for it. Maybe gays will preserve marriage precisely by redefining, expanding, and reforming it—and maybe then it can be palatable to progressives, as one of a multitude of options.

We can entertain these divergent visions of the future because same-sex marriage was really a campaign, not a movement. For a moment, it brought together liberals, progressives, and even some conservatives. *But now that its goal is within sight, the center cannot hold.* And then, things get interesting.[49]

Perhaps "interesting" is not the best word to use. Perhaps "tragically immoral" would be a better description.

Michaelson is absolutely right that "the center cannot hold" and that same-sex "marriage" will serve as "a liberation gateway drug," by which he meant liberation from the bonds of marriage as the lifelong, monogamous union of a man and a woman. This too is an inevitable by-product of the sexual revolution of the '60s, contributing to the increasing sexual anarchy of our society.

CONFIRMATION FROM A HARVARD SOCIOLOGIST

In his magnum opus, *Family and Civilization*, respected Harvard sociologist and historian Carle Zimmerman outlined eight significant indicators of cultural decline. As conveniently summarized on the Institute for Family Studies blog:

- Marriage lost its sacredness; it was frequently broken by divorce.

- Traditional meaning of the marriage ceremony was lost. Alternate forms and definitions of marriage arose, and traditional marriage vows were replaced by individual marriage contracts.

- Feminist movements appeared, and women lost interest in child bearing and mothering, preferring to pursue power and influence.

- Public disrespect for parents and authority in general increased.

- Juvenile delinquency, promiscuity, and rebellion accelerated.

- People with traditional marriages refused to accept family responsibilities.

- Desire for and acceptance of adultery grew.

- Tolerance for sexual perversions of all kinds, particularly homosexuality, increased, with a resultant increase in sex-related crimes.[50]

Does this sound familiar? Unfortunately, yes, it sounds very familiar. But fortunately, we can reverse these trends by emphasizing sexual morality, by esteeming the fundamental importance of marriage, and by ordering our families rightly. The cultural tide can be reversed.

IT'S TIME TO TURN THE TIDE AND REVERSE THE TREND

Things do come in cycles, and this downward trend into sexual anarchy could be the very grounds for the hope for a better future. As noted earlier, Philip Yancey, summarizing the results of J. D. Unwin's study *Sex and Culture*, stated that though "sexual mores would loosen and the societies would subsequently decline," they would "rise again when they returned to more rigid sexual standards."[51]

Today, according to W. Bradley Wilcox, director of the National Marriage Project at the University of Virginia and a senior fellow at the Institute for Family Studies, "the increasingly secular caste of American society has gone hand in hand with a retreat from a family-focused way of life that prioritizes marriage and parenthood. As Americans have become less likely to defer to religious authorities—from the Pope to the pastor—and less likely to darken the door of a church on any given Sunday, they have also become less likely to tie the knot and have that third or fourth child." He demonstrates this with a chart comparing the decline in church attendance in America with the decline in marriages:

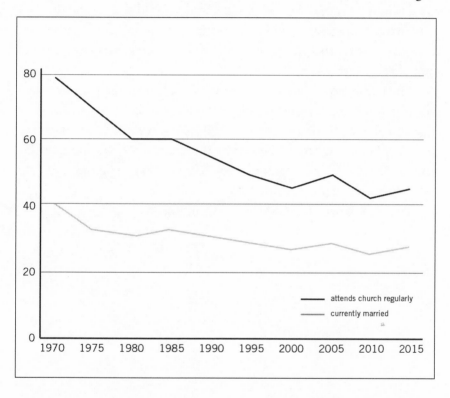

In contrast, Wilcox provides data from fifty-two countries indicating that greater devotion to religion results in more marriages, more solid marriages, and more children per family, noting that "religious traditions also supply family-specific norms, like the importance of marital fidelity, as well as more generic norms, such as the Golden Rule. And they tend to endow these norms with transcendent significance."[52]

This means that the path back to God and biblical foundations—which goes in the exact opposite direction of the path to sexual anarchy—is sexual purity, a greater commitment in marriage, and a greater appreciation for marriage and for stronger, healthier families. And it's a path that each of us can walk as individuals and couples and families, with or without the help of the government. These are choices all of us can make.

Thinking back, then, to Unwin's study, could this be the time for America to rise again? Could it be the time for us to recover the beauty of sexual purity, the power of marital fidelity, and the importance of male-female distinctives?

The bad news is that we cannot continue down the path of sexual anarchy much longer without drastic consequences. The good news is that sexual purity trumps sexual anarchy, and if we will focus on getting our own houses in order, then when the dust settles, we and our kids and grandkids and great-grandkids will be thriving. Then we can help lead our society back to wholeness.

This is how we outlast the gay revolution.[53]

PRINCIPLE #4

REFUSE TO REDEFINE MARRIAGE

Don't ever take a fence down until you know the reason it was put up.
—G. K. CHESTERTON

There is nothing more important for the long-term stability of a society than healthy marriages and healthy families. Healthy marriages will produce healthy families, which in turn will produce a healthy society. Unhealthy marriages will produce unhealthy families, which in turn will produce an unhealthy society. That's why we dare not tamper with the meaning and purpose of marriage. If we do, we tamper with the foundations of society.

Marriage is so foundational to stable societies that even though there have been homosexual men and women through the centuries, and even though some of them engaged in acts of "marriage"—such as Nero "marrying" one of his lovers—there was never a movement to redefine marriage until recent years.[1] And so, despite the presence of all kinds of same-sex relationships over the course of many civilizations, there is no society in recorded history that sought to change the fundamental meaning of marriage.

Consequently, once marriage is fundamentally redefined, it becomes meaningless. Not only that, but basic terms such as *mother* and *father* and *husband* and *wife* become redefined until they too are meaningless. It's like saying that a "couple" can consist of two *or more* people or that a "pair" can consist of two *or more* items. The words become devoid of meaning.

This doesn't mean that there are not very committed same-sex couples or that many of them are not deeply in love. It doesn't mean that they don't want to raise children together. It simply means that no matter how committed and loving they are and no matter how much they're devoted to the kids they raise, their union is not a true marriage (meaning marriage according to its fundamental definition) and it is not a natural marriage (meaning marriage according to our obvious biological design).

That's why we must determine to get our own marriages and families in order—I have often said that no-fault, heterosexual divorce has done more to destroy marriage than all the gay activists combined—and to stand against the redefining of marriage. And that means standing strong even if court cases go against us and even if the Supreme Court rules against us. We're in this for the long haul.

With this in mind, let's take a look at exactly what happens when marriage is redefined.

THE LESBIAN "THROUPLE" AND MUCH, MUCH MORE

Did you hear about the woman who married herself, or the three women who married to form a lesbian "throuple"?

"But that's not marriage," you say. "Marriage is the union of two consenting adults."

Says who? If marriage is not the union of a man and a woman, then why should it be limited to two people (or, for that matter, require two people)? Why can't it be one or three or five? What makes the number two so special if it doesn't refer to the union of a male and a female?

A man and a woman are physically and biologically designed for each other, carrying within themselves the unique components of sperm and egg (the fact remains that there's no such thing as a baby without a male and female involved), and so the two must come together as one to form a marriage. The man and woman also share a unique complementarity emotionally and spiritually—haven't you heard the saying men are from Mars, and women are from Venus?[2] —which is why the union of a man and woman is special, distinctive, and even sacred. And that's why the union of a man and a woman has been recognized as a marriage throughout the ages.

As cultural analyst Robert Knight remarked, "The term 'marriage' refers specifically to the joining of two people of the opposite sex. When that is lost, 'marriage' becomes meaningless. You can no more leave an entire sex out of marriage and call it 'marriage' than you can leave chocolate out of a 'chocolate brownie' recipe. It becomes something else."[3] And when it becomes "something" else, it can become virtually *anything* else.

Really now, how does one limit the possibilities of "marriage" once the concept is fundamentally redefined? Why can't someone "marry" himself or herself? And why can't "marriage" consist of the union of any number or combination of people?

To quote Knight again, "Giving non-marital relationships the same status as marriage does not expand the definition of marriage; it destroys it. For example, if you declare that wine should be labeled identically to grape juice because they have similar properties, you have destroyed the definitions of both 'wine' and 'grape juice.' The consumer would not know what he is getting."[4]

For years now I have been asking the same question to defenders of same-sex "marriage"—namely, if marriage is not the union of a man and a woman, why should it be limited to two people?—and to this day I have not received a single coherent answer. And so, just as $1 + 1 = 2$ is math, not spelling, while *C-A-T* spells *cat* is spelling, not math, so also marriage, by its intrinsic and historic definition, is the union of a man and a woman, not the union of any two people. Consequently, once you redefine marriage, you render it meaningless.

Almost everyone recognized this until very recently, including Hillary Clinton. Not only did she oppose redefining marriage while campaigning as a presidential nominee in 2008, but in 2000, while affirming that homosexual couples should be able to share government and health benefits as married couples do, she could still say, "Marriage has got historic, religious and moral content that goes back to the beginning of time, and I think a marriage is as a marriage has always been, between a man and a woman."[5] Similarly, in 2004 Barack Obama stated, "My religious faith dictates marriage is between a man and a woman, gay marriage is not a civil right"; while in 2008 he opined, "I believe marriage is the union between a man and a woman. As a Christian it's also a sacred union."[6]

As demonstrated in the previous chapter, in today's climate of growing sexual anarchy, the institution of marriage has become less and less important, while rampant no-fault divorce has rendered it flimsy and disposable. But at what cost to future generations?

THE DISINTEGRATION OF MARRIAGE MEANS THE DISINTEGRATION OF THE FUTURE

Peter Hitchens, a British journalist and author, commented on the current situation in the UK in the aftermath of the liberalizing of divorce laws there, but not before reminding his readers how widely accepted these changes were when the laws were first passed. He wrote:

> In every family, every workplace, every school, every pub, every weekend football or cricket team, every political party, every church congregation, there are now large numbers of people who signed up for the Great Cultural and Moral Revolution which was launched in the 1960s and swept through the land like a mighty rushing wind in the 1970s.
>
> The fiery heart of this was the Divorce Law Reform Act of 1969. This change was very popular. . . . Portrayed at the time as a kindness to those trapped in loveless marriages, the new law made it much easier to end a troubled union than to fight to save it.
>
> And once this had become general, marriage changed with amazing speed from a lifelong commitment into a lifestyle choice. . . .
>
> Men began to calculate that marriage wasn't worth it. And the Pill and easy abortion (other parts of the 1960s revolution) put an end to shotgun weddings.

And what are the results today? (Hitchens wrote this in 2013.)

By the end of his or her childhood, a British boy or girl is much more likely to have a TV set in the bedroom than a father at home.

Our 45-year national war against traditional family life has been so successful that almost 50% of 15-year-olds no longer live with both their parents.

He continues:

The cost of our wild, unprecedented national experiment in fatherlessness is now £49 billion each year, more than the defence budget. . . .

Four in ten children being brought up by their mothers—nearly 1.2 million—have no contact with their fathers at all. . . .

Young people from fractured homes are statistically twice as likely to have behaviour problems as those from stable households. They are more likely to be depressed, to abuse drugs or alcohol, to do badly at school, and end up living in relative poverty.

Girls with absent fathers (according to studies in the USA and New Zealand) have teenage pregnancy rates seven or eight times as high as those whose fathers have stayed in meaningful touch with them.

By contrast, the link between marriage and good health is so strong that one study showed the health gain achieved by marrying was as great as that received from giving up smoking.[7]

There are massive societal consequences to tampering with marriage and downplaying the importance of motherhood and fatherhood. And we're not just talking about statistics here. We're talking about people—a whole generation of people. What happens when we go one step further and actually redefine marriage?

BRIDES AND BROOMS, MALE WIVES AND FEMALE HUSBANDS
Prof. N. T. Wright, considered one of the world's top theologians, discussed the serious consequences of changing the fundamental meaning of critical words:

When anybody—pressure groups, governments, civilizations—suddenly change the meaning of key words, you really should watch out. If you go to a German dictionary and just open at random, you may well see several German words which have a little square bracket saying "N.S.," meaning National Socialist or Nazi. The Nazis gave those words a certain meaning. In post-1917 Russia, there were whole categories of people who were called "former persons," because by the Communist diktat they had ceased to be relevant for the state, and once you call them former persons it was extremely easy to ship them off somewhere and have them killed.

When it comes to redefining marriage, Professor Wright explained, "It's like a government voting that black should be white. Sorry, you can vote that if you like, you can pass it by a total majority, but it isn't actually going to change the reality."[8]

That's why we now have cases of a woman "marrying" herself and of three women "marrying" each other, not to mention a whole set of other "marriages," including a woman who "married" her dog, another who "married" a snake, a third woman who "married" a building, and a man who wants to "marry" his computer.[9]

"But that's absolutely crazy," you say. "A person cannot marry an animal or an inanimate object."

Exactly. Neither can a man "marry" a man nor a woman "marry" a woman. Otherwise, words have no meaning at all. As I pointed out in an article in 2013:

> As England moves towards redefining marriage, the *Daily Telegraph* reports that, "The word 'husband' will in future be applied to women and the word 'wife' will refer to men, the Government has decided." According to John Bingham, "Civil servants have overruled the Oxford English Dictionary and hundreds years of common usage effectively abolishing the traditional meaning of the words for spouses."
>
> In the government's proposed guidelines, "'husband' here will include a man or a woman in a same sex marriage, as well as a man

married to a woman. In a similar way, 'wife' will include a woman married to another woman or a man married to a man."

So, a man could be a wife if married to another man (or not), while a woman could be a husband if married to another woman (or not), all of which begs the question: Why use words at all if they have utterly lost their meaning? It's like saying that up is down (or up) and down is up (or down), while north is south (or north) and south is north (or south).

But this is what happens when marriage is redefined.[10]

On August 12, 2010, CNN.com described this somewhat unique "wedding" scene:

> Kirsten Ott walked down the aisle in a white strapless gown with an embroidered bodice and cascading ruffles. Maria Palladino, dressed in a white suit, waited for her at the end of the aisle with a minister. Surrounded by their family and close friends, the women committed to each other for the rest of their lives.
>
> A beautiful reception followed. It had all the makings of a traditional wedding, but instead of calling themselves bride and groom, the couple used the terms bride and "broom."[11]

But of course! How could it be a "traditional wedding" when there were two brides rather than a bride and a groom? (Note also that one of the women wore a gown and the other pants.) That's why this couple was pronounced "bride and broom," underscoring the point that their union, no matter how loving and sincere, could not rightly be described as "marriage" without radically defining the word. (Who ever thought that being called a "broom" would be positive?)

And always leading the way, in July 2014, California passed legislation removing the words *husband* and *wife* from state laws. "California's same-sex couples may now be pronounced spouse and spouse after Gov. Jerry Brown (D) signed a bill Monday eliminating outdated 'husband and wife' references from state laws." Yes, "Senate Bill 1306 was introduced by state Sen. Mark Leno (D-San Francisco) to eliminate confusion and correct discriminatory phrasing in the California Constitution that contradicts state law."[12]

This is an improvement? Pronouncing a couple "spouse and spouse" *eliminates* "confusion"? Has there been a corporate hijacking of our moral sensibility?

On May 5, 2014, I tweeted out this message: "Note to the human race: Regardless of what society says, a man cannot have a husband and a woman cannot have a wife." In response, a man with the Twitter handle "Flying Free" responded mockingly, "Note to the human race. I am a digusting [*sic*] bigot and religion made me this way, ban religion." In other words, only disgusting, bigoted people, brainwashed by religion, would think that a man cannot have a husband and a woman cannot have a wife.

That's how far our society has degenerated in its thinking, and that's how meaningless words have become. And that's why I tweeted later that same day, "Further note to the human race: Despite changes introduced in the UK, a man cannot be a wife or a woman a husband." This too is considered religious bigotry by many today. What in the world is coming next?

WELCOME TO A QUEER NEW WORLD

Actually, we don't have to speculate. It's already here. In fact, it's been here for some time. As I noted in 2011:

> In Ontario, Canada, as a result of the legalization of same-sex marriage, all references to terms like husband, wife, and widow were removed from the law books in 2005. In Spain, birth certificates were changed from "Father" and "Mother" to "Progenitor A" and "Progenitor B," while in America, the State Department made this startling announcement on January 7, 2011:
>
> The words "mother" and "father" will be removed from U.S. passport applications and replaced with gender neutral terminology, the State Department says.
>
> "The words in the old form were 'mother' and 'father,'" said Brenda Sprague, deputy assistant Secretary of State for Passport Services. "They are now 'parent one' and 'parent two.'"

A statement on the State Department website noted: "These improvements are being made to provide a gender neutral description of a child's parents and in recognition of different types of families."[13]

This is what happens when marriage is redefined. You end up with male wives and female husbands, with brooms and throuples, and with parent one and parent two rather than father and mother. You even end up with parents one, two, and sometimes three. As reported by Reuters on February 7, 2013, "A Florida judge has approved the adoption of a 22-month-old baby girl that will list three people as parents on her birth certificate—a married lesbian couple and a gay man."[14]

One year later, on February 11, 2014, the *Huffington Post* reported:

A Vancouver newborn has become the first child in British Columbia, Canada, to have three parents listed on an official birth certificate.

Della Wolf Kangro Wiley Richards is the 3-month-old daughter of a married lesbian couple and their male friend. British Columbia's Family Law Act, which went into effect in March 2013, makes their unique situation possible. The measure allows a child to have three or more legal parents, as long as such a situation is in the best interest of the child.[15]

Note carefully those words "three *or more* legal parents," meaning that the sky is the limit. This puts a whole new meaning on the phrase "Who's your daddy?"

Yet it gets worse. According to a bill passed in the California Assembly in May 2014 (and by a vote of 51 to 13, at that), women can be designated as the "father" on birth certificates while men can be designated as "mother." What was the reason for such an insane piece of legislation? To "modernize" the "definition of the family to reflect same-sex unions."

As explained by the bill's sponsor, Jimmy Gomez, "The definition of a family needs to be more flexible, and same-sex parents should not be discriminated against when filling out a birth certificate. Under AB 1951, same-sex parents will be able to accurately identify each parent as mother, father or parent."[16]

Accurately? A woman—*only* a lesbian, according to the bill—can be Daddy, and a man—*only* a homosexual man, of course—can be Mommy . . . and that is what a more "flexible" definition of family looks like. This is nothing less than social madness.[17]

And so, not only is *marriage* rendered completely ambiguous; not only are the terms *husband* and *wife* emptied of their significance; but now even *father* and *mother* have taken on new (and ridiculous) meanings, making the words absolutely meaningless.

In September 2014 it was announced that two heterosexual men in Australia were going to get "married" since they wanted to win tickets to the Rugby World Cup as a couple. Gay activists were horrified over this. One of them, Alex Greenwich, said, "It essentially makes a mockery of marriage. Marriage is a really important institution about love and commitment and it's sad to see that there are people who are making a joke out of that."[18] He obviously did not realize the irony of his statement.

WHY NOT MARRY YOURSELF?

As for the woman who married herself, Nadine Schweigert, she explained to journalist Anderson Cooper after her "wedding" ceremony in May 2012, "I feel very empowered, very happy, very joyous. . . . I want to share that with people, and also the people that were in attendance, it's a form of accountability. . . . I was waiting for someone to come along and make me happy. At some point, a friend said, 'Why do you need someone to marry you to be happy? Marry yourself.'"[19]

Well, why not? If there can be same-sex "marriage," why can't there be self-"marriage"? As crazy as this sounds, it's happening. An audience member watching the Cooper interview decided that now she wanted to "marry" herself. A thirty-year-old Taiwanese woman "married" herself in 2010, and in 2014, a British woman did the same, with headlines announcing, "Woman Gets Fed Up with Being Single—and Marries Herself!" Why? Because "she didn't have enough time for a 'conventional' relationship."[20]

By the way, isn't it telling that Anderson Cooper's article on

Nadine Schweigert ended with, "What do you think? Is it too much?"[21]

WHAT'S WRONG WITH THREE?

Then there's that lesbian "throuple." According to the *New York Post*, all three wore traditional white wedding gowns at their ceremony, and two of their dads walked them down the aisle. Now "married," the women "sleep together in the same bed, and have sex as a threesome—as well as in pairs." Sadly, adding insult to injury, this very same article's headline, dated April 23, 2014, announced, "Married Lesbian 'Throuple' Expecting First Child."[22]

Was there any LGBT condemnation of this new variation of marriage? After all, gay activists have told us for years that they had no intention of changing the number of those who could marry each other but only the makeup of the couple getting married. Yet now, when we conservatives are watching our slippery-slope predictions fulfilled before our eyes and "marriages" with multiple partners are becoming more common, those same gay activists are strangely silent.

A few years ago, Crystal Tomkins wrote a children's book titled *Oh the Things Mommies Do! What Could Be Better Than Having Two?* with illustrations by her "wife" Lindsey Evans.[23] Perhaps she can write a new book for the child of this lesbian trio since the little one will have three mommies. (Presumably, and tragically, the child will have no connection with the father, an anonymous sperm donor.) Perhaps she could title it, *My Mommies Bring Me So Much Glee! What Could Be Better Than Having Three?* (While we're at it, how about, *Mommies, Mommies, More and More! What Could Be Better Than Having Four?*)

I'm sure that plenty of these lesbian moms are amazing mothers and are devoted to their kids. I'm simply observing that when marriage is redefined, everything related to it must be redefined as well, even to the point of absurdity. "Marriage" can refer to the union of one person, two persons, three persons, or more, while a child can have one parent, which *may* be a female father or a male mother; two parents, both of whom are mothers (or fathers); or three or more legal parents, whether two moms and a dad (or more) or two dads and a mom (or more; in the case of the lesbian "throuple," perhaps three moms and no dad).

This is not a poor joke (how I wish it were). It is an assault on the foundations of human society, not to mention an assault on reason. Marriage either means something very specific, as it has throughout human history, or it can mean virtually anything.[24]

MARRYING YOUR BOX TURTLE?

There is actually a gay watchdog website called BoxTurtleBulletin.com that took its name from this famous (or infamous) comment attributed to Sen. John Cornyn: "It does not affect your daily life very much if your neighbor marries a box turtle. But that does not mean it is right. . . . Now you must raise your children up in a world where that union of man and box turtle is on the same legal footing as man and wife."[25]

In reality, Senator Cornyn never made these remarks. They had been written by a staffer, but the senator dropped them from his speech before delivering it. The original text of the speech, however, got into the hands of a reporter, who filed the article containing this quote.

Yet as Jim Burroway, editor of the *Box Turtle Bulletin*, pointed out all the way back in 2006, the box turtle comments were hardly unique, and he provided the following examples to prove it:

- Bill O'Reilly, interacting pointedly with a guest said: "The people who want to marry a duck can come in, all right. . . . If I want to marry a duck . . . I have a right to marry the duck, alright? . . . And leave my house to a duck."

- In another context, O'Reilly opined: "Somebody's gonna come in and say, 'I wanna marry the goat.' You'll see it; I guarantee you'll see it."

- Sen. Rick Santorum, describing marriage as being between a man and a woman, explained: "It's not, you know, man on child, man on dog, or whatever the case may be."

- Rev. Jimmy Swaggart stated that politicians who supported

redefining marriage "all oughta have to marry a pig and live with him forever."

People marrying ducks, goats, dogs, and pigs? For a literate gay activist like Burroway, this kind of talk only makes the conservative side look foolish. Moreover, as he noted, "since we're really only talking about consenting adults who want to marry each other, comments like these are also irrelevant."

But even Burroway's statement, intended to limit "marriage" to the union of human beings only, opens the door wide to all kinds of abuses. First, by speaking of "consenting adults" without qualifying the number involved, he would have to allow for polygamous unions along with "throuples" and even "quadrouples." Second, if he and his fellow gay activists were "really only talking about consenting adults," that description would have to include adult siblings (or even parents and their adult children), especially two brothers or two sisters, since they could not produce offspring, thereby removing the possibility of genetic defects. (Come to think of it, that could work for a father and his adult son or a mother and her adult daughter, as grotesque as that sounds.)

MARRIAGE EQUALITY "FOR ALL" AND THE "RIGHT" TO INCEST

Not surprisingly, the *Full Marriage Equality* blog advocates for "the right of consenting adults to share and enjoy love, sex, residence, and marriage without limits on the gender, number, or relation of participants. Full marriage equality is a basic human right."[26] There you have it!

At least this website is consistent in using the term *marriage equality*. After all, if "love is love" (as President Obama tweeted when the Supreme Court overturned DOMA on June 26, 2013), and if I have the right to *marry* whomever I love, who can put "limits on the gender, number, or relation" of those lovers as long as they are "consenting adults"? In the words of Monique Pongracic-Speier of the Civil Liberties Association of Canada, "Consenting adults have the right—the Charter protected right—to form the families that they want to form"—and she was advocating for the "right" to polygamy under Canadian law.[27] Why not?

Already in 2007, *Time* magazine raised the question, "Should Incest Be Legal?" The article noted that critics of the Supreme Court's *Lawrence v. Texas* ruling in 2003, which struck down Texas's anti-sodomy law, argued that the ruling would lead to attempts to legalize same-sex "marriage" and polygamy. "It turns out that the critics were right," *Time* observed, adding that plaintiffs were now "using *Lawrence* to challenge laws against incest."[28]

In December 2010, when Columbia University professor David Epstein was arrested for a three-year, consensual affair with his adult daughter, his attorney noted, "It's OK for homosexuals to do whatever they want in their own home. How is this so different? We have to figure out why some behavior is tolerated and some is not." Not surprisingly, some Columbia students asked why any sexual acts committed by consenting adults should be considered a crime.[29] It only follows, then, that any union of consenting adults could be considered "marriage."

According to a July 10, 2014, report from Sydney,

> Judge Garry Neilson, from the district court in the state of New South Wales, likened incest to homosexuality, which was once regarded as criminal and "unnatural" but is now widely accepted.
>
> He said incest was now only a crime because it may lead to abnormalities in offspring but this rationale was increasingly irrelevant because of the availability of contraception and abortion.
>
> "A jury might find nothing untoward in the advance of a brother towards his sister once she had sexually matured, had sexual relationships with other men and was now 'available', not having [a] sexual partner," the judge said.
>
> "If this was the 1950s and you had a jury of 12 men there, which is what you'd invariably have, they would say it's unnatural for a man to be interested in another man or a man being interested in a boy. Those things have gone."

Yes, now that those other social taboos have disappeared—just as I point out in principle 8 on sexual anarchy—why should there be a taboo on consensual, adult incestuous relationships? As the judge said, "we've come a long way from the 1950s—when the position of the English Common Law was that sex outside marriage was not lawful."[30] We have come a long way indeed! Of course, the judge's comments drew outraged responses, but his reasoning, as morally reprehensible as it is, is quite logical given the spirit of the age.

In fact, fewer than four months after the Australian judge made his outrageous comments, the State of New York ruled unanimously that an uncle and niece could be "married." As the *New York Post* reported on October 29, 2014, "The state's highest court has toppled a cultural taboo—legalizing a degree of incest, at least between an uncle and niece—in a unanimous ruling. While the laws against 'parent-child and brother-sister marriages . . . are grounded in the almost universal horror with which such marriages are viewed . . . there is no comparably strong objection to uncle-niece marriages,' [the] ruling reads."[31]

This ruling raises the immediate question, what happens when there is *not* an "almost universal horror" toward "parent-child and brother-sister marriages" in our culture? After all, it wasn't that long ago that the idea of two men or two women "marrying" was viewed with "almost universal horror." If that's the only standard of measurement, what happens when that standard changes?

THE MEDIA'S CELEBRATION OF INCEST

It is not surprising, then, that the same media (and society) that celebrate homosexuality and all kinds of transgender expressions are also beginning to celebrate incest. Consider the following, recent examples:

- In May 2010, Salon.com ran an article on "Gay Porn's Most Shocking Taboo," namely, "Twincest." As expressed by one of the twins, "My brother is my boyfriend, and I am his boyfriend."[32]

- On January 15, 2015, *New York Magazine* featured an upbeat article entitled "What It's Like to Date Your Dad," adorned with a picture of an older man walking off with a younger woman as they held hands. Without a hint of condemnation—actually, there is more justification and even celebration—the article tells the story of "an 18-year-old woman from the Great Lakes region [who] describes her romantic relationship of almost two years with the biological father she met after 12 years of estrangement." She lost her virginity to him—by her explicit choice—and they plan to marry with a formal wedding ceremony.[33]

- In February 2013, Emily Yoffe (aka Prudence, from the "Dear Prudence" advice column) encouraged male fraternal twins who had been living together as lovers to continue doing what worked best for them.[34]

- Promoting his 2013 movie *Yellow*, which features an adult incestuous relationship, director Nick Cassavetes said, "We had heard a few stories where brothers and sisters were completely, absolutely in love with one another. You know what? This whole movie is about judgment, and lack of it, and doing what you want."[35]

- The popular TV series *Game of Thrones* features an incestuous couple (brother and sister) who not only have children together but who also have sex next to the corpse of one of their children after he dies.[36]

- Media analyst Brent Bozell wrote about a new MTV show called *Happyland*, noting, "The female star of the show, actress Bianca Santos, announced the new MTV motto: 'Incest is hot, and we're going to have fun!'"[37]

This is not just being driven by the media. In September 2014, "a government-backed committee in Germany has recommended that the government abolish laws criminalizing incest between siblings, arguing that such bans impinge upon citizens' rights to sexual self-determination. According to findings from the German Ethics Council, that right is a 'fundamental' one, and carries more weight than society's 'abstract protection of the family.'"[38]

Yes, these are the conclusions of a panel of top German ethicists. Need I say more?

And is it any coincidence that the October 9, 2014, article "Should Incest Between Consenting Adult Siblings Be Legalized? Experts Sound Off" was posted in the *Huffpost Gay Voices* section? Jesse Bering, author of *Perv: The Sexual Deviant in All of Us*, explained, "I suppose I take an unpopular view that it's actually moral progress. There are certain caveats that we need to include with our analysis of whether incest is wrong or right, but for me, the biggest point is a matter of harm."

He then referenced Elijah and Milo Peters, "two Czech-born brothers who have performed in gay adult scenes with each other," noting, "The fact that they're violating this . . . taboo notion of your brother or your sister being completely off-limits from a sexual perspective, I think, attracts . . . a large contingency of the viewing public."[39]

Really? Or perhaps we shouldn't be surprised that people already viewing porn (in this case gay porn) are allegedly even more aroused knowing that these are brothers having sex with each other?

Bering added, "It's a carnival-esque affair, but it's actual sexual arousing to us because it probably taps into something, whether we want to admit it or not, deeply unconscious about the possible patterns of attraction to . . . our relatives."

This is sick, but not surprising. That's why I wasn't the least bit surprised when a new website, DebateOut.com (carrying the banner "News for Our Generation"), contacted me about participating in a written debate on whether consensual adult incest should be legal, noting that this was a "hot topic" among young people today. Predictably, out of the five participants in the debate, I was the only one who said that consensual adult incest should remain prohibited by law.[40]

POLYGAMY, POLYAMORY, AND "OPEN" MARRIAGES

It's just not incest that is being celebrated on TV and in the movies and the media. How about shows like *Big Love*, *Sister Wives*, and *My Five Wives*? It looks like polygamy is coming into its own now too. In fact, some members of the *Sister Wives* cast challenged the laws in their home state of Utah, arguing that the prohibition against polygamy was unconstitutional. The judge agreed in part, striking down an important part of the law.[41]

In keeping with the new attitude toward polygamy, feminist Jillian Keenan wrote an article entitled "Legalize Polygamy!" in which she noted:

> Recently, Tony Perkins of the Family Research Council reintroduced a tired refrain: Legalized gay marriage could lead to other legal forms of marriage disaster, such as polygamy. Rick Santorum, Bill O'Reilly, and other social conservatives have made similar claims. It's hardly a new prediction—we've been hearing it for years. *Gay marriage is a slippery slope! A gateway drug! If we legalize it, then what's next? Legalized polygamy?*
>
> We can only hope. . . .
>
> So let's fight for marriage equality until it extends to every same-sex couple in the United States—and then let's keep fighting. We're not done yet.[42]

But of course!

And let's not forget about polyamory, discussed in the previous chapter and glamorized in a new reality TV show called *Polyamory: Married & Dating. Newsweek* reported on this phenomenon in 2009 with an article entitled "Polyamory: The Next Sexual Revolution." The article began, "Only You. And You. And You. Polyamory—relationships with multiple, mutually consenting partners—has a coming-out party." And *Newsweek* actually claimed that there were more than half a million polyamorous households in America.[43] Today some are making the claim that multiple, fluid relationships like this are in the best interest of the kids as well.[44]

There's also the push toward being *monogamish*, to use the term championed by Dan Savage. He argues that monogamy is one of the big reasons for marital unhappiness and even divorce, since it's just not natural for two people to be together for life without having other partners along the way. True to form, in 2013, Savage and his "husband," Terry Miller, freely admitted to having at least nine different sexual partners since they became a couple, which is in keeping with other gay couples who advocate "open marriage."[45]

And it's just not homosexual couples advocating infidelity. Writing for the *Huffington Post* on May 5, 2014, Lisa Haisha asked, "Is It Time to Change Our Views of Adultery and Marriage?" She wrote:

> With today's rate of divorce between 40 and 50 percent, coupled with the prevalence of adultery in many marriages, perhaps it's time for the concept of marriage to continue to evolve. According to Associated Press, Journal of Marital and Family Therapy, 41 percent of spouses admit to infidelity, either physical or emotional. This leads me to ask, "Are we really supposed to be with just one person our whole life? And if not, must we get re-married five times? Are there alternative ways to perceive and participate in a marriage that will guarantee its success?"
>
> Since marriage has evolved so much over the ages, and different cultures have different views of it even today, perhaps it's time for the age-old institution to evolve yet again. Maybe the tenets of a successful marriage should not be whether the couple stays monogamous for decades, but rather whether the couple openly communicates about what their unique marriage will look like, what will be deemed acceptable and what will not, and then honoring that joint decision.[46]

WHAT, THEN, IS MARRIAGE?

All of these radical redefinitions of marriage naturally lead to the question, what, then, is meant by *marriage*? Most couples today have sex before they're married (not to mention having sex with other partners before they were with their present partner); many couples now live together before they're married, with quite a few having children before they're married as well; once married, some advocate "open marriage" or being "monogamish" or "swinging"; and as soon as they tire of each other or have too many conflicts, they get divorced. So what in the world is marriage?

For several decades, marriage has become less and less relevant, being torn asunder and trivialized from every side. In fact, in several Scandinavian countries, most couples live together outside of wedlock, which produces further instability for the children born into such households, not to mention a decline in children born overall.[47]

But now that marriage is being fundamentally redefined, the term (and institution) becomes practically meaningless, to the point that we are hearing more and more examples of people "marrying" animals and inanimate objects. After all, if marriage can be redefined to mean the union of two (same-sex) or more (or less) people, why can't it also mean the union of a person and a _____ (fill in the blank)? If a woman can be a "husband," and a man can be a "wife," then why can't a truck or a tricycle or a household pet be a "husband" or "wife"? If it's all about love anyway, why not marry a dolphin, as Sharon Tendler did, or your cat, as Uwe Mitzscherlich did?[48] (The list goes on and on.) One website lists "13 People Who Married Inanimate Objects," including Amy Wolfe Weber, who is "married" to a roller coaster, and Erika Eiffel, who "married"—you guessed it—the Eiffel tower.[49]

And then there's the man who is fighting for the legal right to "marry" his computer. One report stated, "Man sues for the right to marry his porn-laden Macbook, arguing that if gays are allowed to marry then so should other sexual minorities." As argued by Chris Sevier, the man in question, if gays have the right to "marry their object of sexual desire, even if they lack corresponding sexual parts, then I should have the right to marry my preferred sexual object."[50]

You might question the sanity of some of these people, but what cannot be questioned is that once you redefine marriage, it can soon mean almost anything, which then renders it meaning*less*. And when marriage becomes meaningless, society quickly unravels.

WHEN MARRIAGE UNRAVELS, SOCIETY SUFFERS

Earlier in this chapter, I cited Peter Hitchens's comments about the disastrous effects of fatherlessness in England. Here in America, cultural apologist Dr. Frank Turek pointed out that children from fatherless homes are

- seven times more likely to live in poverty;

- six times more likely to commit suicide;

- more than twice as likely to commit crime;

- more than twice as likely to become pregnant out of wedlock;

- worse off academically and socially;

- worse off physically and emotionally when they reach adulthood.

He also observed that children from fatherless homes account for

- 60 percent of America's rapists;

- 63 percent of America's youth suicides;

- 70 percent of America's long-term prison inmates;

- 70 percent of America's reform school attendees;

- 71 percent of America's teenage pregnancies;

- 71 percent of America's high school dropouts;

- 72 percent of America's adolescent murderers;

- 85 percent of America's youth prisoners;

- 85 percent of America's youth with behavioral disorders;

- 90 percent of America's runaways.[51]

What will kids from motherless homes look like, especially given the fact that, generally speaking, relationships between homosexual men are much less stable than heterosexual unions? The words of founding father John Adams have never been more relevant:

It is by the female world that the greatest and best characters among men are formed. I have long been of this opinion to such a degree that when I hear of an extraordinary man, good or bad, I naturally or habitually inquire who was his mother? There can be nothing in life more honorable for a woman than to contribute by her virtues, her advice, her example, or her address, to the formation of a husband, a brother, or a son to be useful to the world.[52]

Kids raised in motherless homes will not be able to answer the question, "Who is my mother?" Some will not even understand exactly what a mother does and exactly *why* mothers are so special.

And what about kids raised in polyamorous homes? What will happen with this massive, unprecedented social experiment? How do kids even learn how normal male-female relationships work, including husband-wife, mother-daughter and father-daughter, and father-son and mother-son? And what about the kids whose dads are anonymous sperm donors? (Remember that every kid raised in a same-sex household is robbed of a normal relationship with either his mother or father, and that by the choice of the people raising him.)[53]

The next time you have a few minutes, get online and watch some of the old family shows like *Father Knows Best* or *Leave It to Beaver* or *The Adventures of Ozzie and Harriet*, none of which were meant as parodies of a nonexistent, idealist American family but rather as shows that the whole family could enjoy together. Then ask yourself, as distant as that world seems to us today, which model produced more societal stability, more innocence, more trust, more devotion, more loyalty—the old one, with the committed mom and dad raising their own kids together, or our current model, with families fractured by divorce, with fatherless or motherless homes, and with our "anything goes" (really, "everything goes") mentality?

THE CHILDREN OF SPERM DONORS

In 2010 Elizabeth Marquardt and a team of family scholars produced a deeply disturbing 140-page report entitled *My Daddy's Name is*

Donor: A New Study of Young Adults Conceived Through Sperm Donation.
According to the report,

> on average, young adults conceived through sperm donation are
> hurting more, are more confused, and feel more isolated from their
> families. They fare worse than their peers raised by biological par-
> ents on important outcomes such as depression, delinquency and
> substance abuse. Nearly two-thirds agree, "My sperm donor is half
> of who I am." . . . More than half say that when they see someone
> who resembles them they wonder if they are related. Almost as many
> say they have feared being attracted to or having sexual relations with
> someone to whom they are unknowingly related.[54]

This poem, entitled "Uncertainty Is Killing Me," just one of many
on the AnonymousUs.org website, gives us the grown child's perspective. Do we dare to stop, read, and listen?

> Who are you?
>
> Will I pass you in the street?
>
> Will you hold the door for me and smile as I walk into a gas station
> during my travels?
>
> Will you look at me and wonder if I belong to you?
>
> You have the pleasure of knowing I could be here.
>
> For nineteen years, I was denied of knowing you even existed.
>
>
> What was MY grandmother, YOUR mother like?
>
> What about MY grandfather, YOUR father?
>
> Why do you get to selfishly keep them all to yourself?
>
>
> Who are you to deny me half of my family tree—
>
> Branches rich and strong with stories I may never be told?

Who are you to give away my heritage, knowing it will be replaced with something false?

Do I have brothers and sisters with my dark hair, my deep brown eyes?

Will I be attracted to a familiar stranger in my classes?

Will I fall in love with him and kiss him passionately in an act of accidental incest?

Have you told your wife?

Have you told your partner?

What about your children?

Have you told your brothers and sisters about their mysterious niece?

Are you dead?

Will you ever read this?

Have you dismissed it as something in your past that you did to make ends meet?

Did they pay you to give me away?

What did you spend the money on?

Did you buy a sparkly necklace for your ex-girlfriend?

Did you buy books?

(The bank you went to would have paid you half of my College Algebra book for the donation that included me).

Did you buy a candy bar at a gas station?

Was I worth it?

Do you miss me?

Do you ever think of me?

Do I even cross your mind?

Does the uncertainty drive you crazy?

Was it worth it?

Do you wonder when my birthday is?

What color gown I wore to my graduation?

Would you be proud to know I was the Valedictorian of my senior class?

Would you support that I am Christian?

Would you even want me in your life?

I want you in mine.

I will accept anything about you, if I could just get the privilege of knowing who you are, of knowing who my family is.[55]

This poem becomes all the more relevant when we realize that a disproportionate number of babies born to same-sex couples (specifically lesbians) involve anonymous sperm donors. So, by design, there is a whole generation of what some have dubbed "queer spawn" being brought into the world.[56] Do we really think there will be no negative effects on these kids? On the flip side, babies born to gay male couples are separated from their mothers shortly after birth and then, as a general rule, live without a mother for the rest of their lives. Is this right, fair, or even natural?

Some kids are actually the product of donor embryos, meaning that they cannot connect to either their biological mother or father. (This is different from the situation of most adopted children, who can potentially trace their mother, if not mother and father. Here, the history virtually doesn't exist.) One such child, Gracie Crane, now a teenager in England, said, "There are times I've wished I'd never been born—as much as I love my [adoptive] parents, it's just so sad not knowing who I am and where I came from."[57]

And there are other issues as well. According to a 2008 story from Australia,

> One of South Australia's foremost experts in reproductive technology—Andrew Dutney—said that in one reported case, about 30 lesbians were impregnated by sperm from one man, the Advertiser reported.
>
> The mothers then organised picnics with all the children, raising the fear they might socialise with their half-siblings without realising they were related.
>
> In another case, a man's sperm was used to produce 29 children, most of whom were living in Adelaide.
>
> They did not know who their half-siblings are, raising concerns that in a "big country town" like Adelaide, they could accidentally commit incest.[58]

This, in turn, leads to even more tragic consequences and recommendations, as in October 2014: "A Danish professor of criminal justice ethics has stated that he thinks consensual sex between adult siblings should be legal." Why?

> According to Thomas Søbirk Petersen, a professor at Roskilde University, the rise in the number of births resulting from donor sperm, which has the potential to create biological siblings who are born into different families, has created a need to rethink the "old taboos" against incest.
>
> "In a society where more and more children are being conceived using donor sperm, the risk of falling in love with a stranger who turns out to be a biological sister or brother has increased," Petersen told MetroXpress.
>
> Petersen said he believes that siblings who want to have children together can reduce the risk of having a handicapped child by

themselves using donor sperm or eggs—and then there is always abortion as a backup.[59]

Something is terribly wrong with this picture, but it is yet another by-product of the radical redefinition of marriage.

DEFINING MARRIAGE

In 1828 the *Noah Webster Dictionary* defined *marriage* as "the act of uniting a man and woman for life; wedlock; the legal union of a man and woman for life." In 2014 the *Merriam-Webster Dictionary* offered these definitions: "the relationship that exists between a husband and a wife; a similar relationship between people of the same sex; a ceremony in which two people are married to each other."[60]

How long will it be before the number two is dropped from the definition? And how long will it be before the dictionary has to note that the husband could be a woman and the wife a man, or that the "relationship exists between two *or more* husbands and two *or more* wives"? Notice also that there's no mention of the union being "lifelong" in the new (and surely not improved) definition.

Perhaps we should change the wedding vows to sound more like this (with the man speaking here): "I take you as my wife, but probably not for life. I take you as my own, but not just you alone. I pledge myself to you, and perhaps to others too. I take you as my bride, although your name is Clyde."

Is this really so far-fetched? If you can have a bride and a "broom," if "husbands" can be women and "wives" can be men, if you can be "married" and dating and swinging and swapping, if you live together before marriage and end the marriage whenever it suits you best, then what does marriage mean?

Sociologists have underscored the importance of marriage and family for the long-term stability of a culture,[61] and Robert Knight has noted that "marriage is of such importance that it is given special status in the law and culture. It predates the law and the Constitution, and is an anthropological and sociological reality, not primarily a legal one.

No civilization can survive without it, and those societies that allowed it to become irrelevant have faded into history."[62] Do we really want to tamper with something as foundational as marriage?

WHY GAY ACTIVISTS WANT TO REDEFINE MARRIAGE

Almost twenty years ago, gay journalist Andrew Sullivan wrote, "If nothing else were done at all and gay marriage were legalized, ninety percent of the political work necessary to achieve gay and lesbian equality will have been achieved. It's ultimately the only reform that matters."[63] Exactly!

In 1996 gay leader Michelangelo Signorile said that same-sex "marriage" is "a chance to wholly transform the definition of family in American culture. It is the final tool with which to dismantle all sodomy statutes, get education about homosexuality and AIDS into public schools, and, in short, usher in a sea change in how society views and treats us."[64] A sea change indeed.

According to Tom Stoddard, quoted in a task force report for the mayor of San Francisco in June 1990, "Extending the right to marry to gay people—that is, abolishing the traditional gender requirements of marriage—can be one of the means, perhaps the principal one, through which the institution divests itself of the sexist trappings of the past."[65] And divested of those "sexist trappings," it is divested of meaning.

That is why, as much as it depends on us, we must refuse to redefine marriage, even if it means stepping down from a job, as six magistrates did in North Carolina after an activist judge overturned the vote of the people and legalized same-sex "marriage." These magistrates resigned rather than perform wedding ceremonies that were not really marriages, suffering personal loss to avoid contradicting lifelong convictions.[66] Even in our communication, we must not capitulate to gay activism, which is why I encourage other writers and journalists to place the word *marriage* in quotes when referring to gay "marriage." It is not to demean the people but rather to recognize that marriage is only the union of a man and a woman.

To put this in an even larger context, researcher Judith Levine, whom Knight described as "pro-homosexual and pro-pedophile," stated:

> Because American marriage is inextricable from Christianity, it admits participants as Noah let animals onto the ark. But it doesn't have to be that way. In 1972 the National Coalition of Gay Organizations demanded the "repeal of all legislative provisions that restrict the sex or number of persons entering into a marriage unit; and the extension of legal benefits to all persons who cohabit regardless of sex or numbers." Would polygamy invite abuse of child brides, as feminists in Muslim countries and prosecutors in Mormon Utah charge? No. Group marriage could comprise any combination of genders.[67]

Similar quotes could easily be multiplied, but what is undeniable is that once you alter one of the two fundamental, irreplaceable components of marriage, namely, a man and a woman, you fundamentally alter its structure, just as changing one of the components of H_2O (hydrogen and oxygen) renders it into something else, something that will not sustain life.

Ironically, for many years now, conservative thinkers who warned of this descent down the slippery slope were assured that our dire predictions would never be fulfilled.[68] Looking back (and immediately ahead), we see not only that they were fulfilled with striking accuracy but that the slide has been even quicker and steeper than expected, meaning that a societal crash could be near at hand.

WHY MARRIAGE MUST NOT BE REDEFINED

This is yet another reason why the gay revolution will have a hard time enduring through the generations. We can only go on so long with male "brides" and female "fathers," with people "marrying" themselves (or inanimate objects) and three women "marrying" each other. At some point, social sanity will return, and those who have honored true marriage—I mean real, God-ordained, natural, organic marriage—functioning as healthy families with solid male-female role models will show the world the way it's really done. That means that, while standing against the redefinition of marriage, we have a sacred task set before us: making our marriages and families the very best they can be. The lasting rewards are as wonderful as the process itself.

In his famous book *Democracy in America*, Alexis de Tocqueville, the French statesman, historian, and social philosopher, shared his observations about America in the 1830s. He had this to say about marriage and family:

> America is certainly the country where the bonds of marriage are most respected and where the concept of conjugal bliss has its highest and truest expression. In Europe, almost all social disorder stems from disturbances at home and not far removed from the marriage bed. These men come to feel scorn for natural ties and legitimate pleasures. There they develop a liking for disorder, a restless spirit, and fluctuating desires . . . the American draws the love of order from his home which he then carries over into his affairs of state.[69]

Solid and stable marriages make for solid and stable families, which in turn make for solid and stable communities, resulting in a solid and stable nation. Let us give ourselves to the task of rebuilding America one marriage and family at a time. If enough of us do it together, with the help of God, we could spark a whole new revolution.

PRINCIPLE #5

CELEBRATE GENDER DISTINCTIONS

I am Adam. I am Eve. I am me. —TRANSGENDER MODEL CARMEN CARRERA, BORN CHRISTOPHER ROMAN

A s fundamental as marriage is to every society, there is something even more fundamental, namely, male-female distinctions. These distinctions go back to the beginning of our existence as human beings, as stated in the very first chapter of the very first book of the Bible: "So God created man in His own image; He created him in the image of God; He created them male and female" (Genesis 1:27 HCSB).[1] That is why, regardless of the culture, nationality, ethnicity, or skin color, every society has men and women, husbands and wives, sons and daughters, boys and girls. This is another reason why the gay revolution stands on very tenuous ground: it is rendering gender meaningless.

I do realize that there are genuine exceptions to the clear male-female pattern, such as the very rare cases of children born with ambiguous sexual organs or individuals with abnormal chromosomal patterns. I also realize that there are others who are biologically and genetically male or female but are convinced that they were born in the wrong body. I am personally moved when I see or hear the story of, say, a little girl who believed she was a boy and was terribly depressed until her parents began to treat her like a boy, at which point the child came alive.

All these people deserve our compassion and understanding, and we should do whatever we can do to help them find true wholeness, ideally from the inside out. But that does not mean that we look at gender as the enemy or that we seek to eradicate gender distinctions or that we overturn the rights of males and females for the sake of those who identify as transgender or that we make the exception into the rule.

There are blind people in the world, but we don't require everyone to use braille. There are deaf people too, but we don't require everyone to use sign language. But when it comes to the war on gender—a direct result of LGBT activism—the vast majority of people must conform to the needs of the very, very few. And so, a boy who identifies as a girl can use the girls' bathroom in many schools, regardless of how this impacts all the girls and regardless of their parents' concerns, and a teacher must refer to all the children as "friends" rather than "boys and girls" so as not to make a gender distinction.

In Lincoln, Nebraska, a "'gender inclusive' school district" wants to drop terms like "boys and girls" and instead call kids something else, even "purple penguins." A handout for teachers in the Lincoln Public Schools states, "Don't use phrases such as 'boys and girls,' 'you guys,' 'ladies and gentlemen,' and similarly gendered expressions to get kids' attention." As Todd Starnes reported, "The handout was part of an effort to educate teachers and administrators about transgender issues,"[2] meaning again that all the schools must be completely overhauled because of the struggles of a few. How in the world did this happen?

Christin Scarlett Milloy, described as a "human rights activist," went as far as stating that we were doing a terrible disservice to our children by saying, "It's a girl!" or "It's a boy!" at birth. (The article was titled "Don't Let the Doctor Do This to Your Newborn.") Milloy wrote, "Infant gender assignment is a wilful decision, and as a maturing society we need to judge whether it might be a wrong action. Why must we force this on kids at birth? . . . Think carefully. Infant gender assignment might just be Russian roulette with your baby's life."[3]

HOW FAR CAN TRANSGENDER GO?

Not that long ago, gay activists were reluctant to include the *T* word (*transgender*) in the legislation known as ENDA (the Employment Non-Discrimination Act) for fear that it would prejudice lawmakers against their cause.[4] Today, just a few short years later, you are labeled "transphobic" if you have a problem with a boy playing on the girls' softball team or if you object to a male Girl Scout or if you think it's bizarre for a bearded drag queen to win the Eurovision singing contest. Even gay activist Dan Savage, who is totally committed to the LGBT cause, was accused of being "transphobic."[5]

Before you think I'm exaggerating or making a mountain out of a molehill, consider this program that aired on NPR on July 16, 2013, titled "Young People Push Back Against Gender Categories."[6] The show description reads, "As society has become more accepting of gays, lesbians and even transgender people, a new generation of young people is challenging those categories in favor of a more fluid understanding of gender. They refuse to be limited by notions like male and female."

Notice that this is tied directly (and correctly) to the success of the gay agenda. Note also that this is a direct assault on the societal foundations of "male and female." The younger generation is pushing back!

FROM HE/HIM AND SHE/HER TO ZE, ZIM, AND ZIR

The NPR host Audie Cornish introduces the show by explaining, "Americans are becoming more accepting of gays and lesbians and, in some cases, transgendered people. At the same time, a new generation of young people is challenging our understanding of gender. They're calling for more fluid categories beyond just male and female, as NPR's Margot Adler explains."

Adler then shares the experience that opened her eyes:

> It began with a speaking event at Oberlin College in Ohio. I was at dinner with the college chaplain and 16 students on his interfaith council. I was startled when everyone introduced themselves saying their name, what year they were, what they were studying and then

described their preferred gender pronouns. I wasn't taping but it sounded similar to these high school students introducing themselves to me recently in New York.

This was not just one person that Adler encountered; it was sixteen, each of them announcing which gender pronouns they preferred for themselves. A female might have said, "I prefer to be called she/her," or "he/him," or perhaps "ze/zim." And Adler said she had encountered this before, among high school students.

"I admit my first reaction was it felt cult-like," she reported, "and I thought, these people are paying $50,000 a year for college and this is what they care about most—what pronouns you use? When during my college days we were fighting for civil rights, registering voters in Mississippi and facing tear gas and fire hoses. But then I stopped and thought about it."

She then realized that this was their way of standing up for and identifying with transgender individuals, who are often the targets of violence. As Carl Siliciano, another broadcast participant, explained, "It's just so abundantly clear to me that trans kids face an enormously disproportionate burden of the bigotry and the hostility and the hatred that's directed against the LGBT community."

Yet it's more than simply identifying with an abused minority. Adler said that "the fascinating thing with this generation in high school and college is they are going way beyond transgender. They are arguing for a world beyond the gender binary—beyond male and female. And it's something that many people over 30, like myself, are totally unaware of."

What exactly does this "world beyond the gender binary" look like? According to Joy Ladin, described as "a transwoman, a male to female transgender person" and also part of the NPR panel, things have moved way behind simply feeling like a woman trapped in a man's body (or vice versa): "The folks who are cutting edge and exciting, they're gender fluid, they're gender complicated, they're gender queer. They have some kind of much more dynamic relation. But if you are a transsexual, like you just want to relocate yourself from one side of the gender binary to the other. I don't want to blow up the gender binary."

So the younger generation, the ones who are "cutting edge and exciting," want to "blow up the gender binary" (meaning male and female). They are "gender fluid . . . gender complicated . . . [and] gender queer." Is there any limit to where this can go once the categories of male and female are completely "blown up"? The obvious answer is no.

Adler explained that Ladin "went to a Jewish women's retreat; anyone who defined themselves as a woman was welcome—genetic women, trans women. But some of the younger people were uncomfortable. They wanted to get rid of the word woman altogether." Are you beginning to see what I mean when I refer to the war on gender and to LGBT activism making gender meaningless?

Can a society last long and flourish when words and concepts such as *male* and *female*, *man* and *woman*, become antiquated and emptied of all significance? Can this rebellion against biology, genetics, and social sanity sustain itself? According to a high schooler quoted on the show, being queer means "kind of straying from the norm, not being what society tells you to be regarding your sexuality, your gender, who you love." Where does this end?

DOES TOLERANCE REQUIRE SOCIAL INSANITY?

Americans tend to be a tolerant people, often rooting for the underdog and siding with the ones whom others cast out. And so it's understandable that they have wanted to be sympathetic to a child (or adult) who is convinced that he or she is trapped in the wrong body, tormented by the conflict between body and mind, especially if that person has suffered rejection or scorn or even violence from others because of being different.

But our desire to be tolerant and understanding certainly didn't include the complete deconstruction of gender, nor did we expect to be called "transphobic" if we didn't embrace every gender (or nongender) expression imaginable. And are we really being hateful and bigoted if we say that someone who identifies as multiple genders is confused and needs help? If I were absolutely convinced that I was a black man in a white man's body, and I believed that to the core of my being, should I therefore be entitled to some kind of affirmative action for minorities, or should I seek professional help?[7]

I do understand that people are genuinely tormented by the discordance between their bodies and their minds, and I can't imagine the pain they experience. But gender is not whatever we happen to feel that it is, although there's a whole movement that embraces that very concept. As Adler pointed out in the program, "Some students are going further. At one college that Joy Ladin visited, things were so fluid you could make up a different pronoun for a different event."

Ladin explained, "So you can be she/her at one event and then you go to lunch and you say, OK, now I am he/him. And then one charming young woman told me, oh, yes, today, I'm just using made up pronouns." What exactly do these made-up pronouns look like?

At Berkeley, the Gender Equity Resource Center offers definitions for terms such as *gender diverse*, defined as "a person who either by nature or *by choice* does not conform to gender-based expectations of society (e.g., transgender, transsexual, intersex, genderqueer, crossdresser, etc.) preferable to 'gender variant' because it does not imply a standard normativity."[8]

Yes, you can simply choose not to conform to societal norms. After all, who decides what is normal anyway?

REJECTING THE OPPRESSIVE "GENDER BINARY"

Lynn Walker, "a director at Housing Works, an organization that provides housing for those with HIV," joined the NPR discussion, offering perhaps the most extraordinary statement of all: "We encountered high school students who said, I want you to call me Tractor and use pronouns like zee, zim and zer. And, in fact, I reject the gender binary as an oppressive move by the dominant culture."

What? A high school student who would rather be called "Tractor" than be identified as male or female? The "gender binary" is "an oppressive move by the dominant culture" and therefore something to be rebelled against and resisted? This is meant to be taken seriously? And, to repeat, you are branded a "transphobe" if you have any problem with this at all.

Some school systems are even endorsing this, as reported on Canada's *National Post*: "Vancouver School Board's genderless pronouns—xe, xem, xyr."[9] All this leads to unintelligible headlines like this one in the *Washington Post*: "Gender-Neutral Pronouns: When 'They' Doesn't Identify as Either Male or Female."[10]

May God help us before we slide completely off the cliff into a total free fall. Or perhaps we already have. Consider this exchange between Adler and Walker, as Walker spoke of those she deals with on a regular basis:

> WALKER: And then part of the intake is to say, well, what pronoun do you like today? It might be just today.
>
> ADLER: Because Walker has clients who might be Jimmy one day, and Deloris the next.
>
> WALKER: Once you develop the habit of saying, oh, that person, that is a she, that's Delores. It doesn't matter that she looks rather like Jimmy or looks like she was called Jimmy by her parents.

Frankly, if I knew someone who wanted to be called Jimmy today and Delores tomorrow, and if he corrected me when I called him "he," even though the day before he *was* "he" (and he looked like "he" today too), and if he insisted on alternate days that he really was "she," not "he," I would say that he needed professional help. Yet today such a suggestion draws heaps of criticism and charges of bigotry and even extremism, as if we who hold to male-female distinctions and who believe that these people have genuine mental or emotional or spiritual problems are the ones needing help.

Can a society that declares war on gender function with any kind of normality? One headline read: "Transgender Couple Who BOTH Changed Sex Prepare to Explain to Their Two Children How Their Father Gave Birth While Their Mom Provided the Sperm." The story explained, "A transgender couple are preparing to tell their children when they get older that their father actually gave birth to them and the person that they call their mother is in fact their father." What's more, the "father" still has her female organs and the "mother" still has his male organs, since they can't afford sex change surgery—and they're confident their kids will have no problem with any of this.[11]

I was flying through Atlanta one day and noticed that the bathrooms at the Atlanta airport were not just marked "Men" and "Women" and differentiated with stick figures of men (wearing pants) and women (wearing dresses). They were also differentiated by colors, with the little stick figure men lit up in blue and the women lit up in pink. I posted the picture to Facebook and asked sarcastically how long such blatant heterosexist stereotyping would be allowed in the airport until some LGBT advocate complains about it. As facetious as I was being with my terminology, I was not joking about the very real possibility that someone would find it offensive.

DECLARING WAR ON GENDER

In 2012 the largest toy catalog in Sweden went gender neutral. Top Toy Group released a 2012 Christmas catalog featuring girls playing with Nerf guns and boys playing with princess dolls and using blow dryers to dry girls' hair. Matthew Day reported, "In the past the company, which holds the franchise for the Toys"R"Us and BR Toys chains, has fallen foul of regulations in Sweden prohibiting sexist advertising. The advertising standard ombudsman had previously criticised the company for producing a television commercial which spoke of 'cars for boys, princesses for girls.'"

The company has now made its amends, said Jan Nyberg, sales director at Top Toy, explaining that "with the new way of thinking about gender there is nothing that is right or wrong. A toy is not a boy or girl thing; it's a toy for children." Indeed, "The Scandinavian country has strived to foster a culture of gender neutrality, and any advertisement deemed sexist faces legal sanctions or, if not, the wrath of angered Swedes."[12]

In keeping with this, Swedish schools have been charged with the responsibility of breaking down gender stereotypes, a gender-neutral pronoun has been introduced (pronounced "hen," like the bird), and parents are being encouraged to give boys' names to their girls and girls' names to their boys. I kid you not.

As Nathalie Rothschild pointed out in an article on Slate.com,[13]

for many Swedes, gender equality is not enough. Many are pushing for the Nordic nation to be not simply gender-*equal* but gender-*neutral*. The idea is that the government and society should tolerate no distinctions at all between the sexes. This means on the narrow level that society should show sensitivity to people who don't identify themselves as either male or female, including allowing any type of couple to marry. But that's the least radical part of the project. What many gender-neutral activists are after is a society that entirely erases traditional gender roles and stereotypes at even the most mundane levels.

Activists are lobbying for parents to be able to choose any name for their children (there are currently just 170 legally recognized unisex names in Sweden). The idea is that names should not be at all tied to gender, so it would be acceptable for parents to, say, name a girl Jack or a boy Lisa. A Swedish children's clothes company has removed the "boys" and "girls" sections in its stores, and the idea of dressing children in a gender-neutral manner has been widely discussed on parenting blogs. This Swedish toy catalog recently decided to switch things around, showing a boy in a Spider-Man costume pushing a pink pram [baby carriage], while a girl in denim rides a yellow tractor.

And there's more:

The Swedish Bowling Association has announced plans to merge male and female bowling tournaments in order to make the sport gender-neutral. Social Democrat politicians have proposed installing gender-neutral restrooms so that members of the public will not be compelled to categorize themselves as either ladies or gents. Several preschools have banished references to pupils' genders, instead referring to children by their first names or as "buddies." So, a teacher would say "good morning, buddies" or "good morning, Lisa, Tom, and Jack" rather than, "good morning, boys and girls." They believe this fulfills the national curriculum's guideline that preschools should "counteract traditional gender patterns and gender roles" and give girls and boys "the same opportunities to test and develop abilities and interests without being limited by stereotypical gender roles."

As for the new pronoun *hen*, in the online version of the country's *National Encyclopedia*, "the entry defines *hen* as a 'proposed gender-neutral personal pronoun instead of he [*han* in Swedish] and she [*hon*].'" According to Rothschild,

> The *National Encyclopedia* announcement came amid a heated debate about gender neutrality that has been raging in Swedish newspaper columns and TV studios and on parenting blogs and feminist websites. It was sparked by the publication of Sweden's first ever gender-neutral children's book, *Kivi och Monsterhund* (*Kivi* and *Monsterdog*). It tells the story of Kivi, who wants a dog for "hen's" birthday. The male author, Jesper Lundqvist, introduces several gender-neutral words in the book. For instance the words *mammor* and *pappor* (moms and dads) are replaced with *mappor* and *pammor*. [This would be the equivalent of coming up with new terms like moddy and dammy rather than mommy and daddy.]

Despite concerns that "young children can become confused by the suggestion that there is a third, 'in-between' gender at a time when their brains and bodies are developing," the "Swedish school system has wholeheartedly, and probably too quickly and eagerly, embraced this new agenda." Once again, this is a massive social experiment that can end up only in dismal failure. And is it any surprise, given the growing war on gender in America and other nations today, and given the number of homes with nontraditional parents, that more and more kids are gender confused?

In 2012 in Germany, Nils Pickert, hailed as "father of the year," was praised for wearing "women's clothes (including nail polish) to help his five-year-old son feel good about going out in dresses and skirts."[14] The German magazine *Emma* reported that the story had a "happy ending," as Pickert explained: "And what's the little guy doing by now? He's painting his fingernails. He thinks it looks pretty on my nails, too. He's simply smiling, when other boys (and it's nearly always boys) want to make fun of him and says: 'You only don't dare to wear skirts and dresses because your dads don't dare to either.' That's how broad his own shoulders have become by now. And all thanks to daddy in a skirt."[15]

Parental solidarity is one thing. Contributing to a little boy's confusion is another.

And then there is the new children's cartoon show called *Shezow*, featuring a twelve-year-old boy named Guy "who uses a magic ring to transform himself into a crime-fighting girl" wearing "a purple skirt and cape, as well as pink gloves and white boots." And to change from boy to girl, he just says the magic words, "You go, girl!"[16]

Another harmless TV program for the little ones? Not on your life. This is yet another attempt to blur gender distinctions and to celebrate transgender identity. And in this case, the target audience is very young, ages two to eleven.

And let's not forget that the official policy of the Girl Scouts is ambiguous and leaves it up to the local chapters who are free to welcome a boy who identifies and presents himself as a girl. (Is there no thought to how the rest of the Girl Scouts feel about this?) According to their official statement, "Girl Scouts is an inclusive organization and we accept all girls in Kindergarten through 12th grade as members. If a child identifies as a girl and the child's family presents her as a girl, Girl Scouts of Colorado welcomes her as a Girl Scout. Our requests for support of transgender kids have grown, and Girl Scouts of Colorado is working to best support these children, their families and the volunteers who serve them."

As explained by Rachelle Trujillo, vice president of communications with Girl Scouts of Colorado, "We make the distinction that if a child is living life as a girl and the family brings the child to us and says my daughter wants to be a Girl Scout, we welcome her." But there is a line they draw: Trujillo said boys who are living like boys will not be admitted. "The child must be living life as a girl."[17]

And there you have it. A boy who thinks he is a girl and is "living life as a girl" (or his family "presents" him as a girl) can become a Girl Scout, since the organization is "inclusive." This is progress?

FACEBOOK GIVES YOU FIFTY WAYS TO DESCRIBE YOUR GENDER

In February 2014, Facebook announced to its 159 million American users that they could now customize their gender, choosing from fifty different gender descriptions (that's right, fifty). In fact, they could choose up to ten *at once* to describe themselves. Working with Facebook on this new option was the gay activist organization GLAAD (which originally stood for the Gay and Lesbian Alliance Against Defamation but which I have renamed the Gay and Lesbian Alliance Against Disagreement). GLAAD's website announced:

> "This new feature is a step forward in recognizing transgender people and allows them to tell their authentic story in their own words," said GLAAD President Sarah Kate Ellis. "Once again, Facebook is on the forefront of ensuring that the platform is safe and accessible to all of its LGBT users."
>
> Previously, Facebook users were required to select either "male" or "female" in the gender identification field. Users now [have] the option to select "Custom." Once users select custom, they will have the ability to enter up to ten identification terms (e.g., transgender, androgynous, genderqueer, etc.) to better express their gender identities.[18]

GLAAD also noted that, "while the set of [fifty!] options is not comprehensive, the company will continue to work with LGBT organizations to improve the set of options and respond to user need." Not comprehensive? Fifty different ways to describe one's gender (including ten at once) is not enough? This is reminiscent of an ad for "Queer @

Oberlin," posted online by Oberlin's Multicultural Resource Center, listing forty-nine different expressions of sexual orientation or gender, including terms like *boidyke* and *fellagirly*, ending the list with ". . ." since forty-nine variants were not enough.

LGBPTTQQIIAA+

Accordingly, Sam Killerman, in his "Comprehensive List of LGBTQ+ Term Definitions," started with this: "LGBPTTQQIIAA+: any combination of letters attempting to represent all the identities in the queer community, this near-exhaustive one (but not exhaustive) represents Lesbian, Gay, Bisexual, Pansexual, Transgender, Transsexual, Queer, Questioning, Intersex, Intergender, Asexual, Ally."[19]

A 2007 report cited the views of Dr. Barb Burdge, a professor of social work at Manchester University, herself a lesbian, who argues that "the current view of gender—the social construct of dividing humans in to male and female—is oppressive and should be rejected altogether."

She believes that transgendered individuals—which includes a whole range of individuals—should be affirmed and considered to be gender variant, not suffering from gender identity disorders. These individuals include "bigenders, gender radicals, butch lesbians, cross-dressing married men, transvestites, intersex individuals, transsexuals, drag kings and queens, gender-blenders, queers, genderqueers, two spirits, or he-shes."[20]

What does this look like in practical terms? (And remember: If you have any problem with this, you are a certified transphobe.) Let's take the case of writer and porn film director Tobi Hill-Meyer. Is Tobi male or female?

This is Tobi's personal description: "Tobi Hill-Meyer is just about your average multiracial, pansexual, transracially inseminated queerspawn, genderqueer, transdyke, colonized mestiza, pornographer, activist, writer."[21] Do you think there might be some connection between Tobi's gender confusion and the fact that Tobi self-identifies as queerspawn, meaning the child of homosexual parents and (in most cases) an anonymous mother or father?

On a YouTube presentation, Tobi "addresses the similarities between transmisogyny and femmephobia from her perspective as a butch trans woman, and explains the mutual ally relationship that she has formed with the cis femme women in her life." Some of the viewers thought the video was terrific, with comments like this: "This is like ridiculously awesome, as a Tomboy Femme Transwoman, I approve of this extremely." And, "Kudos! I'm a (mostly femme) transguy, and related to a lot of what you had to say—just sort of from a 'reversed' gender experience."[22]

From the bottom of my heart I can tell you that I do not cite these quotes with the least bit of mockery toward Tobi (or others like Tobi), nor do I write these things lightly. To the contrary, I find the situation of these gender-confused individuals to be quite painful to read. (That makes me transphobic too!) But when gender becomes as fluid as "how I feel about myself on a given day" (or in a given situation, or even over the course of many years), with no exterior controls and nothing more authoritative than my own mind, the door has been opened to social anarchy.

You simply cannot declare war on gender without lasting, terribly negative societal effects. But you can expect to find more and more people like the singer La Roux, who "has said she does not feel comfortable openly labeling her sexuality, and embraces androgyny because she doesn't feel man or woman." As she explained in 2010, "I don't have a sexuality. I don't feel like I'm female or male. I don't belong to the gay or straight society, if there is such a thing."[23]

You can also expect to find more people like Richard O'Brien, of *Rocky Horror Show* fame, who says of himself, "I'm 70% man." (You would be mortified to see what this "70% man" looks like wearing a revealing dress.)

What kind of family structures will people like La Roux and O'Brien produce?

WHAT ARE WE REPRODUCING?

In his provocative book *America Alone*, journalist Mark Steyn explains how a dangerously high number of nations in the world today have dipped below the critical number of children born per woman needed to sustain future generations; that is, 2.1. As he noted,

> the salient feature of Europe, Canada, Japan, and Russia is that they're running out of babies. . . . Greece has a fertility rate hovering just below 1.3 births per couple, which is what demographers call the point of "lowest low" fertility from which no human society has ever recovered. And Greece's fertility is the healthiest in Mediterranean Europe: Italy has a fertility rate of 1.2. . . . By 2050, 60 percent of Italians will have no brothers, no sisters, no cousins, no aunts, no uncles.[24]

And so, when the birth rate drops that low, the country will eventually die out, with great hardship experienced by those who grow old without an adequate support system.

What does this have to do with the war on gender? Simply stated, the less we recognize male and female distinctives, the less we will have traditional couples having children, and the less stable our future will be. As world statistics indicate, many countries are already on a precipitous slide away from healthy family reproduction. When you add in another factor, such as the war on gender, you're only speeding up the destruction of normal family life.

"But wait one second!" some protest. "We're talking about a tiny minority of the people who are transgender, and their situation is hardly going to affect the society as a whole or cause a drop in birthrates. You're using scare tactics—and pretty bad ones at that."

I beg to differ, and again, I'm simply stating that the war on gender is yet another factor that will lead to societal (and specifically, reproductive) decline. Note also that gay activism shares a lot of the same goals as radical feminism (for example, most gay activist organizations are also pro-abortion),[25] and so both participate in the larger, cultural war on gender, thereby downplaying the importance of moms and dads and families.[26] (You can rest assured that the average family size of a gay or lesbian couple is smaller than that of a heterosexual couple, if for no other reason than the fact that it is harder for them to bring children into the world.)

And if those who identify as transgender represent such a small percentage of the population, why should we restructure the rest of society to conform to their particular needs? Why must women have to deal with a man who identifies as a woman in their bathroom? Why must companies have to put in place special nondiscrimination policies based on gender identity, meaning that if the male receptionist at the dentist's office begins to dress as a woman—to the discomfort of the employers and patients—the company can't fire that individual? Or why must a nursery school be required to hire a cross-dressing man to teach impressionable little children?[27]

SHE WAS EXPOSING "HER MALE GENITALIA"

In November 2012 there was an uproar at Evergreen College in Olympia, Washington, when young ladies using a college campus swimming pool shared by college and high school students were shocked to see a naked man (who identified as a woman) sitting in their sauna. The police report actually stated that "she" was exposing "her male genitalia." (At the risk of being redundant, I remind you that I'm not making any of this up.)

The girls were traumatized and the parents outraged, but college officials said they could not take action. Why? "'The college has to follow state law,' Evergreen spokesman Jason Wettstein told ABC News affiliate KOMO. 'The college cannot discriminate based on the basis of gender identity. Gender identity is one of the protected things in discrimination law in this state.'"[28]

But this is only the beginning. This individual, now legally a woman and going by the name Colleen Brenna Francis, claims to be a lesbian who is attracted to other women!

I'm a very sexual person and having frequent and regular sexual activity in my life goes far to feel more fully balanced and healthy. While I am not necessarily seeking someone at the moment to be a life partner, I do miss regular and frequent sex. . . . There's no one "type" of woman that I am attracted to, really. I love women and find all kinds of women attractive. I must admit that I have a special affinity for "curvy" girls and those who some might call "natural" girls. I have a thing for "hippie chicks," I have to say! They REALLY get me going! [Here Francis gets very graphic and the comments are not fit to print.][29]

What kind of madness is this? This individual (replete with male "plumbing") has the "right" to be naked in a sauna and locker room with teenage girls? The "rights" of a confused man who believes he is a lesbian transwoman and is madly attracted to other women—and who, by law, can shower next to young ladies and undress in their presence in the locker room, not to mention them having to undress in his presence—override the rights of the high school and college girls? Is this really the America you want for your kids and grandkids?

Yet this is now the law in California with the passage of Assembly Bill 1266, which requires "public K–12 schools to let transgender students choose which restrooms they use and which school teams they join based on their gender identity instead of their chromosomes."[30] Not surprisingly, within months of the bill's implementation at the beginning of 2014, a seventeen-year-old boy who had previously played on the boy's baseball team but who now identifies as a girl became a member of the girls' softball team. And heaven forbid you speak a word of protest over this supposedly enlightened and tolerant bill. Did I say that there was an all-out war on gender distinctions?

"INFINITE" WAYS TO EXPRESS YOUR GENDER

In 2011 the True Tolerance website issued a report about Ally Week, which occurs every year in mid-October. It "is an event sponsored by GLSEN (the Gay, Lesbian and Straight Education Network) for celebration in public schools nationwide." To help facilitate Ally Week,

GLSEN provides a guide to students on "how to be an 'Ally to transgender and gender-nonconforming' people. Students are told that 'Allies to transgender and gender-nonconforming students recognize that there are infinite ways that gender can be expressed. Allies accept this diversity of gender expression and gender identity.'"[31]

There you have it in plain language, confirming what I wrote earlier, namely, that once you deviate from the pattern of male-female, the sky is the limit—in GLSEN's word, *infinite*.

In a section titled "Challenge Gender Assumptions," the Ally Week guide tells students, "Your school is filled with gender! Whether it's the type of sports offered, the colors of the bathrooms, even pictures on school posters, gender is everywhere! Begin to challenge the gender images in your school. Talk with people in your GSA [Gay Straight Alliance] about how gender assumptions can affect students."[32]

Returning briefly to the NPR interview mentioned earlier, perhaps the bizarre comments made by some of the kids are making more sense in light of the mind-set promoted in the schools. To quote again from Margot Adler and Joy Ladin:

ADLER: One of the paradoxes of culture, says Joy Ladin, is that innovation is often driven by young people.

LADIN: And we say, oh, you know, they're pushing the boundaries, they're exploring new ways of being. All of that is true. But part of what enables them to do that is that they're not really sure yet where they are going.

ADLER: Ladin believes that in the future, male and female will always refer to some people but not all. The reins of gender expression will become looser.

Yes, it is young "people pushing the boundaries," and rather than the adults trying to teach them what is right and help them get to the root of their confusion, the older generation is cultivating and encouraging this journey into gender nonconformity. It is even celebrating it.

"TWO HEARTS IN ONE CHEST"

Consider artist Conchita Wurst, whose real name is Tom Neuwirth. Tom/Conchita's website reads:

> "Two Hearts beating in my chest"
> They are a team just working in sync. Although they have never met before—they are constantly missing each other in the mirror. The private person Tom Neuwirth and the art figure Conchita Wurst respect each other from the bottom of their hearts. They are two individual characters with their own individual stories, but with one essential message for tolerance and against discrimination.
>   . . . Because of the discrimination against Tom in his teenage years, he created Conchita. The Bearded Lady, as a statement. A statement for tolerance and acceptance—as it's not about appearances; it's about the human being. "Everybody should live their lifes [*sic*] however they want, as long as nobody else gets hurt or is restricted in their own way of life."[33]

I don't know what Tom went through as a child, and I don't condone bullying or, God forbid, violence against those who are different. But from everything we know, Tom is a man, not a woman, while Conchita, the "bearded lady" character, is not who he really is. As for a society that celebrates a bearded drag queen as its new rising star (in this case, in Europe and beyond), something is terribly wrong. The same can be said for a society (in this case, America and beyond) that celebrates "transgender icon" Carmen Carrera, born Christopher Roman, and now a top female model, recently featured in a nude photo shoot by David LaChapelle, titled (in German) "I am Adam. I am Eve. I am me."[34]

This is the new normal? And you're suffering from transphobia if this troubles you? Really now, if Tom/Conchita believes he has two emotional hearts beating in his chest, shouldn't he be diagnosed with a psychological disorder rather than celebrated?[35]

FROM BRADLEY TO CHELSEA MANNING

Do you remember the name Bradley Manning? Manning was a "United States Army soldier who was convicted in July 2013 of violations of the Espionage Act and other offenses, after releasing the largest set of classified documents ever leaked to the public. Manning was sentenced in August 2013 to thirty-five years confinement with the possibility of parole in eight years, and to be dishonorably discharged from the Army."

That is the description on *Wikipedia* as of February 11, 2015, except it is not listed under "Bradley Manning," but under "Chelsea Manning." The *Wikipedia* article explains that Manning is "a trans woman who, in a statement the day after sentencing, said she had felt female since childhood, wanted to be known as Chelsea, and desired to begin hormone replacement therapy. From early life through much of Army life, Manning was known as Bradley, and was diagnosed with gender identity disorder while in the Army."[36] The rest of the article, along with virtually every news story on all but the most conservative Christian websites, refers to Manning as "she" or "her," simply because this is what he perceives himself to be.

Initial reports stated that Manning, who identified as gay and was involved in gay activist causes, was angry with the military for a number of reasons, and after a breakup with his boyfriend, he released almost one hundred thousand classified documents. (He also reported being bullied and even attacked because of his homosexuality.)[37] Now we are told that he is actually Chelsea, and the military is providing him with hormone treatment and sex change surgery while in prison. And somehow this troubled individual, who endangered the lives of American troops and was guilty of espionage, has become a celebrity in LGBT circles, named as the honorary grand marshal to the annual San Francisco gay pride event in 2014.[38]

So, no matter what biology and genetics say, no matter what your birth certificate says, you can simply announce to the world, "I'm not Bradley; I'm Chelsea," and this becomes the new reality. And what if he decides in a few years that he's actually Bradley after all?[39]

SEX CHANGE REGRET

This actually happened to Brad (aka Ria) Cooper, who at eighteen was set to be Britain's youngest sex change patient. An October 28, 2012, headline in the *Mirror* read, 'I Was a Boy . . . Then a Girl . . . Now I Want to Be a Boy Again': Agony of Teen Who Is Britain's Youngest Sex-Swap Patient."

According to the article:

> Teenager Ria Cooper has spent the last year having hormone injections to turn her from a boy into a girl.
>
> Formerly named Brad, she has already developed breasts, dresses in glamorous outfits, wears her hair in a feminine bob and has dated several young men.
>
> At 18, she is Britain's youngest sex-swap patient.
>
> Yet despite thousands of pounds worth of NHS treatment, as well as psychiatric and doctors' assessments, Ria has now decided she wants to go back to being a BOY.
>
> Her decision, which comes after two suicide attempts, calls into question whether she was too young to be allowed to swap sexes in the first place. And notice that despite Ria's desire to be Brad again, he is consistently referred to as "she/her" in the article.[40]

There was also the tragic story of sports columnist Mike Penner, who became Christine Daniels, only to revert back to Mike Penner before taking his own life.[41] Obviously there were deeper issues going on inside him, but for any of us to suggest that his gender confusion could have been the result of some kind of mental disorder would be considered hateful and transphobic.[42]

The same could be said for TV news producer Don Ennis, married for seventeen years and with three kids, who then became Dawn Stacey Ennis, before reverting back to Don, after which he reverted back to Dawn. In May 2013, when he first surprised everyone at work by showing up in a little black dress, he claimed that he had an "unusual hormone imbalance" and felt more comfortable living as a woman.

"Please understand," he said in a statement, "this is not a game of dress-up, or make-believe, it is my affirmation of who I now am and what I must do to be happy, in response to a soul-crushing secret that my wife and I have been dealing with for more than seven years, mostly in secret."

Three months later Dawn Stacey Ennis arrived at work as Don again. He said that he had amnesia, claiming his wife dressed him in a wig and created a fake ID card bearing the name "Dawn"

"I am now totally, completely, unabashedly male in my mind, despite my physical attributes," he said in an email to colleagues.

Ennis said that while his memories of the past 14 years had returned, his female identity did not.[43]

Then, in June 2014, he returned to work as Dawn, after which he was fired for performance-related issues (not gender-related issues, we were told). Remarkably, a *New York Daily News* article reporting on his firing stated, "Dawn Ennis was canned weeks after her latest transition from her male persona, Don Ennis."[44] Why in the world are they calling him "her"? Rather than colluding with this social madness (as the *Daily News* does with its headline), it would be a lot more compassionate to help Don to get to the root of his mental or emotional issues.

WHY DON'T WE HEAR MORE ABOUT SEX CHANGE REGRET?

Sadly, we are now told by the media that transgender is the new civil rights movement, with new programs celebrating the wonders of sex change surgery and the glories of transgender life.[45] Why don't we hear more about the many failures? Why don't we hear more about trans-gender struggles?

A November 11, 2014, article posted on *The Federalist* blog gives us some of the answer. The headline announces, "Trouble in Transtopia: Murmurs of Sex Change Regret. Transgender People Who Regret Their Sex Changes Typically Get Buried in Venom Rather Than Loved."

Stella Morabito, author of the article, cited the experience of Alan Finch, an Australian who decided when he was nineteen to transition from male to female, and in his twenties had genital surgery. But then, at age thirty-six, Finch told the UK's *Guardian* in 2004:

[T]ranssexualism was invented by psychiatrists. . . .You fundamentally can't change sex . . . the surgery doesn't alter you genetically. It's genital mutilation. My "vagina" was just the bag of my scrotum. It's like a pouch, like a kangaroo. What's scary is you still feel like you have a penis when you're sexually aroused. It's like phantom limb syndrome. It's all been a terrible misadventure. I've never been a woman, just Alan . . . the analogy I use about giving surgery to someone desperate to change sex is it's a bit like offering liposuction to an anorexic.

Note carefully those words: "transsexualism was invented by psychiatrists."

Morabito also cited a more deadly account:

Another heart-wrenching story, of a female-to-male transgender, is that of Nancy Verhelst in Belgium. She was aghast after her surgery, saying she felt more like a "monster" than a man. She also spoke of her sad childhood, in which her mother rejected her in favor of her brothers, and isolated little Nancy in a room over the garage. Nancy was so distraught that she asked doctors to put her to death under Belgium's lax euthanasia laws. They coldly complied.[46]

Adding to the tragedy—and giving insight into why Nancy wanted to try to become a man—were the comments Nancy's mother made after hearing about her daughter's suicide: "When I first saw 'Nancy' [at birth], my dream was shattered. She was so ugly. I had a ghost birth. Her death does not bother me."[47]

In spite of all this, online articles continued to refer to Nancy as "he," not even bothering to reflect on the obvious causes of her gender confusion and shame. Morabito concluded her article with these sage remarks: "Biological truth has a way of outing itself. The hard reality of it is written right into our DNA as 'male' or 'female.' In the end, transgender activists and their media enablers won't be able to drown that massive iceberg."[48]

LET'S NOT BE A SOCIETY BENT ON SELF-DESTRUCTION

Is gender now entirely a matter of how you feel and identify yourself? Is there nothing to biology, nothing to chromosomes, nothing to anatomy? Is an all-out war on gender in the best interest of the vast majority of men, women, boys, and girls who are not confused about their identity?

As noted by conservative journalist Erick Erickson,

> Across the country, the left has decided our sexual preference is something we are born with, but our gender is something we get to decide. Anyone who thinks otherwise is threatened and harassed. Several thousand-year-old pillars of society are being shoved aside in the name of tolerance. Those who speak up for sanity, tradition and faith are treated scornfully.
>
> This will not end well for any of us. . . . A society that willfully undermines perpetuating itself is a society bent on suicide.[49]

Things have gotten to the point that now, in a number of states, someone who identifies as transgender can have his or her birth certificate changed to reflect his or her new identity, in some cases without even undergoing sex change surgery.[50] In fact, according to Assembly Bill 1121 in California, which was passed in 2013 but didn't go into effect fully until 2014, those wanting to have their birth certificates changed "now have the option to just submit a form and a doctor's letter directly to the state Department of Public Health along with a $23 fee."[51] So, even though the child really was born a boy (this is now referred to as the "birth gender"[52]), and in every testable way genuinely was a male, his birth certificate will now say that he was born a girl, and he can make this change when he's sixteen years old.

Just think of what the mother and father might have to say about that. Their child's birth certificate has been altered to change reality, almost as if by time travel. And this is the law in a growing number of states, while in Canada, a twelve-year-old girl who identifies as a boy has been officially recognized as a boy, with her birth certificate changed accordingly—based solely on her own self-perception.[53] (Remember: she's just twelve.)

What, then, sets her apart from those suffering from what is called "species dysphoria," where people are convinced that they are part (or all) animal, become more convinced of their animal identity as they get older, and dress up like animals and legally change their names to fit their animal identity?[54] And is it a coincidence that it was Logo TV, the gay TV channel, that began airing a series in 2013 called *What? I Think I'm an Animal*? As the blurb explained, "*I Think I'm an Animal* reveals the truth behind the Otherkin movement's furry costumes and explores what it's like to inhabit an animal identity."[55]

One young man explained in the documentary series, "Basically, other than the fact that I have a human body and human flesh, I am a wolf." He said that, for him, this was spiritual, psychological, and behavioral, and that going through school was a living hell since others didn't recognize his real identity. He also claimed that he was personally aware of communities numbering in the hundreds of thousands who also identified as animals, including wild cats, domestic cats, flies, and even insects.[56] (They call themselves "therians."[57])

This may be a brave new world for some, but for the rest of us, this is societal madness, a surefire way to undermine civilization by tampering with the most basic of all foundations: God made us male and female in His image: "Then God said, 'Let us make mankind in our image, in our likeness, so that they may rule over the fish in the sea and the birds in the sky, over the livestock and all the wild animals, and over all the creatures that move along the ground.' So God created mankind in his own image, in the image of God he created them" (Genesis 1:26–27). This means that there really is a divinely intended order for the human race, a male-female, heterosexual order, which "explains why a man leaves his father and mother and is joined to his wife, and the two are united into one" (Genesis 2:24 NLT; literally, "the two become one flesh")—uniquely fit for emotional and spiritual unity, uniquely fit to reflect the image of God together, uniquely fit to reproduce and bring forth new life, to "be fruitful and multiply" (Genesis 1:28)—which is more than just a biological process. It is a man and woman giving themselves to one another for life, becoming one in body and spirit, joining together in sexual love, producing a brand-new life within the womb, then watching with wonder as the baby grows in its mother's belly, feeling it kick and move, counting the days until delivery, and then experiencing what truly feels like a miracle as a new human being bursts forth from the womb and is soon in the arms of its mom and dad, who are laughing and crying for joy and wonder.

This is why God made us male and female, and this is why the natural family is the ideal place for a child to be nurtured and raised, the daughters mentored by their mothers and the sons mentored by their fathers, with both mom and dad uniting to set an example for their children.[58] It truly is a beautiful picture.[59]

It's time we get back to the basics and recover our foundations. We can have compassion on those who struggle without redesigning the very fabric of humanity.

PRINCIPLE #6

KEEP PROPAGATING THE TRUTH
UNTIL THE LIES ARE DISPELLED

In a time of universal deceit—telling the truth is a revolutionary act. —GEORGE ORWELL

What if it turns out that America has been conned? What if we discover that an entire movement—a revolution—has been built on lies, exaggerations, and deception? What if we learn that we have been duped by the mainstream media and deceived by the propagandizing press? As author Robert Reilly noted, "Illusions ultimately lead to disillusion. Reality always wins."[1]

There was a day when communism ruled much of the world, with more and more nations coming under its sway every decade, and with Nikita Khrushchev's words, "I will bury you" echoing around the planet.[2] And that was not so long ago. It was in 1982 that President Reagan gave his famous "evil empire" speech. Yet today that empire has been massively reduced, and even in China, capitalism is more powerful than communism.[3]

What caused this dramatic shift? Communism did not deliver on its promise of economic equality and social egalitarianism, producing instead a harvest of poverty, starvation, inequality, and injustice.[4]

Simply stated, the communist revolution failed because it was built on lies and false expectations, and ultimately, any revolution built on lies will fail, no matter how powerful and widespread it may appear at a given point in time.

"PROPAGANDA FED TO THE NATION VIA THE MEDIA"

In the late 1980s, gay activists laid out one of their major strategies for changing public opinion about homosexuality, calling for the "conversion of the average American's emotions, mind, and will, through a planned psychological attack, in the form of propaganda fed to the nation via the media."[5] And they were quite candid about their approach, explaining that since gays had often been portrayed in false and unflattering terms, it was fine to exaggerate in the other direction, presenting overly positive and embellished depictions of gays and gay culture. In other words, balance out the bad lies with good lies.

Today Americans have believed those "good lies" beyond all reasonable expectation. We have been duped and brainwashed, plain and simple. I can prove it to you.

Beginning with the influential publications of Alfred Kinsey in 1948, it has been widely reported that "one in ten people is gay," although gay activists have acknowledged for years that this figure is way too high.[6] But since it seemed like a good figure to use—who cares about truth and accuracy?—it has been disseminated as one of those "good lies," with movie and TV scripts echoing the "one in ten" claim.[7]

Yet the media hasn't stopped there. Instead, they have flooded us day and night with gay images and themes, from news stories to characters in sitcoms and from reality TV shows to the sports world. Gay is virtually everywhere, giving the average American a totally false impression as to the real number of those who identify as gay, lesbian, or bisexual in our country. Would you like to know the truth?

HOW GAY IS THE USA?

According to a major health study released in July 2014 by the CDC

(Centers for Disease Control and Prevention), "Less than 3 percent of the U.S. population identify themselves as gay, lesbian or bisexual." To be exact, "1.6 percent of adults self-identify as gay or lesbian, and 0.7 percent consider themselves bisexual,"[8] which means the total of those identifying as gay, lesbian, or bisexual is just 2.3 percent, which is less than one in forty people. Other studies have reached similar conclusions, give or take a percentage point in either direction. (A 2014 survey conducted by the Office of National Statistics in the UK yielded the exact same result: 1.6 percent of the population identified as gay or lesbian.[9]) So forget about one in ten being gay. Not even one in fifty identifies as gay and not even one in one hundred as bisexual.

What do Americans believe about the number of gays and lesbians in our country? According to a Gallup poll released May 27, 2011, "U.S. Adults Estimate That 25% of Americans Are Gay or Lesbian."[10] Yes, Americans believe that one in four people is gay whereas the actual number is less than one in forty. That is absolutely extraordinary.

Where in the world did we get such an idea? The poll explains that "those with lower incomes, the less educated, women, and young people give the highest estimates," with those aged eighteen to twenty-nine believing, on average, that the number was 29.9 percent, meaning almost one in three. (No other age group put the figure this high.)[11] Confirming this was an informal poll I conducted while speaking at a Christian youth conference, asking these committed young people what percentage of the population was gay. (Some of these kids were homeschooled, and most seemed less aware of the more notorious cable TV shows, so they were less worldly wise than your average young people.) The first teen answered, "Thirty percent." The second said, "Forty percent."

How could our perceptions be that far off?[12] How could we think that one in four people (or one in three people) was gay when the number is less than one in fifty (or, based on higher estimates, still less than one in thirty)? Gallup stated, "This suggests Americans have had even more exposure to gays and lesbians, be it in their personal lives or *through entertainment* or other means."[13]

There you have it. We have been brainwashed by the media, which is why, in particular, those who are less educated, along with young people, were the most misled. Just watch some episodes of *Glee*, a favorite among young teens today, and tell me if you'd come away thinking that less than one person in fifty was gay. In fact,

> according to GLAAD, 31% of the original primetime programming on HBO is LGBT-inclusive. Shows like "Looking" and "True Blood" and the film "The Normal Heart" helped boost its ranking this year. By GLAAD's measurements, MTV is even more inclusive, with nearly half (49%) of its primetime original programming, most notably the scripted series "Teen Wolf" and reality show "The Challenge," deemed LGBT-inclusive.[14]

No wonder our young people in particular have such dramatically skewed perceptions of reality.

FALSE IMPRESSIONS LEAD TO FALSE CONCLUSIONS

There are implications to these false impressions as well, as noted by Gerald Bradley, professor of law at Notre Dame University and an expert in constitutional law:

> Gay Americans are afforded all their rights. They can vote, can have almost any job they are qualified for, live where ever they want to, travel unburdened, just like everyone else. Demographics show they are among the wealthiest and best educated people in the United States. No one wants to take anything away from them. But the question becomes, can a tiny sliver of our population change the definition of marriage not only for the 243,000,000 adult Americans alive today, but for all those who will come after us?[15]

Clearly, gay activists have succeeded in bringing about the "conversion of the average American's emotions, mind, and will, through a planned psychological attack, in the form of propaganda fed to the nation via the media." Otherwise, if we simply based things on our personal experiences, namely, on how many gays and lesbians we knew in our families, schools, places of business, neighborhoods, and congregations, on average, we never would come up with the one-in-ten figure, let alone the one-in-four (or -three) figure.[16]

To quote once again the top gay strategists writing in the late 1980s, their plan was "to desensitize straights to gays and gayness, inundate them in a continuous flood of gay-related advertising, presented in the least offensive fashion possible. If straights can't shut off the shower, they may at least eventually get used to being wet."[17] In short, they explained, "The main thing is to talk about gayness until the issue becomes thoroughly tiresome. . . . If you can get [straights] to think homosexuality is just another thing—meriting no more than a shrug of the shoulders— then your battle for legal and social rights is virtually won."[18]

Many years ago on TV I saw a professional magician and pickpocket tell the host of the show that he was going to take off the man's wristwatch, shirt, and T-shirt as they talked, and the host wouldn't even realize what was happening. To my shock, he did that very thing, right in front of the TV host's eyes. In similar fashion, gay activists told us they were going to brainwash us and dupe us without us realizing what was happening, and right in front of our eyes, they did that very thing.

HOW BRAINWASHED ARE WE?

This media brainwashing affects us in more ways than we realize. For example, over the last twenty years, American views on same-sex "marriage" have shifted dramatically. As noted by Dawn Michelle Baunach, a sociologist at Georgia State University, "There's just been a real huge sea change in how people view gay marriage. In 1988, we had 72 percent of people who said they disapproved of gay marriage, and only 13 percent approved. But by 2010, we had cut disapproval almost in half, and approval has quadrupled."[19]

Yet that shift didn't happen in a vacuum, and it was not only due to Americans now knowing gay couples personally (as if none of us knew gay couples in the past). Instead, the media have helped change public perception in this area too, thereby helping to drive the polls by pushing an aggressively pro-homosexual viewpoint. As reported in June 2013, "In a period marked by Supreme Court deliberations on the subject, the news media coverage provided a strong sense of momentum towards legalizing same-sex marriage, according to a new study by the Pew Research Center. Stories with more statements supporting same-sex marriage outweighed those with more statements opposing it *by a margin of roughly 5-to-1.*"[20] So, while the nation was evenly divided over the question of same-sex "marriage," news coverage was totally slanted in favor of redefining marriage.

And this is just the influence of the news coverage. What about the influence of the TV dramas, sitcoms, movies, reality shows, and commercials, along with Hollywood films? Several years ago, I documented the media's widespread celebration of queer, but if you're a regular TV viewer or moviegoer, you don't need my documentation. You can simply ask yourself, "How many times have I seen a story painting same-sex couples or same-sex 'marriage' in a negative light?" Perhaps none? In contrast, how many times did you see conservative Christians—especially those who opposed the normalizing of homosexuality—portrayed in a negative light?[21]

Why then should we be so impressed with polls that point to shifting American attitudes toward homosexuality and gay "marriage," as if those shifts were the result of careful, rational thought? The reality is that people, to a great extent, are being indoctrinated by the media, which means that under different circumstances—including confrontation with the truth—their views could easily shift again.

Am I saying that there's a media conspiracy to promote homosexuality? Yes and no. I say no because networks, producers, directors, screenwriters, and advertisers are ultimately free to do what they want to do, so in that sense there is no conspiratorial movement controlling them, as if there were a gay illuminati of sorts. But I say yes because (1) there is a disproportionately large presence of gay men and women in the Hollywood and TV industry; (2) organizations such as GLAAD and People for the American Way (PFAW) monitor new shows and movies to ensure that they are gay-positive; and (3) there is a well-known liberal bias in both the news and entertainment.

THE GAY-DOMINATED MEDIA

Let me unpack the reasons why I believe that there is a pro-gay media conspiracy of sorts. First, with regard to the gay presence in movies and TV, already in 1996, gay writer David Ehrenstein boasted in *Los Angeles Magazine* that "there are openly gay writers on almost every major prime-time situation comedy you can think of. . . . In short, when it comes to sitcoms, gays rule."[22] It is surely not a demographic coincidence that "West Hollywood recently got a perfect score on the Human Rights Campaign's Municipal Equality Index," and that "it's known to Angelenos as the place where LGBT people from all over Greater Los Angeles gather for community protests and celebrations," and that "gay and bisexual men comprise 41 percent of the city's population."[23] To my knowledge, gay activists do not deny this strong gay presence in Hollywood.

Second, with regard to gay activism's monitoring of the media, rather than repudiating such activities, organizations like GLAAD boast about such work in order to raise funds.[24] In fact, they have been so successful that a May 2013 article argues that "the best thing the organization [GLAAD] could do is dissolve—not because it is actively harmful, but rather because it is a victim of its own success." According to James Kirchick, writing in the *Atlantic*, whereas twenty-five years ago gays were often marginalized and demonized in the media, today, "not only are media representations of gays plentiful, they are almost overwhelmingly positive."[25] GLAAD, Kirchick opines, has worked itself out of a job.

As for PFAW, founded by Normal Lear, it uses subgroups like Right Wing Watch (RWW) to attack conservative Christians in the media, exerting enough pressure that, in some cases, shows have been pulled based on their negative reports. Take, for example, the story of Jason and David Benham, best known today as the Benham Brothers (they are also good friends of mine, so I know their story well). Jason and David are committed Christians, great husbands and dads, former athletes (having played professional baseball), successful businessmen, and twins who were about to star in a reality TV show on HGTV in which they helped people in need flip homes for a profit. It was HGTV that approached them about doing the show—the Benhams were initially approached by an agent who thought they had a good story—and they were vetted before any contracts were signed. So their strong, even outspoken Christian beliefs were well known to HGTV execs.

Taping had already begun when HGTV announced its new roster of shows, and as soon as GLAAD got word that the Benhams were being featured in a show, they put the network under pressure. But after further interaction with Jason and David, HGTV held its ground, deciding to go on with the show. Unfortunately, when Right Wing Watch released an extremely biased report on the Benhams, one that included the beliefs of their father, Flip, known for his more militant public stands, HGTV got cold feet and pulled out.[26] It turns out that Right Wing Watch, although little known to the general public, carries a lot of weight with Hollywood.[27]

Third, in terms of liberal media bias in the news, this has been documented for several decades, beginning in 1981, when professors S. Robert Lichter and Stanley Rothman "released a groundbreaking survey of 240 journalists at the most influential national media outlets—including the *New York Times*, *Washington Post*, *Wall Street Journal*, *Time*, *Newsweek*, *U.S. News & World Report*, ABC, CBS, NBC and PBS—on their political attitudes and voting patterns." The survey found these "media elites" to be shockingly liberal, to the point that "54 percent did not regard adultery as wrong, compared to only 15 percent [of the general public] who regarded it as wrong," while "ninety percent agree that a woman has the right to decide for herself whether to have an abortion; 79 percent agree strongly with this pro-choice position."[28] Today websites such as Newbusters.org are devoted exclusively to "exposing and combating liberal media bias," and on a regular basis, they have a lot to report.

The sad fact is that most Americans are far more influenced by the media than they realize, believing what the media want them to believe and thinking what the media want them to think. And given the strong gay presence in the media, along with the strongly liberal leanings of many in the "media elite," this has been a great tool of gay activism, with the media *affecting* society more than *reflecting* society.

So, if the media have shaped your worldview, it's time to wake up, my friend. You have been conned. Sold a bill of goods. Duped. How does that make you feel?

Are you ready, then, for a serious dose of truth? Here's a short list of some of the most widely believed LGBT lies.[29]

LIE #1: HOMOSEXUAL RELATIONSHIPS ARE NO DIFFERENT FROM HETEROSEXUAL RELATIONSHIPS

In 2014, Prof. Jay Michaelson, a leading gay Jewish intellectual, wrote an article for the *Daily Beast* titled "Were Christians Right about Gay Marriage All Along?" In it, he expressed his opinion that gay "marriage" would help redefine heterosexual marriage, ultimately leading away from monogamy into various forms of acceptable promiscuity within wedlock. Almost twenty years earlier, gay activist Jack Nichols wrote, "Nonprocreative same-sex relationships have a particularly redeeming quality, namely, that they take place between people who are the same and can therefore, theoretically at least, welcome others into affectional relationships that bypass exclusivity. This, conceivably, could promote a maximization of affection through communal contact, replacing today's failing models of exclusive, neurotic, narrow, monogamous duos."[30]

To be sure, there are many gay couples who have been committed to each other for years and who do not believe in undermining marriage or even in being "monogamish" (to use gay sex columnist Dan Savage's term), but the undeniable fact is that there is more promiscuity among gay couples, especially men, and it is an accepted part of the culture.[31] Lesbian author Camille Paglia actually expressed admiration for the ability of gay male couples to have their flings: "A fling for a lesbian couple is a betrayal. . . . It's a betrayal of intimacy. Whereas the gay men, possibly because of the compartmentalization of male sexuality that I talked about in *Sexual Personae*, where it's just a matter of . . . the random, mischievous sex organ just doing its thing, and it's like, it doesn't go very deep. . . . It's one of the many things I've envied about gay men."[32]

Even the noted gay strategists Kirk and Madsen, whom I've quoted several times in this book, admitted that "sooner or later, the roving penis rears its ugly head." They further noted that "yes, that wayward impulse is as inevitable in man-to-man affairs as in man-to-woman, only, for gays, it starts itching faster." Thus, "many gay lovers, bowing to the inevitable, agree to an 'open relationship,' for which there are as many sets of ground rules as there are couples."[33]

"That's certainly not a message you'll get from gay activists or the media, who are constantly showing us touching pictures of Jim and John who have been together for the last thirty years and now at last can seal their love with marriage," a Hollywood actor told me recently. "Well, faithful, truly monogamous, long-term Jim and John may exist, but they are quite a rare species in the gay male world."

He continued, "A gay colleague once told me, 'For every ten men I'm with (sexually), I'll only see one of them again. And for every ten of those men, only one of them will end up being my friend.'"[34]

Consider also the sentiments expressed by Russian human rights activist and lesbian Masha Gessen, honored by Secretary of State Kerry in June 2014 for her opposition to Vladimir Putin. She said gays

> should have the right to marry, but I also think equally that it is a no-brainer that the institution of marriage should not exist. . . . Fighting for gay marriage generally involves lying about what we're going to do with marriage when we get there, because we lie that the institution of marriage is not going to change, and that is a lie. The institution of marriage is going to change, and it should change, and again, I don't think it should exist.[35]

In the words of Dan Savage, certainly one of the most influential gay activists in America and the founder of the "It Gets Better" campaign, endorsed by President Obama himself:

> Absolutely we need to rethink love and commitment. You know 60 years ago was when we decided that men had to be monogamous too. Men were not monogamous. For all of recorded human history men had concubines and whores, and 60 years ago straight relationships began to become more egalitarian and it was less of a property transaction—a marriage had been a property transaction for most of recorded human history—and it became a union of two equals. And at that moment instead of deciding to allow women to have the same sort of freedom and leeway that men did we decided to let men have the same limitations, impose the same limitations what women had and we put monogamous sexual commitment at the heart of all relationships, all long-term commitments, all marriages and we have watched.
>
> We should now be able to recognize the consequences of that, which are a lot of short-term relationships, a lot of divorce. Because monogamy is ridiculous and people aren't any good at it. We're not wired for it. We didn't evolve to be. It's unnatural and it places a tremendous strain on our marriages and our long-term commitments to expect them to be effortlessly monogamous. . . .
>
> We need to talk about monogamy the way we talk about sobriety, which you can be monogamous and fall off the wagon and then sober back up. You can monogamous back up and get back on the wagon. And the truth of the matter is that if you're with someone for forty, fifty years and they only cheated on you a few times they were good at being monogamous not bad at being monogamous, they were good at it. But I do think there needs to be some leeway and a lot of really good loving relationships are destroyed because somebody wants a little variety or isn't getting a need met and feels they have to step out and it exploded the relationship. I'm conservative. I think that we should do what we can to preserve marriages and long term relationships and one way to do that is to encourage people to have more realistic attitudes about sexual exclusivity.[36]

So monogamy is ridiculous, and to preserve marriages, we should encourage at least a little adultery along the way. Thus says Dan Savage. There is also a lot more "intergenerational intimacy" that goes on in homosexual relationships, in particular among the men, although, to be perfectly clear, every gay man I have ever spoken to about pedophilia *deplores it and renounces it* every bit as vehemently as I do. (Tragically, there *are* some male homosexual activists who push for "consensual" pedophilia as well, including leading academics, but I believe—and certainly hope—that this represents a tiny minority.[37]) But when it comes to more acceptable forms of "intergenerational" relationships, like men in their thirties having sexual and romantic relationships with teenage boys, that's another thing. In fact, it is all too common in male homosexual circles.

That's why almost no one in the gay community bats an eyelash when they hear about Harvey Milk's sexual history (yes, I'm talking about the slain political leader who has taken on iconic status in our culture). To be specific, according to acclaimed gay journalist Randy Shilts, at age eleven, Milk began attending performances of the New York Metropolitan Opera, where he met with "wandering hands" and soon was engaged in "brief trysts [with grown men] after the performances." While still in junior high, he "dove headfirst into the newly discovered subculture," and by fourteen, Milk was "leading an active homosexual life." As he grew older, the pattern reversed itself to the point that, at age thirty-three, Milk hooked up with a sixteen-year-old named Jack McKinley, one of a number of younger men with whom he was intimate.[38]

Has this tarnished his legacy? Not at all. Why? Because it is not that unusual. As gay journalist and radio host Michelangelo Signorile explained:

> [W]e've been so focused in recent years on how we're all the same [meaning as heterosexuals]—we want many of the same things in life, including a job, a home, a relationship—that we've obscured some real differences in how we've constructed our community and

our relationships. Historically, gay men have engaged in intergenerational sexual encounters, brief romances and long-term relationships— among consenting adults—probably much more than straight people have.[39]

And those "consenting adults" were often men in their teens. (The situation that Signorile was defending involved Hollywood screenwriter Dustin Lance Black, age thirty-nine, and British diving champion Tom Daley, age nineteen. Other gay leaders were critical of the relationship.) That's why it was not surprising to hear that Terry Bean, one of the founders of the influential HRC—and a major player in Democratic politics and gay activism—was arrested on November 19, 2014, "on charges of sex abuse in a case involving a 15-year-old boy. [Bean was 66 at the time.] . . . The arrest comes after a five-month investigation that began with allegations Bean secretly made video recordings of men having sex in his bedroom."[40]

As argued by conservative journalist and law professor Matt Barber, "The cases of Bean and [Larry][41] follow a long-established pattern as old as the ancient Greek bathhouse. It's not just homosexual priestly predators on the prowl in the Catholic Church. From pedophile 'LGBT' hero Harvey Milk, to high-profile 'gay activists' like Duke University's Frank Lombard and USC's Walter Lee Williams, the homosexual lust for young flesh seems insatiable."[42]

In support of this statement, which some would find extreme and unfair, Barber cited Harry Hay, the iconic pioneer of the gay rights movement, who (in)famously said, "It seems to me that in the gay community the people who should be running interference for NAMBLA [the North American Man/Boy Love Association] are the parents and friends of gays. Because if the parents and friends of gays are truly friends of gays, they would know from their gay kids that the relationship with an older man is precisely what 13-, 14-, and 15-year-old kids need more than anything else in the world."

The point I'm making is simple: because the combination of two men or two women is not really the same as the combination of a man

and woman, there will be more deviations from the norm in those relationships,[43] especially among the males, including more promiscuity and
even "intergenerational" relationships. This too will provide a reminder
that homosexual relationships are not identical to heterosexual relationships, and since they are not identical, it is wrong for society to try to
treat them as if they were.

As noted by social worker Luis Pabon in his web article "I No Longer
Want to Be Gay":

> The self-loathing in this community forces you to encounter a series
> of broken men who are self-destructive, hurtful, cruel and vindictive
> towards one another. I have struggled to adapt my moral code to fit
> the behaviors concomitant with the lifestyle but it seems that the
> lifestyle is forcing me too far away from everything I love and value.
> No matter how many times I try to purge my perception of its firmly
> held beliefs and skewed biases, the same classic stereotypes of gay men
> keep rearing their ugly heads. The indiscriminate sex, superficiality,
> unstable relationships, self-hatred, peter pan syndrome, closeted con-
> nections, ageism, shade, loneliness, preoccupation with sex, prejudice,
> aversion to intimacy all seem to come out of the ground I thought
> they were buried under. Gay men just seem to find it difficult to
> transcend the stereotypes and clichés attached to the life and it is
> becoming disheartening.[44]

This is much more common than many gays want to admit, and
you certainly won't hear it broadcast by gay activists.

LIE #2: GAY SUFFERING IS PRIMARILY DUE TO HOMOPHOBIA

The more our society accepts and even celebrates homosexuality (and
bisexuality and transgenderism), the harder it will be to blame the higher
incidences of depression, suicide, substance abuse, and STDs in the
LGBT community on alleged societal homophobia.

I don't dispute for a moment that societal rejection, especially among
family members and close friends, has caused a great deal of suffering

among those who identify as LGBT, including some negative, antisocial, even self-destructive behavior. Common sense would tell you that this is so, and I do not minimize the tragic consequences of antihomosexual hatred, particularly from family. But it is also indisputable that societal acceptance of homosexuality does not greatly diminish these self-destructive LGBT behaviors, which have remained disproportionately high in countries and cities that have long embraced LGBT culture.

As noted by a team of conservative researchers:

> The usual hypothesis is that societal discrimination against homosexuals is solely or primarily responsible for the development of this pathology. However, specific attempts to confirm this societal discrimination hypothesis have been unsuccessful, and the alternative possibility—that these conditions may somehow be related to the psychological structure of a homosexual orientation or consequences of a homosexual lifestyle—has not been disconfirmed. Indeed, several cross-cultural studies suggest that this higher rate of psychological disturbance is in fact independent of a culture's tolerance of—or hostility toward—homosexual behavior. We believe that further research that is uncompromised by politically motivated bias should be carried out to evaluate this issue.[45]

The recent CDC study, cited earlier in this chapter, found a higher percentage of substance abuse in gay and lesbian circles, while other recent studies have found a higher percentage of mental and emotional disorders.[46] Simply blaming this on homophobia doesn't make it go away, while refusing to look for deeper causes to these problems does a disservice to the LGBT community. Similarly, the steady trend of high health risks for gays and bisexuals cannot be blamed on homophobia.

Could it be that men are not designed to be with men and women are not designed to be with women? Could that be part of the problem? Is the high incidence of STDs society's fault or a result of homosexual behavior?

A 2014 report in the UK pointed to much higher drug use among LGB people than among the general population:

In response to questions on drugs, 76% replied they had used them recreationally while 31% said they spent between £100 and £300 on average every month on illegal substances.

On what drugs they took before sex, 56% answered poppers, 48% cannabis, 41% cocaine, 40% MDMA/ecstasy, 32% Viagra, 12% crystal meth, 11% ketamine and 10% mephedrone.

When asked if recreational drugs would make them more likely to have sex with a stranger, 60% said it would.[47]

A gay leader in England, Monty Moncrieff, responded with concern, noting:

> Our primary association by identity as LGB people is done in bars and clubs, and we can usually stay at play longer than our hetero-sexual counterparts with responsibility for childcare still less common. Certainly we normalise longer partying behaviour, and more recently drugs have crept increasingly into our bedrooms with chemsex noticeably on the rise amongst some gay and bi men. When drugs are used less for fun but to self-medicate we know all too well that the reasons—depression, anxiety, prejudice—are more prevalent in our populations too.[48]

This is a very telling admission for a gay man. And note that "homophobia" (which would implicitly be the cause of "prejudice" in particular) wasn't on the list of reasons to self-medicate. In fact, the word wasn't used in the article at all.

All this underscores the fact that there are differences in the life-styles of homosexuals and heterosexuals, and while the media want us to think that the vast majority of gay men and women want to get "married" and live a quiet life together, there's actually a lot more partying going on among gays than straights, which is consistent with higher rates of drug use and promiscuity. That's why drug users have often known that the best place to get certain kinds of drugs was in the gay community, not because they were medicating because of societal rejection, but because they partied more.

A recent study from Australia confirms that homophobia is not the principal cause of gay suffering:

> While many assume that family rejection is the leading cause of depression among LBGTI individuals, a new study has found that in fact the problem appears to stem predominantly from the higher incidence of relationship problems among homosexuals.
>
> Dr. Delaney Skerrett led a team of researchers from the Australian Institute for Suicide Research and Prevention (AISRAP) in studying suicides in Queensland. He found that a leading cause of suicide among "lesbian, gay, bisexual, transgender, and intersex" (LGBTI) people is stress from their romantic partners.
>
> "We tend to assume that the psychological distress LGBTI people are often going through is due to family rejection. But it seems that's not so much the case. The conflict seems to be largely related to relationship problems, with partners," Dr. Skerrett said.[49]

When it comes to those who identify somewhere in the spectrum of "transgender," again, I don't doubt that societal rejection plays a significant role here, sometimes leading to depression, substance abuse, and even suicide. But, as I noted earlier in the book, many of those who go as far as having sex change surgery live to regret it deeply. This points to other issues in these people's lives that never got addressed, and so the "cure" is worse than the "sickness."

As I noted in my June 19, 2014, article "Sex Change Regret":

> Dr. Paul McHugh, formerly chair of the Johns Hopkins psychiatric department and a longtime opponent of sex-change surgery, penned an op-ed piece for the *Wall Street Journal*, arguing that "policy makers and the media are doing no favors either to the public or the transgendered" by not treating transgender "confusions . . . as a mental disorder that deserves understanding, treatment and prevention."
>
> He cited a 2011 study from Sweden that followed the lives of 324 "sex-reassigned" persons over a 30-year period (from 1973–2003),

noting that "beginning about 10 years after having the surgery, the transgendered began to experience increasing mental difficulties. Most shockingly, their suicide mortality rose almost 20-fold above the comparable nontransgender population."

This confirmed a similar study McHugh had commissioned decades earlier at Johns Hopkins, and for opposing sex-change surgery, he is vilified to this day.

Is it possible that something other than transphobia is driving him?

Walt Heyer has lived through this himself, undergoing years of hormone treatments and then sex-change surgery to become a woman, only to realize over a period of years that he was, in fact, a man and that there were other issues he needed to address in his life.

To help others, he has launched the SexChangeRegret.com website, featuring articles like, "The insanity of hormone blockers for kids," and "1,500 Sex Changers Request Surgical Reversals" (this was in one center in Belgrade alone), and "Regret Is Real—and Transgenders Are Going Back."[50]

And this is just the tip of the iceberg.

In short, the more our society embraces homosexuality, bisexuality, and transgenderism, from childhood through adulthood and through all sectors of our society, the harder it will be to blame mental, emotional, and physical problems experienced in higher proportion in the LGBT community on alleged homophobia and transphobia.

Once again, the success of the gay revolution will reveal some of its greatest weaknesses.

LIE #3: HOMOSEXUALITY IS INNATE AND IMMUTABLE

This has been one of the most fundamental gay activist arguments and one of the most effective: "We are born this way and we cannot change, and since there's nothing inherently wrong with homosexuality and we didn't choose it, it is cruel and bigoted to find fault with us for simply being who we are. This would be just as wrong as claiming that heterosexuals chose to be heterosexual and that they are now required to become homosexual. How ridiculous is that?"

To be sure, there is solid evidence that homosexual desires are often so deeply rooted in some people's lives that they genuinely believe they were born gay.[51] And there is no doubt that many gays and lesbians tried desperately to change and were unable to do so. I don't doubt this at all. But the fact remains that there is no reputable scientific evidence that anyone is born gay, to the point that the very liberal, pro-gay American Psychological Association stated:

> There is no consensus among scientists about the exact reasons that an individual develops a heterosexual, bisexual, gay, or lesbian orientation. Although much research has examined the possible genetic, hormonal, developmental, social, and cultural influences on sexual orientation, no findings have emerged that permit scientists to conclude that sexual orientation is determined by any particular factor or factors. Many think that nature and nurture both play complex roles; most people experience little or no sense of choice about their sexual orientation. [52]

This admission becomes all the more remarkable when you read the publication in which this statement is found: "Answers to Your Questions for a Better Understanding of Sexual Orientation & Homosexuality," which is as pro-gay as possible. The APA website, in promoting the brochure, even states that

> since 1975, the American Psychological Association has called on psychologists to take the lead in removing the stigma of mental illness that has long been associated with lesbian, gay, and bisexual orientations. . . . This pamphlet is designed to provide accurate information for those who want to better understand sexual orientation and the impact of prejudice and discrimination on those who identify as lesbian, gay, or bisexual. [53]

And still, the APA must say that no one knows for sure what causes homosexuality. Had there been the slightest possible hint of definitive evidence pointing to people being "born gay," the APA would have been all over it.

Similarly, in England, the decidedly pro-gay Royal College of Psychiatrists backtracked on an earlier statement that homosexuality was biologically determined, now saying that "sexual orientation is determined by a combination of biological and postnatal environmental factors." And while they stated clearly their belief that homosexuality was not a mental disorder and that it should be accepted, they added, "It is not the case that sexual orientation is immutable or might not vary to some extent in a person's life."[54]

What? A consortium of fifteen thousand British psychiatrists now admits that homosexuality may not be innate and it may not be unchangeable? You had better believe it took a lot of evidence to convince them to make this shift. As John D'Emilio, a gay activist and a professor of history and of gender and women's studies at the University of Illinois, wrote, "What's most amazing to me about the 'born gay' phenomenon is that the scientific evidence for it is thin as a reed, yet it doesn't matter. It's an idea with such social utility that one doesn't need much evidence in order to make it attractive and credible."[55]

The fact is, more and more studies point to sexual fluidity, especially among women but among men as well, as documented by researcher Lisa Diamond, a lesbian herself. A 2009 interviewer with her wrote, "The queer community has been obsessed with cultivating the idea that we all have fixed sexual identities. We've crafted terrific narratives and political platforms based on the notions that all gays are 'born that way.' But what if sexuality is more complex? What if biology actually intersects with environment, time, culture, and context? Could we possibly be more fluid than we've supposed?"[56]

At that time, Diamond was more focused on gay female sexuality, but more recently she has argued for sexual fluidity among gay men as well.[57] In that light, it's not surprising to hear stories like that of Chirlane McCray. McCray, wife of New York City mayor Bill de Blasio, said, "In the 1970s, I identified as a lesbian and wrote about it. In 1991,

I met the love of my life, married him."[58]

More recently, lesbian activist Rebby Kern wrote an op-ed for the *Advocate*, a flagship gay publication, entitled "I'm Going Back to Bi: Confessions of a Former Lesbian." The subtitle stated, "Rebby Kern dated women for most of her adult life but is now understanding the *fluidity of her sexuality*" (my emphasis). Kern herself had this to say:

> I have to accept that I am growing and changing. The kinds of people I spend time with have shifted over the years, my hairstyle and my body have definitely changed, and my attractions have changed.
>
> When I came out as lesbian I felt I checked the box in ink, and now that I am dating someone who identifies as male I find myself needing to change my answer. I'm finding myself in a self-conflict just as difficult as when I came out as nonhetero.[59]

And could there be more to the story of Jason Collins, the NBA's first openly gay basketball player? He has an identical twin brother who is not gay, pointing once again to the nongenetic causes of homosexuality (otherwise both identical twins should have been gay), and when he came out in 2013, Carolyn Moos, his girlfriend of eight years, said she never suspected he was gay. I'm aware, of course, that Collins says he was wearing a mask all that time, denying his true identity. But if he could be in an ostensibly healthy (and presumably sexually active) heterosexual relationship for eight years, perhaps his sexuality was more complex and fluid than even he acknowledges?

Of course, these days it is considered heretical to question the prevailing orthodoxy of "innate and immutable," as I noted in principle 1, discussing the attack on New York Giants' football hero David Tyree. But as more and more people come out of homosexuality, either through midlife changes, new romantic attractions, professional therapy, or spiritual conversion, as more of them demonstrate different aspects of sexual fluidity, and as science continues to fail in its attempts to locate that elusive "gay gene," it will be impossible to hold to this "born this way and can't change" mantra.

More than twenty years ago, the influential lesbian author Camille Paglia had this to say about the "born gay" myth: "Homosexuality is not normal. On the contrary it is a challenge to the norm. . . . Nature exists whether academics like it or not. And in nature, procreation is the single relentless rule. That is the norm. . . . Our sexual bodies were designed for reproduction. . . . No one is born gay. The idea is ridiculous . . . homosexuality is an adaptation, not an inborn trait."[60]

But she was just getting started as she asked:

> Is the gay identity so fragile that it cannot bear the thought that some people may not wish to be gay? Sexuality is highly fluid, and reversals are theoretically possible. However, habit is refractory, once sensory pathways have been blazed and deepened by repetition—a phenomenon obvious with obesity, smoking, alcoholism or drug addiction—helping gays to learn how to function heterosexually, if they wish is a perfectly worthy aim. We should be honest enough to consider whether or not homosexuality may not indeed, be a pausing at the prepubescent stage where children band together by gender. . . . Current gay cant insists that homosexuality is not a choice; that no one would choose to be gay in a homophobic society. But there is an element of choice in all behavior, sexual or otherwise. It takes an effort to deal with the opposite sex; it is safer with your own kind. The issue is one of challenge versus comfort.[61]

No wonder many gay activists are uncomfortable with her candor. Freelance journalist Blake Adams noted, "It is not an overstatement to say that the gay's most robust platform, as well as the stronghold for their sense of identity, is entrenched in a well-developed yet deliciously simple fatalism," namely, that of biological determinism.[62] What happens, then, when this foundational linchpin of gay activism disappears?

LIE #4: THE TRAGIC MURDER OF MATTHEW SHEPHARD WAS AN ANTIGAY HATE CRIME

Nothing can possibly minimize the horrible nature of young Matthew Shepard's death, as he was tied to a fence with his hands behind his back, savagely beaten with a pistol until his skull was crushed, and left alone to die in the freezing cold of Laramie, Wyoming, ultimately succumbing to his wounds less than a week later in a local hospital. And to the extent that his death has called attention to the mistreatment of other gays and lesbians, that is certainly positive. In that sense, he did not die in vain.

But is it right to pass national legislation in the name of a myth? Is it right to perpetuate a media-created lie? It is right to base a civil rights movement on falsehood? The truth is that the Matthew Shepard Act, passed by Congress in 2007, is founded on fabrication.

The much-publicized, standard narrative alleges that Matthew met two strangers a bar, Aaron McKinney and Russell Henderson, and when they found out he was gay, they beat him to death. In reality, there is no evidence that is why he was killed and abundant evidence that Aaron and Matthew knew each other before that fateful night. There's even evidence that they had been sexually involved with each other.

All this, and much more, has been documented in devastating detail by award-winning journalist and TV producer Stephen Jimenez in his 2013 book *The Book of Matt: Hidden Truths about the Murder of Matthew Shepard*, the result of thirteen years of painstaking research.[63] And Jimenez is openly gay. He was hardly looking to stir up controversy, but he realized that something was amiss in the standard narrative once he began to look into it more deeply.

Not surprisingly, there has been great resistance to his findings. As noted by Julie Bindel in the *Guardian*, "Jimenez has been accused of being a revisionist, a criticism usually reserved for extreme rightwing ideologues that deny the Holocaust, and labeled a homophobe. 'People object to the idea of the book, rather than what is in the book,' says Jimenez. 'The anger directed at me has been pretty extreme.'"[64]

Already in 2004, when Jimenez worked with ABC's *20/20* to provide documentary evidence to refute the antigay hate crime narrative, gay activist organizations sought to squelch the show, led by the Human Rights Campaign and GLAAD.[65] The myth must not be touched! (Note also that David Sloan, executive producer of *20/20*, was gay, yet he too was more interested in the truth than in perpetuating a falsehood.)

Appearing in the *20/20* documentary was respected gay journalist Andrew Sullivan, who stated, "If you're going to base a civil rights movement on one particular incident, and the mythology about a particular incident, you're asking for trouble, because events are more complicated than most politicians or most activists want them to be."[66] Exactly so.

To repeat: none of this minimizes the tragedy of Matthew's murder or mitigates the loss experienced by his parents and friends, and to the extent that we have greater awareness of the suffering of LGBT people because of this, that is a positive development. But it is very telling that the iconic story behind antigay hate crimes legislation is itself a larger-than-life lie.

LIE #5: GAY IS THE NEW BLACK

One of the most common questions I'm asked is, how could such a tiny percentage of the population bring about such radical change to society in such a short period of time? The answer is that they didn't do it alone; they did it with the help of their straight allies who perceived the LGBT struggle as the new civil rights movement, as if gay were the new black. And given our country's history of slavery and segregation, this is a very compelling line of thought.

I'm aware that there are black leaders today, some of whom were even involved in the civil rights movement, who say that gay is the new black (Sen. John Lewis would be a prime example). But whenever I mention this topic on my radio show, asking my listeners if they believe it is fair to equate the black civil rights movement with today's gay rights movement, I am flooded with African American callers who take strong exception to this comparison.

Some of them remind me of public lynchings, of blacks being hosed down with fire hoses and attacked by police dogs, of families having to spend the night sleeping in their cars because the hotels wouldn't serve them, of water fountains marked "No coloreds"—not to mention the horrible history of African slavery in our nation.

They feel that gays and lesbians are hijacking their movement, even if they recognize that many LGBT individuals have experienced real suffering. They simply do not believe that the comparison is fair, also pointing out that the financial situation of the average gay or lesbian in America today is far better than the average situation of an African American during the days of segregation (or perhaps even today, for that matter).

Looking at Out.com's list of the fifty most powerful gay Americans[67] and using 1964 as an end date for official segregation (with the passing of the Civil Rights Act), would someone please be kind enough to tell me who the pre-1964 African American equivalents were for the following gay leaders?

- Suze Orman, the national TV host and respected financial guru

- Anderson Cooper, one of the most familiar faces on CNN, and Rachel Maddow, of MSNBC fame

- Annise Parker, mayor of Houston

- David Geffen, one of the most powerful media moguls

- Tim Cook, CEO of Apple

What? No well-known pre-1964 financial guru comes to mind? No prominent black newscasters or black mayors of major cities either? And you can't think of a single black media mogul or Fortune 500 CEO in America before 1964? Hmm . . .

When Jason Collins came out as the first openly gay NBA player, he received a congratulatory call from the president. Is that what happened to Jackie Robinson when he broke the color barrier in Major League Baseball? Not on your life. And did Robinson just come out as black one day, to the surprise of many of his closest friends, as did Collins, or was he subjected to hatred and even death threats for years because of the color of his skin? Just as it is ludicrous to make Jason Collins into the new Jackie Robinson, it is equally absurd to make sexual orientation the new civil rights battle.

Here's a brief summary of why gay is not the new black:

1. There is no true comparison between skin color and behavior. Although gays and lesbians emphasize identity rather than behavior, homosexuality is ultimately defined by romantic attraction and sexual behavior. How can this be equated with the color of someone's skin? Skin color has no intrinsic moral quality, and there is no moral difference between being black or white (or yellow or red). In contrast, romantic attractions and sexual behaviors often have moral (or immoral) qualities, and there is no constitutional "right" to fulfill one's sexual and romantic desires.

2. The very real hardships endured by many gays and lesbians cannot fairly be compared with the monstrous suffering endured by African Americans. As expressed by conservative gay journalist Charles Winecoff, "Newsflash: blacks in America didn't start out as hip-hop fashion designers; they were slaves. There's a big difference between being able to enjoy a civil union with the same sex partner of your choice—and not being able to drink out of a water fountain, eat at a lunch counter, or use a rest room because you don't have the right skin color."[68]

In contrast with the horrific suffering of black Americans in our past, where in America are gays and lesbians being lynched today with societal approval? And what is the LGBT equivalent to the American slave trade?

3. Skin color is innate and immutable; sexual orientation is not. We discussed this in the previous section, so I won't repeat it here, but let's remember that the "innate and immutable" lie is what fuels the fire of the "gay is the new black" concept. Suffice it to say that, contrary to popular opinion, there are former homosexuals but there are no former blacks. This also underscores the fact that skin color cannot be compared to behavior, since even someone who remains same-sex attracted can modify his or her sexual behavior. A black person cannot modify his or her blackness. Stated another way, genetics determine skin color, not behavior.

4. Removing the unjust laws against miscegenation (interracial marriage) did not require a fundamental redefinition of marriage and family; legalizing same-sex "marriage" does. Marriage between a black person and a white person always included the two essential elements of marriage, namely, a man and a woman (as opposed to just two people), and as a general rule, interracial marriage could naturally produce children and then provide those children with a mother and father. In contrast, same-sex "marriage" cannot produce children naturally and can never provide children with both a mother and a father.

Removing the laws of miscegenation simply required the removal of antiblack bigotry (since a white man could marry a Native American woman but not a black woman), whereas legalizing same-sex "marriage" requires the redefinition of marriage (opening the door to polyamorists, polygamists, and advocates of incestuous "marriages," who are already mounting their legal and social arguments) and the normalizing of homosexuality (beginning with elementary school education), among other things.

There is more, but this is enough to demonstrate that the idea that "gay is the new black" is fundamentally flawed.

STRAIGHT OUT OF HOLLYWOOD

There are many more lies and misconceptions that could be addressed, including: gays are all peace-loving, tolerant people; attempts to change sexual desires are always dangerous and harmful; there is no such thing as ex-gays; those who speak out against homosexual practice are closeted homosexuals—among others. But let me focus on one example of a blatant lie being instrumental in passing an oppressive gay activist bill. At some point, these lies will be exposed in the light of the truth, and this can mean only major setbacks for the gay revolution.

I'm speaking of one particular testimony before the New Jersey Senate that allegedly detailed the dangers of "gay conversion therapy." It was so riveting that it sounded like something taken straight out of a

Hollywood script. That testimony proved pivotal in the push to outlaw professional counseling for minors with unwanted same-sex attraction, discussed in principle 1. Unfortunately, from everything we can tell, it *was* taken straight out of Hollywood.

I'm referring to the testimony of Brielle Goldani, born male but now identifying as female, who described how he/she was sent by his/her parents to a religious camp in Ohio called True Directions, allegedly run by the Assemblies of God, a conservative Christian denomination. "Goldani told lawmakers she was given electric shocks and drugs to induce vomiting as part of the treatment."

Christopher Doyle, a professional counselor and himself a former homosexual (yes, these do exist, by the thousands), testified before the Senate against the bill, but he was deeply troubled by Goldani's story, prompting him to do further research. Here's what he uncovered: (1) "According to the office of the Ohio secretary of state and attorney general, no such camp called True Directions has ever existed." (2) The Assemblies of God, including the local church that allegedly sponsored the camp, never heard of it and would never sanction such barbarous treatment. (3) Licensed therapists in Ohio completely disavowed such treatments.

So where did Goldani's horror story come from? Doyle reports that "it came from a 1999 film titled 'But I'm a Cheerleader,' starring RuPaul. In the film, the main character is suspected of being a lesbian by her family, who then proceeds to send her to a 'conversion therapy' camp called True Directions."[69] Amazing! Yet New Jersey passed this bill, with Goldani's apparently fabricated testimony certainly playing a role, and Governor Christie signed it into law.

Sadly, this is not the first such instance of fabricated testimonies on the alleged danger of professional counseling for those with unwanted same-sex attractions (meaning the counselor talking with the client, not giving him or her shock therapy).[70] But what we now have is this: lies, falsehoods, and misconceptions have greatly advanced the gay revolution to the point that the argument has gone from "Gay is good" to "You can do nothing to stop being gay, and we'll make it illegal if you dare try." Talk about the suppression of all contrary values and ideas!

A HOUSE BUILT ON LIES WILL COLLAPSE

The question before us is not whether these lies are true. They are not. Rather, the question is this: What will happen when the public realizes they have supported a cause based on lies more than truth and that they have been conned by the media? Of course I care about treating all people fairly, and of course I want to see all people receive equal treatment under the law. But I categorically oppose using lies to advance an agenda, and I will continue to do my best to expose those lies.

Someone once said that if you tell a lie big enough and keep repeating it, people will eventually come to believe it. The lie can be maintained only for such time as the State can shield the people from the political, economic, and/or military consequences of the lie. It thus becomes vitally important for the State to use all of its powers to repress dissent, for the truth is the greatest enemy of the State.

But what happens when the lie is exposed? What will happen when people realize that opposition to the normalizing of homosexuality and the redefining of marriage is not based on hate but on concern for what is best for society—and that those who have been branded homophobes and bigots are actually caring and compassionate people? How will they react when they learn that there are often serious differences between homosexual relationships and heterosexual relationships, that gay suffering is not primarily due to homophobia, that homosexuality is not innate or immutable, and that gay is not the new black (let alone transgender being the new black) and therefore the battle for gay rights is not the same as the civil rights struggle?

How will people respond when they realize they have been duped? Only time will tell, but of this we can be sure: a revolution built on lies will ultimately fail, and those who stand on the side of truth will outlast the lies. As John wrote in his Gospel, "And the light shines on in the darkness, but the darkness has not mastered it" (John 1:5 NET).

So speak the truth and write the truth and proclaim the truth and spread the truth without fear. Propagate the truth with wisdom and love and boldness, however and wherever and whenever you can.

Don't back down when you're ridiculed on social media, when you're singled out for criticism in the workplace, when your denomination censures your words, when family members call you hateful. Just stay the course and speak the truth in love. People may *mock* your words for the short term, but they will *mark* your words over the long term.

PRINCIPLE #7

FACTOR IN THE GOD FACTOR

The church is too far gone ever to be redeemed. —SUPREME COURT CHIEF
JUSTICE JOHN MARSHALL, WRITING TO BISHOP MADISON OF VIRGINIA, EARLY 1800S

James Edwin Orr (1912–1987) was one of the leading authorities on spiritual awakenings. He taught that, in the mid-1850s, while immorality, violent crime, spiritualism, corruption, and atheism were on the rise, America's churches were becoming worldly and internalized. Then, in 1857, a great prayer movement began in New York City (it began quite inauspiciously, the truth be told, before spreading like fire across the country), and the nation was greatly impacted.[1] As Mary Stewart Relfe explains, "The Revival of 1857 restored integrity to government and business in America once again. There was renewed obedience to the social commandments. An intense sympathy was created for the poor and needy. A compassionate society was rebirthed. The reins of America were returned to the godly. Yet another time, Revival became the solution to the problems, the remedy for the evils, the cure of all ills."[2]

Within a few years, President Lincoln freed the slaves and the Civil War broke out, meaning that massive cultural change followed on the heels of a powerful spiritual awakening, ultimately with positive results that we commemorate to this day. And this was not the first time America had been changed by a religious revival, as historians of the

First and Second Great Awakenings have documented.[3]

Could it be that there is another great awakening at hand? Could our nation be transformed again by a spiritual renewal movement? Before we answer that, let's look at this from a more secular perspective, seeing exactly where we stand in our society today.

THE GAY REVOLUTION AND YOUNG AMERICA

Perhaps the strongest argument in favor of the assured success of the gay revolution is the demographic argument. Whereas the older generation strongly opposes gay activists' goals, the younger generation strongly supports them. This is even true in the Republican Party. As reported on March 11, 2014, "A new poll from the Pew Research Center reports that only 39% of Republicans overall support same-sex marriage; however, the youngest generation, the so-called Millennials aged 18–29, support same-sex marriage by 61%."[4]

The logic is clear and convincing. Soon enough, the older generation, representing the main opposition to gay activism, will die out, to be replaced by the younger generation, which supports gay activism. In turn, the following generation will be even more firmly pro-gay, having grown up in a new, tolerant era, one in which kids raised by two moms or two dads will be as American as apple pie. As reported by the *New York Times* on February 26, 2013, "A majority of Americans now favor same-sex marriage, up from roughly one third in 2003. While Republicans lag behind the general population—the latest New York Times survey found a third of Republicans favor letting gay people marry—that too is changing quickly as more young people reach voting age. Several recent polls show that about 70 percent of voters under 30 back same-sex marriage."[5]

Thus the triumph of the gay revolution is assured—or at least we are told it is assured. As *Time* magazine proclaimed on April 8, 2013, with a double-cover story (each cover featuring a gay couple kissing, one male, the other female), "Gay Marriage Already Won: The Supreme Court Hasn't Made Up Its Mind—But America Has."[6] This, of course, was before the Supreme Court overturned DOMA in June 2013, which was another major landmark in the gay revolution.

Eleven months later, in May 2014, an article by Sarah Posner in Al Jazeera America declared, "A decade later, same-sex marriage tide has almost completely turned." Posner quoted the pessimistic outlook of columnist Rod Dreher, writing in the *American Conservative* in March 2014: "It's time for social conservatives active in politics to start thinking about what the post-SSM landscape looks like." Dreher "acknowledged that even within the conservative movement, many libertarians are trending toward approval of same-sex marriage," as he lamented, "This was a major battle . . . and we lost it decisively. . . . We have lost American culture, no question about it."[7]

There you have it. America has made up its mind, the conservative side has lost decisively, and there's nothing further to discuss—or so we are told, even by conservative pundits.

Religion writer Jim Hinch underscored this in his June 2014 article titled "Evangelicals Are Changing Their Minds on Gay Marriage. And the Bible Isn't Getting in Their Way." Hinch stated:

> Over the past decade, evangelical support for gay marriage has more than doubled, according to polling by the nonpartisan Public Religion Research Institute. About a quarter of evangelicals now support same-sex unions, the institute has found, with an equal number occupying what researchers at Baylor University last year called the "messy middle" of those who oppose gay marriage on moral grounds but no longer support efforts to outlaw it. The shift is especially visible among young evangelicals under age 35, a near majority of whom now support same-sex marriage. And gay student organizations have recently formed at Christian colleges across the country, including flagship evangelical campuses such as Wheaton College in Illinois and Baylor in Texas.
>
> Even some of the most prominent evangelicals—megachurch pastors, seminary professors and bestselling authors—have publicly announced their support for gay marriage in recent months. Other leaders who remain opposed to gay unions have lowered their profiles on the issue.[8]

IS THE BATTLE REALLY OVER?

So the battle is over, gay activists have won the culture wars, and Christians should just throw in the towel, right?

Gay activist Wayne Besen argues that there is another nail in the coffin of the conservative Christian side: "An ultimately fatal problem for anti-gay marriage activists is that conversions appear to be a one-way street," he wrote. "For example, in 2011, Louis Marinelli, a former organizer for the National Organization for Marriage reversed his opposition, explaining: 'Too many see support for gay rights as strictly a liberal issue. That's a mistake. Supporting the constitutional rights of all citizens is a conservative issue, too.'"

Besen then pointed to several other significant converts to the same-sex "marriage" cause, including David Blankenhorn, "the lead expert [witness] defending California's Proposition 8, [who] rethought his opposition and spoke out in favor of gay marriage in a *New York Times* editorial," and Ted Olsen, who served in the Reagan and George W. Bush administrations before helping overturn California's Proposition 8. Worse still for the conservative side, Besen noted that there are "virtually no defections on the pro-same-sex-marriage side. Once people see the light on this issue, they have no desire to return to darkness."[9]

As the argument goes, once society becomes more enlightened and same-sex "marriage" becomes the law of the land, there is no way to reverse the tide. And as we have seen, even in the world of religion, which is the last organizational bastion of opposition to homosexual activism, we are told that more and more leaders are seeing the light, renouncing their antigay positions, and embracing a new understanding of the Scriptures. As gay bishop Eugene Robinson proclaimed in the title of his book—a book endorsed by President Obama—*God Believes in Love*, and therefore it is self-evident that He believes in same-sex "marriage" too. At least, that's what we are told.[10] Indeed, some ministers proclaim that homosexual practice is not a sin. It is homophobia that is a sin.[11]

This, then, is where we find ourselves today, and it is understandable why even some conservative leaders have reluctantly acknowledged that we have lost the culture wars. Yet as I have argued throughout this book, such a conclusion is completely premature, even if it may seem accurate for the present and for the immediate future.

IT'S NOT TIME TO THROW IN THE TOWEL

I have suggested that the backlash against gay bullying will only increase as our freedoms of speech, religion, and conscience continue to be attacked. I also have argued that our society's acceptance of homosexuality is part and parcel of its larger decline into sexual anarchy. And since a society that gives way to sexual anarchy cannot thrive, our country will need to make a course correction.

I have noted that the redefining of marriage has rendered it virtually meaningless, which could well lead us back to marriage as God intended it (and virtually all civilizations have recognized it). In the same way, I believe that the war on gender will defeat itself when tolerant, loving Americans realize that the gay revolution is going places they never intended to go. And because so many of the main pillars of the gay revolution are based on falsehood, misrepresentation, or exaggeration, persistent propagating of the truth will ultimately expose the lies. All this means that even the younger generations could have a shift in perspective as a direct result of the gay revolution coming into its fullness.

This would be similar to what has happened with perspectives on abortion, as today's younger generation, the one we were told years ago would be totally embracing of abortion, has become increasingly pro-life.[12] As Austin Ruse noted in the very article that announced growing support for same-sex "marriage" among GOP youth, "Social conservatives point out that the number of young people opposed to abortion used to be equally bleak among the young but is now trending their way."[13] Why can't the same thing happen with homosexual activism?

When the Supreme Court passed *Roe v. Wade* in 1973, pro-life forces were in disarray, yet they quickly mounted "a push for a constitutional amendment affirming that life begins at conception." But, Nina Martin reported in the *New Republic*, "that first effort fizzled, and it's only in recent years that a new wave of pro-life activists—many of them born after *Roe* and educated in fundamentalist Christian settings—have once again seized on personhood as a way not just of weakening *Roe*, but of overturning it. In state after state, they have been pushing to have their beliefs enshrined in policy."[14]

Did you catch that? Many of those leading the pro-life charge today were born after 1973 and were raised in conservative Christian homes. Again I ask, why can't the same thing happen when it comes to turning the tide of homosexual activism? These recent years have been marked by major gay activist victories, but again, this is the beginning of the story, not the end.

THE FUTURE IS FULL OF SURPRISES

The very day I started writing this chapter, some unexpected, even unprecedented news came from Virginia. Republican Congressman Eric Cantor was defeated in the primaries by an almost unknown candidate, an economics professor named David Brat. This marked the first time in American history that the House majority leader lost in a primary. Ever. Unexpected things do happen! Cantor had outspent Brat by roughly fifty to one, and internal polling by Cantor's team had him up by thirty points shortly before the primary. AP News called it "an upset for the ages," while Brat proclaimed, "This is a miracle from God that just happened."[15]

Virtually no one saw it coming, which reminds us that the pollsters and the social prognosticators are not always right. The startling outcome prompted journalist Ron Fournier to write, "Elites Beware: Eric Cantor's Defeat May Signal a Populist Revolution." He added, "A violent revolution is unconscionable. But what may be in the air is a peaceful populist revolt—a bottom-up, tech-fueled assault on 20th-century political institutions."[16]

Things can sometimes turn on a dime, a lesson we learned from the tumultuous decade of the '60s, another time the pollsters were not able to predict what was about to come. I was there when it happened.

So dramatic was the cultural shift because of the counterculture revolution that author David G. Meyers stated that if you fell asleep in the year 1960 and woke up in the year 2000, you would be awakening to a:

- Doubled divorce rate.

- Tripled teen suicide rate.

- Quadrupled rate of reported violent crime.

- Quintupled prison population.

- Sextupled (no pun intended) percent of babies born to unmarried parents.

- Sevenfold increase in cohabitation (a predictor of future divorce).

- Soaring rate of depression—to ten times the pre–World War II level by one estimate.[17]

THE POLLSTERS MISSED AN IMMINENT REVOLUTION

The dramatic moral shift that took place in the '60s has been familiar to me (and many others) for years. But what I didn't know until recently was that the pollsters did not see this rebellious youth movement coming, a movement marked by the proverbial sex, drugs, and rock 'n' roll (plus some Eastern religion thrown in). In fact, their analysis of the social data pointed in the exact opposite direction. I learned of this through a fascinating book by Larry Eskridge titled *God's Forever Family: The Jesus People Movement in America.* (Dr. Eskridge has been on the staff of the Institute for the Study of American Evangelicals at Wheaton College since 1988.) According to Eskridge,

> Going into the 1960s, there was little indication of the cultural turmoil that would swarm around a sizable segment of the Baby Boom generation later in the decade. In fact, if the experts were to be believed, the rising generation of adults-to-be appeared to fit in quite nicely with their elders' values and expectations. That was certainly

the thrust of a late-1961 survey of American youth by pollsters George Gallup and Evan Hill. . . . Their research indicated that American teenagers were happy with their world, if not downright complacent.[18]

What exactly did the polls reveal? According to Gallup and Hill, "The typical American youth shows few symptoms of frustration and is most unlikely to rebel or involve himself in crusades of any kind."

This is utterly remarkable. Yes, "the typical youth demonstrated 'little spirit of adventure'; most simply wanted 'a little ranch house, an inexpensive new car, a job with a large company, and a chance to watch TV each evening after the smiling children are asleep in bed.'" And these young people were quite religious: "[M]ore than 75% firmly believed in God, and nearly two-thirds believed that the Bible was 'completely true.'"

Eskridge further noted that "Gallup and Hill's findings were very similar to those put forth in a 1962 article by Harvard sociologist Talcott Parsons. 'The general orientation,' he said of American teenagers, appeared to be 'an eagerness . . . to accept higher orders of respectability' and a 'readiness to work within the system.'"

In retrospect, these observations seem almost comical, but this is how the younger generation appeared to be in 1962—and even beyond. As Eskridge explains, "Two years later, [Parsons] found the situation to be much the same. Indeed, he believed that youth were generally becoming more conservative and, perhaps most important, seemed more amenable to adult control. Parsons's sentiments were echoed in a statement by one university administrator who opined in the early 1960s that 'employers will love this generation. . . . They are going to be easy to handle.'"

Yes, the generation that within a few years would be in full-scale rebellion (think "generation gap"), burning draft cards, gathering in droves for the Summer of Love in San Francisco, wreaking havoc at the Chicago Democratic Convention in 1968, and celebrating a mass orgy at Woodstock—*that* generation was deemed "unlikely to rebel or involve [themselves] in crusades of any kind." According to the pollsters, the young generation of the 1960s was even "going to be easy to handle." How incredible it is to read these words with the benefit of hindsight.

Who could have predicted the nation-shaking events that were about to transpire: the assassinations of President Kennedy, Martin Luther King Jr., and Robert Kennedy, all within a five-year span; the rise of the civil rights movement; the dramatic shift in sentiment regarding the Vietnam War; the impact of the British Invasion; the explosion of the drug culture; and so much more that shaped that tumultuous decade? All of which goes to show that radical, cultural shifts can happen on a dime, and without much warning at that.

The very subject of this book, namely, the gay revolution, would be a case in point. America has never seen such rapid changes in such a short period of time.

CULTURAL REVOLUTIONS CAN COME OUT OF NOWHERE

Writing in 2014, Mark Engler and Paul Engler noted:

> It can be difficult to remember how hostile the terrain was for LGBT advocates in even recent decades. As of 1990, three-quarters of Americans saw homosexual sex as immoral. Less than a third condoned same-sex marriage—something no country in the world permitted. In 1996, the Defense of Marriage Act, which defined marriage as a union between a man and a woman and denied federal benefits to same-sex couples, passed by an overwhelming 85-14 margin in the U.S. Senate. Figures including Democratic Sen. Joe Biden voted for it, and Democratic President Bill Clinton signed the act, affirming, "I have long opposed governmental recognition of same-gender marriages."

All of this pointed back to a time when conservative resistance to same-sex "marriage" was a positive political strategy, with thirteen states voting against the redefinition of marriage in 2004. "Today," the authors note, "these seem like scenes from an alternate universe," especially Republican presidential candidate Gary Bauer's comment that the Vermont Supreme Court's decision in 1999 to recognize homosexual civil unions was "in some ways worse than terrorism."

They continued:

What is striking about this is not just the seeming suddenness of the reversal. It is that the rapidly expanding victory around same-sex marriage defies many of our common ideas about how social change happens. . . . For the tradition now known as "civil resistance," the triumph of same-sex marriage in the United States is a remarkable example of what happens when a critical mass of people withdraws its willingness to cooperate with an existing state of affairs, and when the support of social institutions for an idea or a regime falls away.[19]

Just think. Speaking to a major gay publication in 1996, President Clinton said, "I remain opposed to same-sex marriage. I believe marriage is an institution for the union of a man and a woman. This has been my long-standing position, and it is not being reviewed or reconsidered."[20] Today he is a champion of redefining marriage.

Similarly, in 2004, then senator Barack Obama said, "My religious faith dictates marriage is between a man and a woman, gay marriage is not a civil right." And in 2008 he reiterated, "I believe marriage is the union between a man and a woman. As a Christian it's also a sacred union." That same year he even said to the very pro-gay MTV, "I believe marriage is between a man and a woman. I am not in favor of gay marriage."[21] Today he can be described as militantly pro-gay "marriage."[22] What a difference just a few short years make!

DRAMATIC AND UNEXPECTED SHIFTS IN THE WORLD OF RELIGION

In the world of religion, ultra-Orthodox Judaism, in particular Hasidic Judaism, seemed all but dead after the Holocaust, with the major religious communities utterly decimated. Now these expressions of Judaism are rapidly growing while other, more liberal expressions are in steady decline, and in the State of Israel (which did not even exist at the time of World War II), the *Haredim* (ultra-Orthodox, meaning "God-fearers") are growing by leaps and bounds.[23]

Even more astounding, though, is the growth of Christianity worldwide, something that may surprise many Americans and Europeans given the decline of the Church in recent decades and the rise of an increasingly militant atheism. The facts are utterly astonishing:

During the twentieth century, Christian numbers expanded mightily around the world, but especially in the Global South. According to the respected World Christian Database, since 1900 the number of African Christians has grown by an incredible 4,930 percent, and the growth in Latin America was 877 percent. The increase for particular denominations was even more startling. During the twentieth century, Africa's Catholic population grew from 1.9 million to 130 million— an increase of 6,700 percent.

The total number of African believers of all shades soared, from just 10 million in 1900 to almost 500 million today, and (if projections are correct) to an astonishing billion by 2050. Put another way, the number of African Christians in 2050 will be almost twice as large as the total figure for all Christians alive anywhere in the globe back in 1900.[24]

Who knew? The truth is, from a global perspective, atheism is on the wane and religion is on the rise, with Christianity leading the way.[25] One British intellectual even wrote a book in 2006 titled *The Twilight of Atheism: The Rise and Fall of Disbelief in the Modern World*.[26]

IS GOD DEAD? NO!

Bringing this closer to home, on April 8, 1966, the cover of *Time* magazine asked in stark red-on-black lettering, "Is God Dead?" Looking back in 2009, theologian Albert Mohler noted that the feature article, written by John T. Elson after more than a year of research, "became an icon of the rebellious and increasingly secular sixties. For the first time," he continued, "TIME published the magazine cover without a photograph or drawing. The question, 'Is God Dead?,' was all that mattered."[27]

Five years later, on June 21, 1971, *Time* ran another striking cover story, this time featuring a hippie-like depiction of Jesus, with the caption "The Jesus Revolution."

The article described a remarkable spiritual movement among the psychedelic generation—the hippies, the rockers, the rebels, the druggies, the kids into Transcendental Meditation and pot and LSD and the Beatles and the Grateful Dead—with thousands coming to faith in Jesus and becoming born-again Christians. I was one of those kids, experiencing a radical and quite unexpected (not to mention fervently resisted) conversion experience as a sixteen-year-old, heroin-shooting, LSD-using, proud, rebellious, rock-drumming Jew.

Time got its answer. No, God was not dead! In fact, this extraordinary spiritual awakening among the rebellious young generation was as unexpected and unpredicted as the youth rebellion itself, having its origins in none other than the city of San Francisco in 1967, just one year after the "Is God Dead?" feature story. Who saw *that* coming?

THE JESUS REVOLUTION

Many of those who came to faith at that time are leaders in the Church today, not just in America, but in many nations where the Jesus revolution was also taking place. (A spiritual movement is not limited by geographical or ideological borders.) Many of them have served for years on the front lines of compassionate, humanitarian efforts, while others have become pastors and educators, and still others have become leaders in conservative social movements—meaning that radical rebels of the counterculture revolution became the committed, biblical conservatives of the Jesus revolution.[28]

As *Time* reported in 1971:

Jesus is alive and well and living in the radical spiritual fervor of a growing number of young Americans who have proclaimed an extraordinary religious revolution in his name. Their message: the Bible is true, miracles happen, God really did so love the world that he gave it his only begotten son. In 1966 Beatle John Lennon casually remarked that the Beatles were more popular than Jesus Christ; now the Beatles are shattered, and George Harrison is singing My Sweet Lord. The new young followers of Jesus listen to Harrison, but they turn on only to the words of their Master: "For where two or three are gathered together in my name, there am I in the midst of them."

What exactly did this look like? The article continues:

Christian coffeehouses have opened in many cities, signaling their faith even in their names: The Way Word in Greenwich Village, the Catacombs in Seattle, I Am in Spokane. A strip joint has been converted to a "Christian nightclub" in San Antonio. Communal "Christian houses" are multiplying like loaves and fishes for youngsters hungry for homes, many reaching out to the troubled with round-the-clock telephone hot lines. Bibles abound: whether the cherished, fur-covered King James Version or scruffy, back-pocket paperbacks, they are invariably well-thumbed and often memorized. "It's like a glacier," says "Jesus-Rock" Singer Larry Norman, 24. "It's growing and there's no stopping it."[29]

Who is to say another, even more profound and far-reaching Jesus revolution can't happen again in our day? Revival historians will tell you that stranger things have happened in the past, and that's what I refer to when I speak of the God factor, meaning something that transcends logic and often defies the predictions of the wisest prognosticators, a season of divine intervention resulting in unexpected cultural shifts sparked by religious awakenings.

To speak of such things is not a matter of cognitive dissonance or spiritual denial, of refusing to accept the inevitable. It is a matter of confident faith, of trust in the goodness of God, of firm belief that His ways are best and that they will triumph in the end, of deep-seated assurance that He will hear the prayers that His people have been praying for many years, in some cases literally day and night. History tells us that religious awakenings have helped shape American life and culture, and as it has happened in the past, it can happen again. Why not?

WHO IS ON THE WRONG SIDE OF HISTORY?

In a very important article entitled "Marriage and the 'Wrong Side of History,'" Jeff Jacoby painted a fascinating picture of where we stand today, raising important questions about where we might stand tomorrow.

"Marriage has got historic, religious, and moral content that goes back to the beginning of time," said Hillary Clinton in 2000, "and I think a marriage is, as a marriage has always been, between a man and a woman." Even after the Massachusetts Supreme Judicial Court ruled that legal objections to same-sex "marriage" were irrational, many liberals stood pat. Leading Democratic presidential candidates in 2004—John Kerry, John Edwards, Joseph Lieberman, Dick Gephardt—ran as gay "marriage" opponents. So did Clinton and Barack Obama in 2008.

As we asked earlier, Jacoby also wondered, "Has there ever been an issue so elemental on which the tide turned so swiftly?

"Overnight, same-sex marriage has gone from all-but-unthinkable to all-but-unstoppable," he went on. "So what do those marchers in Washington think they're going to accomplish? Don't they have better things to do with their lives than fight for a cause that, if not yet entirely lost, is surely down for the count?

"Why don't they wake up and smell the historical inevitability?"

Yes, why don't people like Jacoby and me just "wake up and smell the historical inevitability"? Why do we stubbornly position ourselves on the wrong side of history? Why do we stubbornly position ourselves on the wrong side of history?

Jacoby looks back in order to look ahead:

> History is littered with causes and beliefs that were thought at one point to be historically unstoppable, from the divine right of kings to worldwide Marxist revolution. In the relative blink of an eye, same-sex marriage has made extraordinary political and psychological gains. It is on a roll, winning hearts and minds as well as court cases. No wonder it seems to so many that history's verdict is in, and same-sex marriage is here to stay.
>
> Maybe it is.
>
> Or maybe a great national debate about the meaning of marriage is not winding down, but just gearing up. And maybe those marchers in Washington [speaking of a conservative, pro-family, pro-marriage March in Washington, DC], with their "simple and beautiful message," will prove to be not bitter-enders who didn't know when to quit, but defenders of a principle that history, eventually, will vindicate.[30]

LEARNING FROM WILLIAM WILBERFORCE

On February 24, 1791, just six days before his death at age eighty-eight, John Wesley wrote a letter to Parliament member William Wilberforce, a convert through Wesley's ministry. Wilberforce had been campaigning for years to abolish slavery and the slave trade in the British Empire, but it seemed like a hopeless, uphill climb. Slavery was not just an accepted part of life. It also played an important national and international economic role, and all of Wilberforce's efforts to date had resulted in failure.

Wesley wrote these words to him:

Dear Sir:

Unless the divine power has raised you up to be as "Athanasius against the world" [Athanasius was a courageous church leader who stood his ground against great odds], I see not how you can go through your glorious enterprise in opposing that execrable villainy, which is the scandal of religion, of England, and of human nature. Unless God has raised you up for this very thing, you will be worn out by the opposition of men and devils. But if God be for you, who can be against you? Are all of them stronger than God? O be not weary of well-doing! Go on, in the name of God and in the power of His might, till even American slavery (the vilest that ever saw the sun) shall vanish away before it.

Reading this morning a tract wrote by a poor African [speaking of a man who had been kidnapped and sold for a slave in Barbados], I was particularly struck by the circumstance, that a man who has a black skin being wronged or outraged by a white man, can have no redress; it being a LAW in all of our Colonies that the OATH of a black man against a white goes for nothing. What villainy is this!

That He who has guided you from youth up may continue to strengthen you in this and all things is the prayer of, dear sir,

Your affectionate servant,

John Wesley[31]

Wilberforce persevered, and after more years of defeat and frustration, his cause finally prevailed. Wesley's words proved prophetic, not only with the abolition of slavery and the slave trade in Great Britain, but two generations later, in America as well. And this was all done against what seemed like insurmountable odds.

IT'S TIME FOR ANOTHER GREAT AWAKENING

That should bring great encouragement to those of you today who are standing for marriage and family as God intended them to be, who are standing against sexual anarchy and the war on gender, who refuse to bow down to bullying and intimidation, and who are determined to uphold the truth regardless of cost or consequences.

Prof. Donald Whitney recounted, "A terrible declension of Christianity followed the War of Independence. The outer ripples of the First Great Awakening were still seen as late as the 1770s when as much as 40 to 50 percent of the population attended church. But by the 1790s only 5 to 10 percent of the adult population were church members." Revival historian J. Edwin Orr wrote:

> The Methodists were losing more members than they were gaining. The Baptists said they had their most wintry season. The Presbyterians met in general assembly to deplore the ungodliness of the country. The Congregationalists were strongest in New England. [And yet] Rev. Samuel Shepherd, pastor of a typical church in Lennox, Massachusetts, said in sixteen years he had not taken one young person into the fellowship. . . . The Lutherans were so languishing they discussed uniting with the Episcopalians, who were even worse off. The Protestant Episcopal bishop of New York, Bishop Samuel Provost, quit functioning. He had confirmed no one for so long, he decided he was out of work, so he took up other employment. The Chief Justice of the United States, John Marshall, wrote to Bishop Madison of Virginia and said, "'The church is too far gone ever to be redeemed.'"

But that was only the beginning. Whitney continued:

Orr further notes that for the first time in American history, women were afraid to go out at night for fear of assault. Out of five million citizens, 300,000 were drunkards, and increased sexual immorality multiplied the numbers of illegitimate births and sexually transmitted diseases. Bank robberies were a daily occurrence. Dueling, wrote Daniel Dorchester a century later, "had become a great national sin. With the exception of a small section of the Union, the whole land was deeply stained with blood."

The overall situation seemed so hopeless that a friend wrote to George Washington in 1796, near the end of his two terms as president, "Our affairs seem to lead to some crisis, some revolution; something that I can not foresee or conjecture. I am more uneasy than during the war." Washington replied, "Your sentiment . . . accords with mine. What will be is beyond my foresight."[32]

What a hopeless, depressing description, but that was the state of the nation toward the end of the eighteenth century.

According to Whitney, five major factors contributed to this spiritual backsliding: (1) the divisive effect of the war itself, since the war had fractured the nation; (2) "the impact of Tom Paine and rationalistic Deism" (Deism believes that God created the universe and set it in motion but has not been involved in His creation in a personal way since); (3) the influence of French unbelief; (4) Unitarianism, a heretical, humanistic form of Christianity that denied certain foundations of the faith; and (5) the westward expansion of the population, depleting churches in the East and leading to lawlessness in the West.

And so, "nothing less than a sovereign act by an omnipotent God could effectively deal with the situation. Revival was the church's only hope."

And revival was what God sent. A spark that He kindled in the 1790s burst into flames in the early 1800s as the Second Great Awakening, both in the apathetic, skeptical east and in the lawless, godless west.

The preaching of the Law of God awakened people's consciences, laid upon them an unrelenting conviction of sin, and terrified them with the realities of judgment and eternal punishment. Such preaching, followed by the application of the Gospel of Jesus Christ, resulted in the conversion of hundreds of thousands in the early decades of the nineteenth century. The wind of God's Spirit blew almost everywhere. New congregations began dotting the churchless western landscape. Bible-preaching churches back east were filled again. Christians hungered for the teaching of God's Word. Holy living became their passion. They delighted in prayer meetings and worship services.[33]

But it was not just church buildings that were filled. The society was impacted positively as well, with many claiming that it was this revival movement that tamed the Wild West.[34]

This is a big part of the reason I am not in the least bit discouraged today, despite so many negative spiritual and social indicators that surround us. Societies have turned around before, quite unexpectedly, and as quickly as the gay revolution has spread across the nation (and other nations), it could dissipate. Yet my trust is not placed in the shifting sands of human society but in the unchanging God of truth and justice, and as He acted before in our history—the God factor!—I believe we will see Him act again.

PRINCIPLE #8

BE DETERMINED TO WRITE THE
LAST CHAPTER OF THE BOOK

One thing is for sure—a faith that survived its followers being used as torches to light the streets of Rome will survive a modern age hell bent on ruthlessly stamping it out. —ERICK ERICKSON

There is a remarkable quote in Prof. Elaine Showalter's book *Sexual Anarchy*, where she states that the '80s and '90s,

in the words of novelist George Gissing, were decades of "sexual anarchy," when all the laws that governed sexual identity and behavior seemed to be breaking down. As Karl Miller notes, "Men became women. Women became men. Gender and country were put in doubt. . . ." During this period both the words "feminism" and "homosexuality" first came into use, as New Women and male aesthetes redefined the meanings of femininity and masculinity. . . .

Especially there was a call to reaffirm the importance of the family as the bulwark against sexual decadence.[1]

You might be thinking, "What's so remarkable about that quote?" The only thing odd is her claim that the words *feminism* and *homosexuality* first came into use in the 1980s and 1990s. They're older than that!

Precisely so. Showalter was talking about the *1880s* and *'90s* in Europe and America, not the *1980s* and *'90s*. Now go back and read the quote again and see if it is not remarkable.

How many of us knew that in parts of Europe and America, the late nineteenth century was marked by "sexual anarchy"? That men became women and women became men, and "all the laws that governed sexual identity and behavior seemed to be breaking down"? Or that in response to this social decline, "there was a call to reaffirm the importance of the family as the bulwark against sexual decadence"?

This reminds me of a verse in a fascinating book of the Bible called Ecclesiastes, which says, "History merely repeats itself. It has all been done before. Nothing under the sun is truly new. Sometimes people say, 'Here is something new!' But actually it is old; nothing is ever truly new" (Ecclesiastes 1:9–10 NLT).[2]

To be sure, technology is new, and there are things we can do today in travel and communication and many other areas that would have been inconceivable in past generations. But when it comes to human nature, there really is nothing new under the sun.

For example, the apostle Paul condemned homosexual practice (both male and female) in very categorical ways, but there are some who claim today that Paul was exposed only to really bad forms of homosexuality, like pederasty and temple prostitution and the like, and that he didn't understand contemporary concepts like having a homosexual orientation. Is this an accurate observation? Was homosexuality back then totally different from homosexuality today?

Actually, scholars have pointed out that in the Greco-Roman world in which Paul lived, he would have been exposed to all kinds of homosexual practice, including long-term, same-sex relationships. There were even ancient discussions as to whether homosexual desires were inborn.[3] As noted by respected New Testament scholar Anthony Thiselton, commenting on Paul's first letter to the Corinthians, "Paul witnessed around him both abusive relationships of power or money and examples of 'genuine love' between males. . . . The more closely writers examine Graeco-Roman society and the pluralism of its ethical traditions, the more the Corinthian situation appears to resonate with our own."[4] In other words, people are people.

That's why author Amy Orr Ewing could state, "While recognizing that what the Bible says about homosexual practice may seem controversial and unpopular, it is important to remember that it would also have seemed so at the time it was written." And so, "although the Bible may seem 'out of date,' the culture in which it was written was not so dissimilar from our own."[5]

That means that while human beings today might have cell phones and computers and airplanes and even rocket ships, we're still human beings, and the issues faced by past generations, even if they didn't look exactly the same, are strikingly similar to ours. It also means that there were societies that openly engaged in homosexual practice, but they did not stand the test of time.

WHAT DID THE ANCIENT RABBIS KNOW ABOUT SAME-SEX "MARRIAGE"?

Confirmation for this comes from a surprising source, namely, the ancient rabbinic writings, reflecting traditions that go back to the time of Jesus and, in some cases, centuries before. Several of these writings actually addressed the issue of same-sex "marriage," which raises the obvious question, how did they know about this phenomenon so long ago?

The first text we'll look at begins with a verse from Leviticus 18, which forbade the Israelites from participating in pagan practices when they entered the promised land:

> "According to the doings of the Land of Egypt . . . and the doings of the Land of Canaan . . . you shall not do" (Leviticus 18:3): Can it be (*that it means*) don't build buildings, and don't plant plantings? Thus it (*the verse*) teaches (*further*), "And you shall not walk in their statutes." I say (*that the prohibition of the verse applies*) only to (*their*) statutes—the statutes which are theirs and their fathers and their fathers' fathers. And what did they do? A man got married to a man, and a woman to a woman, a man married a woman and her daughter,

and a woman was married to two (*men*). Therefore it is said, "And you shall not walk in their statutes."[6]

Did you follow that? The ancient rabbis were asking what God intended when He commanded the Israelites not to do what the pagans did. Did this mean they shouldn't build and plant, since the pagans did those things too? Certainly not! It meant that the Israelites were not to follow their sinful customs, which included, in so many words, same-sex "marriage" and polygamy. Did I just say that there is nothing new under the sun?

This rabbinic text is more than eighteen hundred years old, and it's very possible that it reflects traditions hundreds of years older than that. Furthermore, it's speaking about Israel's exodus from Egypt, roughly thirty-five hundred years ago, and claiming that even way back then, the people of Canaan and Egypt practiced same-sex "marriage" and other forbidden relationships. How extraordinary.

Another ancient rabbinic text, this one a few decades later than the first one but also containing older traditions, claims that God did not send the flood in Noah's day until things reached a particular breaking point: "Rabbi Huna in the name of Rabbi Yosef (*said*): The generation of the Flood was not wiped out until they wrote *gemumasi'ot* for (the union of a man to) a male or to an animal."[7] What were these *gemumasi'ot*? They were marriage contracts!

These ancient rabbis claimed that the straw that broke the camel's back, causing God to send a flood to wipe out everyone but Noah's family, was "marriages" conducted between two men or between a man and an animal. Shades of what we described earlier in this book (see principle 4). Who knew?

But there's more. According to a statement in the Babylonian Talmud, which is the most foundational compilation of rabbinic tradition, although God gave thirty specific requirements for the Gentile world (in contrast with Israel, which received 613 commandments), they kept only three of them, one of them being "that they do not write a marriage contract for males."[8] And this comment is more than fifteen hundred years old, reflecting, as I have said, much earlier Jewish traditions.

Where did these traditions come from? There are really only two logical choices: (1) the rabbis actually had access to traditions going back to the time of Israel's exodus from Egypt and even back to the time of Noah's flood;[9] or (2) the rabbis projected back into ancient times things they witnessed in their own day (or knew about from recent, previous generations). In either case, the conclusions are the same: they were aware of the concept of same-sex "marriage," it represented an especially debased behavior, and the societies that engaged in this sinful practice no longer existed.

Based on these rabbinic writings, Gail Labovitz, senior research analyst in Brandeis University's Feminist Sexual Ethics Project, concluded:

> What all of these sources suggest is that in the rabbinic mindset giving societal recognition to same-sex marriage is among the most egregious violations that human beings can commit. Only non-Israelites might be suspected of sanctioning such relationships; there is no suggestion that Israelites would ever consider such a thing. Indeed, Israelites are to avoid this in no small measure precisely because it is the (imagined) practiced of the Other. Homosexual contact, especially between men, is already highly stigmatized in rabbinic literature and is often associated with non-Jews (see, as just one example, Sifra *Acharei Mot*, *perek* 13:8). Marriage between members of the same gender, however, goes beyond forbidden sexual acts between individuals to the level of societal approval of this sin. When sin is no longer recognized as sin by a society, the rabbis would assert, that society loses its right to existence—like the generation of the Flood, or the defeated Egyptians and Canaanites, such a society deserves to be swept away.[10]

Now, aside from these texts being absolutely astounding, reminding us that there is, indeed, nothing new under the sun—it's even possible Jesus Himself was familiar with some of these traditions—they also tell us something else: societies that engage in same-sex "marriages" appear doomed to fail.

DAYS OF NOAH?

Interestingly, there are some Bible teachers who are convinced that the end of the world is very near and that America's slide into sexual anarchy (among other things) is a clear sign of impending doom, meaning that the return of Jesus is at hand. And they believe that when Jesus said, "For as were the days of Noah, so will be the coming of the Son of Man" (Matthew 24:37 ESV), He was speaking of the great evil that existed in Noah's day, which, according to these ancient Jewish texts, included same-sex "marriage."

In other words, these teachers believe that as it was in the end of Noah's day, that's how it will be at the end of the world, and they see the sudden, widespread embrace of same-sex "marriage" as yet another sign that Jesus is about to return.[11] If they are right and Jesus could return any minute, then you might want to put this book down and tell everyone you know to get ready to meet God face-to-face.[12]

If they are not right, then there will be plenty of time to put into practice the eight principles laid out in this book, including this final one: be determined to write the last chapter of the book, which means having a multigenerational vision and strategy, refusing to quit just because the tide has temporarily turned against many of our values.

I truly believe that our society can deviate only so far before it either totally collapses or makes a massive course correction (or Jesus returns!). That's why the ancient rabbis could talk about past civilizations that engaged in all kinds of sexual practices, including homosexual "marriages." Those civilizations are gone, while the Jewish people remain.[13]

There is, indeed, nothing new under the sun, and while in one way the growing acceptance of same-sex "marriage" in America and other nations is unprecedented, in another way it is hardly unprecedented, having either existed in different forms historically (meaning without being called "marriage" but being practiced in the society) or else having existed in the form we see today, but in cultures that have been largely lost to history. No matter how you look at it, though, the historical lesson is the same: this will be a social experiment that will ultimately fail. The real question is, what will be left when it fails? And further, who will be the last man standing?

Before I share some final strategies for preserving a godly, moral legacy for the long term, I want to make two important observations.

SOME SOLID REASONS FOR HOPE

First, things are not as bleak as they may appear. Not only is a Bible-based, conservative Christian faith rising rapidly around the globe (as noted in principle 7), meaning that the adherents to this faith will neither sanction nor celebrate homosexual practice, but even in America, many young people are standing strong in their moral convictions. A new study released in July 2014 indicated that "young evangelical Christians are defying America's sexual liberalism despite predictions to the contrary." The article continued:

> Some Americans outside conservative Christianity have forecast young evangelicals soon will reject the church's standards and join the culture in its liberal views on such issues as same-sex marriage, premarital sex and gender identity, Russell D. Moore [president of the Southern Baptist Convention's Ethics & Religious Liberty Commission (ELRC)] and Andrew Walker [ERLC's director of policy studies] wrote Wednesday (July 9) in a piece at National Review Online. That is not what research by a University of Texas sociologist indicates, they say.
>
> A study by Mark Regnerus, an author and associate professor of sociology at the University of Texas–Austin, suggests "churchgoing Evangelical Christians are retaining orthodox views on Biblical sexuality, despite the shifts in broader American culture," Moore and Walker wrote.[14]

Some of the most significant findings of the study were the following:

- Only 11 percent of evangelicals between the ages of 18 and 39 say they support same-sex marriage, while a "solid majority" of self-identified atheists, agnostics, liberal Catholics and liberal Protestations back it.

- About six percent of evangelicals support abortion rights, while more than 70 percent of their non-believing peers agree with such rights.

- Only five percent of evangelicals believe cohabitation by unmarried couples is acceptable, but about 70 percent of those who are religiously unaffiliated or consider themselves "spiritual but not religious" agree with cohabitation.[15]

Based on statistics like these, Moore and Walker concluded, "The Sexual Revolution marches on, but it doesn't move forward without dissent. On any given Sunday morning, in your community, young Evangelicals are telling America that a sexual counter-revolution is ready to be born, again."[16] This sounds like a new version of that Jesus revolution we were just talking about!

Interestingly, about the same time this article came out, there was a large gathering of young United Methodists in the Philippines, representing many nations. They discussed and voted on a number of controversial issues, including redefining marriage. John Lomperis, a United Methodist leader, reported that "the vote totals from GYPCLA [Global Young People's Convocation and Legislative Assembly] 2014 reveal that redefining marriage was ultimately rejected by quite the multicultural coalition of young United Methodists from Africa, America, Eurasia, and the Philippines."[17]

So, here you have a strong coalition of young United Methodists, representing the next generation of that denomination's leaders, and they strongly affirm that marriage is the union of one man and one woman. And they did this despite the fact that in the States, United Methodists are deeply divided over this issue.

Could it be, then, that the success of the gay revolution and the capitulation of the next generation is not really a given? Could the constant media bombardment that has negatively colored our thinking, along with the "trash talk" of gay activists (to borrow a sports term), be nothing more than a ruse to make us believe we may as well give up since our cause is already lost?

THE MISLEADING MEDIA

In principle 7 we demonstrated that the media have greatly shaped public opinion about homosexuality, to the point that many Americans think that more than 30 percent of the population is gay (whereas the real number is less than 2 percent). It appears to be the same with abortion (albeit not to the same extent), with a Gallup poll reporting that in 2013, America was almost equally divided between pro-life and pro-choice, yet when people were asked for their impression of how Americans felt about this issue, they thought the country was strongly pro-choice (as are the media elite!).

So, while the real stats showed that Americans were more pro-life than pro-choice (48 to 45 percent), those polled thought that it was dramatically reversed (51 percent pro-choice to 35 percent pro-life). Not only that, but the real stats pointed to a strong and growing pro-life trend from 1995, when, according to Gallup, 56 percent of Americans were pro-choice as opposed to only 33 percent who were pro-life.[18]

From this we can take away some encouragement: Public perception is often driven by the media, meaning that things might not be as bad as they seem, since perception often does *not* correspond to reality. And just as the pro-life movement has made progress when it seemed dead in the water—or, at the least, when the media elite wanted us to feel that way—it continues to make progress today. The same can happen with the pro-family, pro-marriage, pro–sexual purity movement—the *new* counterculture revolution.

HAS GAY ACTIVISM GONE CONSERVATIVE?

My second observation is that the gay revolution has succeeded only to the extent it has become conservative in terms of family values and being "just like everyone else." In other words, it has succeeded to the extent it has emphasized the importance of marriage and sexual morality, of not being different. This is in stark contrast with many pioneer gay activists who opposed marriage entirely and who flaunted homosexual immorality and gloried in their "differentness."

But it was a strategy doomed to failure, and so, in 1989, gay strategists Kirk and Madsen wrote:

> The gay revolution has failed.
>
> Not completely, and not finally, but it's a failure just the same. The 1969 Stonewall riot—in which a handful of long-suffering New York drag queens, tired of homophobic police harassment, picked up rocks and bottles and fought back—marked the birth of "gay liberation." As we write these lines, twenty years have passed. In those years, the combined efforts of the gay community have won a handful of concessions in a handful of localities. Some of those concessions have been revoked; others may be. We should have done far better.[19]

This is what the authors were really saying:

- "We're here; we're queer; get used to it" wasn't cutting it.

- "Zaps," those strategically timed, carefully staged, flamingly gay, hit-and-run protests widely used in the 1970s, had run their course.

- In-your-face sexual displays at gay pride events were counterproductive.

- A new strategy needed to be employed.

You see, in the early days of gay activism, marriage was largely despised, viewed as the vestige of a backward, patriarchal culture, and the gay attack on conventional marriage was part of the larger attack on other cultural boundaries. This was reflected in some of the goals presented in the 1972 Gay Rights Platform, including these:

> Repeal of all state laws prohibiting private sexual acts involving consenting persons; equalization for homosexuals and heterosexuals for the enforcement of all laws. (1972 State-2)

> Repeal of all state laws prohibiting transvestism and cross-dressing. (1972 State-6)

Repeal of all laws governing the age of sexual consent. (1972 State-7)

Repeal of all legislative provisions that restrict the sex or number of persons entering into a marriage unit; and the extension of legal benefits to all persons who cohabit regardless of sex or numbers. (1972 State-8).[20]

Other gay activists trashed marriage in the strongest of terms, even claiming that to seek gay "marriage" was an act of self-hatred. As expressed by Carl Wittman in his famous document "Refugees from Amerika: Gay Manifesto," dated Thursday, January 1, 1970:

> Marriage is a prime example of a straight institution fraught with role playing. Traditional marriage is a rotten, oppressive institution. Those of us who have been in heterosexual marriages too often have blamed our gayness on the breakup of the marriage. No. They broke up because marriage is a contract which smothers both people, denies needs, and places impossible demands on both people. And we had the strength, again, to refuse to capitulate to the roles which were demanded of us.
>
> Gay people must stop gauging their self-respect by how well they mimic straight marriages. Gay marriages will have the same problems as straight ones except in burlesque. For the usual legitimacy and pressures which keep straight marriages together are absent, e.g., kids, what parents think, what neighbors say.
>
> To accept that happiness comes through finding a groovy spouse and settling down, showing the world that "we're just the same as you" is avoiding the real issues, and is an expression of self-hatred.[21]

What has become of these militant expressions? They have largely disappeared, replaced by a push to institutionalize same-sex "marriage" to the point that gay activists claim they are "pro-marriage," while those of us who want to uphold the institution of marriage are branded "anti-marriage."[22]

And that's how the gay revolution has found success: by saying that, aside from some variations in private sexual practices (along with plenty of standard sexual practices), gays are just like straights—as individuals, as couples, as parents, as families. Therefore, as Judge Henry Floyd wrote in overturning the ban on same-sex "marriage" in Virginia, "Denying same-sex couples this choice prohibits them from participating fully in our society, which is precisely the type of segregation that the Fourteenth Amendment cannot countenance."[23]

NOT ALL GAY ACTIVISTS ARE HAPPY

To a certain extent, this was the very thing that pioneer gay activists like Carl Wittman opposed, the very thing that some contemporary gay activists feel has taken away the cutting edge of their movement, the very thing that steals their counterculture distinctives. That's why a radical gay group—but one that would have been in lockstep with the gay pioneers—vandalized a Human Rights Campaign store in June 2011, announcing, "ROWDY QUEERS TRASH AND GLAMDALIZE HUMAN RIGHTS CAMPAIGN GIFT SHOP IN WASHINGTON, DC ON THE 42nd ANNIVERSARY OF THE STONEWALL RIOT." (The HRC, it will be recalled, is the world's largest gay activist organization, featuring President Obama as a regular speaker at their annual DC fund-raising dinner.)

The group that took responsibility for this, called "The Right Honorable Wicked Stepmothers' Traveling, Drinking and Debating Society and Men's Auxillary," shared their disgust with the HRC in a vulgar press release, which said in part, "The modern LGBT movement owes its success to three days of smashing, burning, punching, and kicking—all of it happily indiscriminate—and the confrontational tactics of groups like ACT-UP that followed in the decades since. Yet, somehow we've forgotten our riotous roots."[24]

Similarly, in October 2009, the HRC headquarters in DC was vandalized by a group that left this message:

Communique from the Forgotton:

Human Rights Campaign HQ Glamdalized By Queers Against Assimilation

HRC headquarters was rocked by an act of glamdalism last night by a crew of radical queer and allied folks armed with pink and black paint and glitter grenades. Beside the front entrance and the inscribed mission statement now reads a tag, "Quit leaving queers behind."

The HRC is not a democratic or inclusive institution, especially for the people who they claim to represent. Just like society today, the HRC is run by a few wealthy elites who are in bed with corporate sponsors who proliferate militarism, heteronormativity, and capitalist exploitation. . . .

The queer liberation movement has been misrepresented and co-opted by the HRC. The HRC marginalizes us into a limited struggle for aspiring homosexual elites to regain the privilege that they've lost and climb the social ladder towards becoming bourgeoisie. . . .

REMEMBER THE STONEWALL RIOTS! On the 40th anniversary of Stonewall, pigs raided a queer bar in Texas, arrested and beat our friends, and we looked towards politicians and lawyers to protect us. This mentality is what keeps the money flowing to the HRC and their pet Democrats, and keeps our fists in our pockets.

Most of all we disagree that collective liberation will be granted by the state or its institutions like prisons, marriage, and the military. We need to escalate our struggle, or it will collapse.[25]

What an eye-opening "communique"! These "Queers Against Assimilation" are fighting *against* the very thing that almost all major gay activist organizations today are fighting *for*, namely, the institutional right to be just like the prevailing, straight, married-with-kids society.

On the one hand, this does represent a definite change in strategy in order to influence public opinion, since plenty of gays have no desire to "marry" and settle down, and highlighting their lifestyles would hardly advance the gay cause. On the other hand, this is not just a matter of strategy, since there has, in fact, been a domesticating of many in the LGBT community, just as there has been a domesticating of most gay pride events. (Some would argue that rather than this reflecting a "domesticating" of the movement, it points to the conservatives triumphing over the radicals.)[26]

WHEN HOMOSEXUALS EMULATE HETEROSEXUALS

This points to something very profound: *It is only by seeking to become just like the heterosexual society that homosexual activism has made so much progress.* If gay activists emphasized their queerness, like their Stonewall forebears did, their revolution would have petered out a long time ago. (Ironically, they still celebrate and commemorate the Stonewall Riots every year.) Instead, they have had to recognize the importance of the foundations of heterosexual society in order to succeed.

But alas—and I genuinely mean "alas," since I write this with sadness, not with joy—two men cannot produce their own child and two women cannot have a baby, and so every year at Mother's Day or Father's Day, kids raised in gay homes are reminded that something fundamental is missing.[27] And every time a homosexual couple wants to have a child, they are reminded that, in a very important way, they are not like everyone else.

In light of this, it appears that one of two scenarios will play out:

1. As the LGBT community gets more and more domesticated, the gay revolution will lose its purpose and vision (just like GLAAD has worked itself out of a job; see principle 6), and with gay families being massively outnumbered by straight families, "heteronormativity" will again be the societal norm.[28]

2. To the extent that the more promiscuous, radical elements of the LGBT community become dominant, perhaps feeling they have less reason to be discreet about their lifestyles, this sexual anarchy will drag their whole community down, to be rejected by a society increasingly longing for sexual purity.

Either way, this does not bode well for the gay revolution.

Regardless, though, of the successes or failures of the gay revolution, it is our responsibility to do our part to bring about positive change. Here's what that means:

1. Never compromising our moral convictions

2. Being people of light, not of darkness

3. Living in sexual purity

4. Making solid marriages a priority

5. Recognizing the importance of male-female distinctives

6. Continuing to propagate the truth

7. Looking to God for His intervention

8. Persevering to the end so *we* can write the last chapter of the book

STAND FIRM

I know how easy it is to get worn out with the constant culture wars, especially when many Christian leaders have lots of other ministry concerns, whereas for gay activists, this *is* their concern. And so, while a major Christian ministry like Focus on the Family never spent more than 3 percent of its annual budget on homosexual issues,[29] organizations such as the HRC and NGLTF and Lambda Legal and GLAAD and GLSEN and a host of others *invest their entire budgets* in the gay activist cause. And they are joined by massively funded organizations like the ACLU and the SPLC, both of which are deeply invested in the gay activist cause.

Then there is the Obama administration, which has been aggressively pro-gay, with the president himself inviting gay activists to the White House on the anniversary of the Stonewall riots in June, along with proclaiming June gay pride month; signing into law an unprecedented pro-LGBT, antireligious executive order; speaking at HRC fund-raising events; using his second inaugural speech as a bully pulpit; reaching out personally to openly gay athletes—and much, much more.

The president has been joined by Vice President Joe Biden, now a vocal champion for gay activism, along with former secretary of state Hillary Clinton, who put pressure on other countries to bow to gay activist pressure. There is also former attorney general Eric Holder, who actually instructed other attorneys general not to defend so-called antigay laws in their states if they personally objected to them, making clear that he himself would not defend them.

Added to this is the never-ending media bombardment, coupled with corporate America's embrace of "gay rights" as the new civil rights movement. And did I mention that the National Education Association is also aggressively pro-gay activist? The list seems almost endless, and it's easy to get weary with the battle, especially when it seems that our side has already sustained so many losses.

But, as I have argued throughout this book, the cultural battles are hardly over—in many ways, they have just begun—and if we look at the example of history, it is only those who have held their ground against seemingly insurmountable odds who have a made lasting impact. (I remind you again that pioneer gay activists did this very thing themselves, and while I differ with many of their goals, I commend them for their persistence.)[30]

In principle 1 I quoted Billy Graham, who once said, "Courage is contagious. When a brave man takes a stand, the spines of others are often stiffened." Why not determine to be that brave man or woman, that person who will do what is right even if it means losing your reputation or your job or your social status or your pension or your tax exemption? Believers in other countries are literally losing their heads for their faith. Surely we shouldn't be afraid of losing our popularity for ours.

Of course, being brave does not mean being nasty, and I for one am glad to live in a society that does not sanction gay bashing, let alone gay killing, as still happens in other parts of the world with societal approval. God forbid that we associate boldness with cruelty. We simply need to come to a firm conviction about what we believe to be right and best for our nation when it comes to marriage and family and sexual morality. And once we have come to that conviction, we each need to proclaim and live out the words of that old hymn "I Shall Not Be Moved." As Paul exhorted his readers, "Let us not grow weary of doing good, for in due season we will reap, if we do not give up" (Galatians 6:9 ESV). And, "be steadfast, immovable, always abounding in the work of the Lord, knowing that in the Lord your labor is not in vain" (1 Corinthians 15:58 ESV).

Forward without flinching! It is by going through the fire that we come out shining brightest.

GOD'S WAYS ARE BEST

One of the most famous verses in the Bible is found in Psalm 37 and is quoted again by Jesus in the New Testament. It states that the *meek* will inherit the earth (Psalm 37:11; Matthew 5:5), something that is totally counterintuitive, since we would think that the toughest and most aggressive will inherit the earth. After all, isn't it the nation with the most powerful military that takes over the most territory? Isn't it the strongest who survive? And isn't it human nature to be selfish, combative, and dominating?

The author of this psalm, traditionally thought to be King David, who lived about three thousand years ago, brought a very different perspective. He wrote:

Wait for the LORD and keep his way,

  and he will exalt you to inherit the land;

  you will look on when the wicked are cut off.

I have seen a wicked, ruthless man,

  spreading himself like a green laurel tree.

But he passed away, and behold, he was no more;

  though I sought him, he could not be found.

Mark the blameless and behold the upright,

    for there is a future for the man of peace.

But transgressors shall be altogether destroyed;

    the future of the wicked shall be cut off. (Psalm 37:34–38 ESV)

In the same way, Psalm 1 states that the person who spurns the counsel of the wicked and lives by God's principles would be "like a tree planted beside streams of water, which yields its fruit in season, whose foliage never fades, and whatever it produces thrives." In contrast, the wicked would be "like chaff that wind blows away" (vv. 3–4 NJV).

Am I referring to homosexual men and women as "wicked" and looking forward to the day they will be "cut off"? That is not the point I am making here at all.[31] Am I anticipating some kind of fiery divine judgment that will consume the gays? Actually, I'm anticipating the day when countless thousands of LGBTs receive God's love into their hearts and experience true wholeness in Him.[32]

The point I am making—really, that the Scriptures are making—is that those who honor the Lord and live by His standards will, in the end, outlast those who don't, since God's ways are best. That's why people who don't drink or smoke will, on average, live longer than those who do, while people who wear seat belts and obey traffic laws will, on average, live longer than those who don't. Even insurance companies recognize this to be true.

In the same way, married couples who are faithful to each other and devoted to their children will, over the course of generations, leave a much greater legacy than those who give birth to kids out of wedlock or are serial adulterers or deadbeat dads. One outstanding example of this principle is the Christian leader Jonathan Edwards (1703–1758), America's greatest philosopher and theologian in the eighteenth century. He was married to his wife, Sarah, for thirty years, and they had three sons and eight daughters. The legacy they left behind was remarkable.

A CONTRAST IN LEGACIES

This was confirmed by American educator and pastor A. E. Winship, who, at the turn of the twentieth century, "decided to trace out the descendants of Jonathan Edwards almost 150 years after his death. His findings are astounding, especially when compared to a man known as Max Jukes. Jukes' legacy came to the forefront when the family trees of forty-two different men in the New York prison system traced back to him."[33]

The name of Winship's book was *Jukes-Edwards: A Study in Education and Heredity*, and the results of his study were astonishing.[34] The descendants of Edwards, fewer than 150 years after his death, included

1 US vice president

3 US senators

3 governors

3 mayors

13 college presidents

30 judges

65 professors

80 public office holders

100 lawyers

100 missionaries

The legacy of Max Jukes was the polar opposite. His descendants included

7 murderers

60 thieves

50 women of debauchery

130 other convicts

310 paupers (with over 2,300 years lived in poorhouses)

400 who were physically wrecked by indulgent living.[35]

How absolutely tragic and pitiful, yet had Edwards been a drunkard or a philanderer or a thief—or simply an abusive father—his legacy might have looked closer to that of Jukes, which leads to a question: Based on the lifestyle choices *you* are making today, what will *your* legacy look like tomorrow (meaning, in the generations to come)?

Our job is to concentrate on doing what is right, even if same-sex "marriage" becomes the law of the land, even if gender distinctions are all but erased in many sectors of society, even if we can't rely on the public school systems at all and we have to come up with creative educational alternatives that work for the poor as well as the rich.

We need to walk in sexual purity whether we're single or married. We need to be true to our wedding vows and really mean it when we say, "Till death do us part." We need to celebrate motherhood and fatherhood and the beauty of gender distinctions. We need to make our kids a priority rather than a distraction, recognizing that we have no more precious gift in this world than our children and that, one day, they will be the leaders of the society.

We need to embrace wholesome values in our personal lives and inculcate those in our families. We need to be positive influences in the secular society, with reputations for integrity, generosity, compassion, and honesty. And we need to celebrate life to the full, beginning with the sanctity of life in the womb, thereby swimming against the tide of the culture of death.[36]

If we do this, not only will God's blessing be on us, since His ways are ways of life, but with our roots down deep and our branches spread wide (to borrow an agricultural image), we will endure the coming storms as well as continue to reproduce through the many seeds we have planted.

GOD WILL RESPOND TO THE PRAYERS OF HIS PEOPLE

In the previous chapter I described how our nation has been deeply impacted by spiritual awakenings in the past, and they always came when things looked very bleak. But that's the very reason why people started to pray so earnestly. They realized that the country was in serious moral and spiritual decline (which often results in economic decline as well), and the desperate situation drove Americans to their knees. Of course, skeptics could claim that these so-called awakenings were nothing but emotionalism or even mass hysteria, but to an unbiased observer, the most logical conclusion would be that something very supernatural happened.

Before the First Great Awakening, which lasted from the 1730s into the mid-1740s, Jonathan Edwards wrote a short book with a long title, calling on Christians worldwide to unite in prayer for a divine visitation. The title says it all: *A Humble Attempt to Promote the Agreement and Union of God's People Throughout the World in Extraordinary Prayer for a Revival of Religion and the Advancement of God's Kingdom on Earth, According to Scriptural Promises and Prophecies of the Last Time.*

What were some of those "scriptural promises"? They included famous verses like these:

> If my people who are called by my name humble themselves, and pray and seek my face and turn from their wicked ways, then I will hear from heaven and will forgive their sin and heal their land. (2 Chronicles 7:14 ESV)

> For I know the plans I have for you, declares the LORD, plans for welfare and not for evil, to give you a future and a hope. Then you will call upon me and come and pray to me, and I will hear you. You will seek me and find me, when you seek me with all your heart. (Jeremiah 29:11–13 ESV)

Many Christians took these words to heart and cried out to God to have mercy on our nation (in Edwards's day, we were still British colonies), and the results were nothing short of dramatic. Edwards, ever the careful intellectual, described what he witnessed in detail.[37]

Prior to the Second Great Awakening, which began in the early nineteenth century, an Episcopal minister bemoaned the sorry state of affairs in his region, the Carolinas: "How many thousands . . . never saw, much less read, or ever heard a chapter of the Bible! How many Ten thousands who never were baptized or heard a Sermon! And thrice Ten thousand, who never heard of the name of Christ, save in Curses . . . ! Lamentable! Lamentable is the situation of these people."[38]

That actually sounds worse than the situation today, but once again, in those times of great spiritual declension, Christians cried out to God, recognized and renounced their own sins (how can we help others live right when we're not living right ourselves?), and prayed for a great awakening. Once again, the results were dramatic, and those results could be traced back directly to the prayers of God's people—desperate prayers, fervent prayers, heartfelt prayers.

GIVE YOURSELF TO PRAYER

With this in mind, let me make a heartfelt appeal to each of you reading this book. If you knew that if you prayed for $1 million for just five minutes a day and skipped two meals a week, after one year, you would get the money, would you do it? I imagine so, even if your motivation was to give the money to the poor. Well, there's nothing in the Bible promising us financial results like this, but there are many promises assuring us that if we ask God to have mercy and restore and bring change, He will answer, even though we can't set a specific timetable for those answers. What is sure is that if we cry out—in citywide rallies, in church prayer meetings, in our homes, with our families, or all alone—and we do not give up, the Lord Himself will answer, and the nation will be shaken.

Jesus emphasized this theme to His disciples with "a parable to the effect that they ought always to pray and not lose heart."

> He said, "In a certain city there was a judge who neither feared God nor respected man. And there was a widow in that city who kept coming to him and saying, 'Give me justice against my adversary.' For a while he refused, but afterward he said to himself, 'Though I neither fear God nor respect man, yet because this widow keeps bothering me, I will give her justice, so that she will not beat me down by her

continual coming.'" And the Lord said, "Hear what the unrighteous judge says. And will not God give justice to his elect, who cry to him day and night? Will he delay long over them? I tell you, he will give justice to them speedily."

But He also asked this probing question: "Nevertheless, when the Son of Man comes, will he find faith on earth?" (Luke 18:1–8 ESV).

That is a question only we can answer, but it's a good question to ask even now. Are we putting our faith in God? Do we believe His promises? Are we convinced that if we cry out to Him, He will answer? If so, then let's do it, starting now and not stopping until justice and equity and morality reign in the land.

WE MUST NOT FALL INTO THE HEZEKIAH SYNDROME

Hezekiah (ca. 715–687 BC) was one of the greatest kings in Judah's history, a man who put his trust in the Lord and who helped spark a national reformation movement. But later in life, he made one of the most selfish, shortsighted statements recorded anywhere in the Bible. We cannot afford to make the same tragic mistake he made.

According to Isaiah 39, after Hezekiah was miraculously healed and his life extended fifteen years, envoys from Babylon came to visit him in honor of his recovery. Their motivation, although not recorded explicitly in the chapter, was obvious. They had a common enemy in the nation of Assyria, and they were obviously looking to gain Hezekiah as an ally.

Hezekiah greeted them warmly and "showed them his treasure house—the silver, the gold, the spices, and the precious oil—and all his armory, and everything that was found in his treasuries. There was nothing in his palace and in all his realm that Hezekiah did not show them" (v. 2 HCSB).

After they left, the prophet Isaiah came to the king and asked him about these visitors: "'Where did these men come from and what did they say to you?' Hezekiah replied, 'They came to me from a distant country, from Babylon'" (v. 3 HCSB).

Isaiah then asked, "'What have they seen in your palace?' Hezekiah answered, 'They have seen everything in my palace. There isn't anything in my treasuries that I didn't show them'" (v. 4 HCSB).

Isaiah then delivered a devastating prophetic word to Hezekiah: "'The time will certainly come when everything in your palace and all that your fathers have stored up until this day will be carried off to Babylon; nothing will be left,' says the LORD. 'Some of your descendants who come from you will be taken away, and they will become eunuchs in the palace of the king of Babylon'" (v. 6 HCSB).

What terrible news! Everything the past generations had worked for would be carried off to Babylon, and even the king's own offspring—his sons or grandsons or great-grandsons—would go into exile. Some of them would even be castrated.

And how did Hezekiah respond to this dreadful word? Did he turn to the Lord and weep, as he did when he was told by the prophet that he was about to die? (See Isaiah 38:1–3.) Did he go to God in desperation, as he did when the Assyrians were threatening to destroy the nation? (See Isaiah 37:1–4.)

No. He responded with these shocking words: "'The word of the LORD that you have spoken is good,' for he thought: There will be peace and security during my lifetime" (v. 8 HCSB). In other words, "Praise the Lord! As long as I'm going to be all right, it doesn't matter what happens to my kids and grandkids. That's a good word, Isaiah, since there will be *shalom* during my lifetime."

What a shortsighted, self-centered mind-set. It was the polar opposite of the words spoken by Thomas Paine twenty-five hundred years later: "If there must be trouble, let it be in my day, that my child may have peace." (And Paine was hardly an orthodox believer either.)

Is it any wonder, then, that Manasseh, the son born to Hezekiah after he was healed, ended up being the most wicked king in Judah's history? Could it be that Hezekiah failed to be a godly father? Could it be that he failed to have a vision for the next generation?

WHAT IS OUR LASTING LEGACY?

According to Dietrich Bonhoeffer, "The ultimate test of a moral society is the kind of world that it leaves to its children." This forces us to ask ourselves, what kind of world are we leaving to our children and grandchildren?

Many religious leaders today are afraid to (or, at the least, reluctant to) address the most pressing social issues, not wanting to get caught up in controversy, to offend their congregants, to stir up opposition, to risk their tax-exempt status, or to rock the boat. After all, they think, "Our congregation is healthy and the ministry is bearing fruit. Why should I jeopardize this by taking a stand for righteousness? And why should I risk pushing the seekers away?"

The answer is simple: It is our holy calling to stand for what is right (joining grace together with truth and compassion together with justice). It is our responsibility before God as the moral conscience of society, the salt of the earth and the light of the world, a prophetic voice to a confused and self-destructive world. It is also our sacred responsibility to the next generation.

Otherwise, if we fall short of our calling here, our children and grandchildren will have every right to say to us one day, "Mom! Dad! (or "Grandma! Grandpa!"). What were you doing when America changed so radically, when our freedoms were taken away, when marriage became all but meaningless, when tens of millions of babies were killed in the womb? How did you let this happen on your watch?"

What will we say to them on that day? And what will we say to the Lord when we stand to give account? Where is our generational vision?

And so I say to every leader and to every parent: please, consider your ways, and save yourself from the Hezekiah syndrome. The discomfort of swimming against the tide today will be worth it all tomorrow. And in the coming years, your kids and grandkids will honor you and thank you. The legacy of the righteous is blessed (see Psalm 112:2).

FINAL THOUGHTS ON THE COMING COURSE CORRECTION

In principle 4 I cited a powerful article by Peter Hitchens, a former atheist and the brother of the late famous atheist Christopher Hitchens, as he lamented the effects of fatherlessness on his home country of England. As for the importance of fathers in our history and culture, he pointed out that "the fundamental prayer of the Christian church begins with the words 'Our Father'. Americans speak of their 'founding fathers'. The father has since human society began been protector, provider, source of authority, bound by honour and fidelity to defend his hearth." This led him to ask the question: "If he is gone, who takes his place?"

Hitchens described how enthusiastically the previous generation in Great Britain embraced the concept of no-fault divorce, with little or no vision for the disastrous consequences this would have for the family, in particular the children. He wrote, "Now we are finding out. And a generation which has never known fathers, or family life, or fidelity or constancy, is now busy begetting children of its own. What will become of them? How will boys who have never seen a father learn to be fathers?"

Yet he was not completely without hope, as he expressed with real candor, "I'd have a moral panic at this stage, if I thought it would do any good. But perhaps it will be the victims of this selfish generation, our children and grandchildren, who—having suffered its effects—will re-establish stable family life in our country."[39]

That is exactly my hope today, except there is nothing stopping us from beginning to make that course correction ourselves rather than waiting for our kids or grandkids to do it. We can join this new revolution by being people of integrity and faith, by refusing to compromise our convictions, by exemplifying courage joined with compassion, by upholding the beauty of true marriage, by praying for divine intervention, by living in such a way that we will leave a wonderful legacy to the next generation.

THE WRONG SIDE OF HISTORY?

Writing in October 2014, conservative journalist Ben Johnson noted that "among the stratagems employed by the cultural Left to discourage, dispirit, and dissuade the plurality of culturally sane Americans from opposing same-sex 'marriage' is the all-encompassing insistence that the fight has already been lost. The phrase of choice has been to say that proponents of traditional marriage are on 'the wrong side of history.'"

But, he continued, "with at least 5,000 years of Western civilization normalizing monogamous heterosexual marriage, and the American experiment with redefining marriage a mere 10 years old, it certainly seems like I'm on the right side of history—the long one . . . the one authenticated by every society that produced human flourishing."

Johnson made clear that he wasn't in the least bit concerned with allegedly being on the wrong side of history, explaining, "I spent the first part of my life being told that the global triumph of Communism was 'inevitable.'"[40] How things change!

In light of the sudden, dramatic, and often unexpected twists and turns of history, Johnson made this important observation:

> It may be that in the Left's cultural conquest of marriage, we are closer to 1917 than 1989, that a cocksure, opaque, malicious spirit is inexorably advancing rather than retreating. Those who defend the superiority of the natural family face social, economic, and (increasingly) legal censure. We have only the truth of science, human development, and children's social well-being on our side. And we must never tire of repeating it, whatever the outcome. But it is not hard to imagine that the worst is yet before us.
>
> Where we stand in the mystery of iniquity and redemption is known only to their Master. But we may take to heart the words of the famed dissident Aleksandr Solzhenitsyn, who lived to see the fall of the Gulag Archipelago that once imprisoned him: "One word of truth shall outweigh the whole world." And the words of another, greater Authority: "In the world ye shall have tribulation: but be of good cheer; I have overcome the world."[41]

The bottom line is that we do what is right because it is right, leaving the results to God. But we take our stand with hope and confidence, knowing that in the end, we will be vindicated by the verdict of history.

A TIME FOR CERTAINTY

Writing in *First Things*, Andrew Walker stated that "if I were writing the Art of Cultural War, this is the strategy I'd use to bring the opposing side to heel. The steps look something like this: Relativize the [controversial moral/social/spiritual] issue with other issues. Be uncertain about the issue. Refuse to speak publicly on the issue. Be indifferent toward the issue. Accept the issue. Affirm the issue. Require the issue."

And with that, the cultural flip-flop is complete. For Walker, the church that starts down this path quickly becomes a church in retreat. "A church in retreat doesn't give answers," he noted. "It doesn't storm the gates of Hell. It settles and makes peace where there is no peace (Ezekiel 13:10)."

Instead, he argues, we must live like the Church in exile, "one that is faithful amidst the culture, regardless of whether that culture looks more like America or more like Babylon. It knows that it may lose the culture, but that it cannot lose the Gospel. So be it."

This much is sure, Walker concludes, "The good news is that the truth of Christianity outlasts the untruths of man's applause."[42] And that is the certainty that fuels the stands we take. Whether we "win" or "lose" in the short term, we will certainly "win" in the long term. And since, in many ways, the battle over marriage and morality has just begun, there's no reason to be discouraged with short-term setbacks.

MORDECAI WILL NOT BOW

All this reminds me of a famous account in the book of Esther involving a Persian official named Haman and a Jewish man named Mordecai who was living as an exile in Persia. Now, to be perfectly clear, I am *not* comparing Haman, who wanted to slaughter all the Jews, to gay activists, as if they want to slaughter their enemies. That is *not* the point I am making, nor do I believe it to be true. Instead, I want to point out an interesting psychological parallel between Haman's attitude and the attitude of many gay activists, also pointing to Mordecai as an example to follow.

According to the book of Esther, although Haman had become a highly exalted official in the Persian Empire, with all citizens having to bow down to him on sight, Mordecai refused to bow down, which really riled Haman (see Esther 3). The adulation of all the people was not enough for Haman. This one Jew also had to bow the knee—or be killed—or Haman would not be satisfied.

In the same way, gay activists will not be satisfied with victory after victory as long as there is a group that refuses to bow down to their agenda, a group that is even allowed legally to dissent, which is why our religious freedoms are now under constant attack.[43] *I'm here to declare that Mordecai will not bow.*[44]

I BELIEVE GOD!

Twenty centuries ago, in the midst of a life-threatening storm at sea, the apostle Paul, who was a prisoner of Rome, received a supernatural word of assurance that, despite suffering great loss, not one person on board would die. And he brought a word of encouragement to all those on the ship, saying, "So take heart, men, for I have faith in God that it will be exactly as I have been told" (Acts 27:25 ESV).

I am not claiming to have received a supernatural revelation like Paul did, but I am saying that, to the core of my being, I'm convinced that a spiritually based, moral and cultural revolution is at hand and that the success of the gay revolution is but one short chapter in a very long book. Shall we join together, with God's help, and write the chapter that comes next?

To my fellow cultural revolutionaries I say: *On with it!*

NOTES

PREFACE

1. Dennis Prager, "Judges, Hubris, and Same-Sex Marriage," February 18, 2014, townhall.com/columnists/dennisprager/2014/02/18/judges-hubris-and-samesex-marriage-n1796339.

2. Melissa Moschella, "A Time for Heroism," Public Discourse (The Witherspoon Institute), August 6, 2014, http://www.thepublicdiscourse.com/2014/08/13486/ The article was adapted from a graduation address delivered at Tyburn Academy in Auburn, NY.

3. Cited in Joe Dallas, "Assessing Matthew Vines 'God and the Gay Christian' Pt. VII," May 26, 2014, http://joedallas.com/blog/index.php/2014/05/26/assessing-matthew-vines-god-and-the-gay-christian-pt-vii/.

INTRODUCTION: THE DAY THE LINE WAS CROSSED

1. Michael Brown, "Pastors of Houston, Shout It from the Rooftops This Sunday," Charisma News, October 15, 2014, http://www.charismanews.com/opinion/in-the-line-of-fire/45769-pastors-of-houston-shout-it-from-the-rooftops-this-sunday.

2. "Sen. Cruz: City of Houston Has No Business Asking Pastors for Sermons," press release, October 15, 2014, http://www.cruz.senate.gov/?p=press_release&id=1805.

3. "Attorney General Greg Abbott Asks Houston City Attorney to Withdraw Subpoenas Seeking Sermons, Other Documents from Houston-Area Pastors," news release from the office of Ken Paxton, Attorney General of Texas, October 15, 2014, https://www.texasattorneygeneral.gov/oagnews/release.php?id=4880.

4. Benjamin L. Hall, "Reckless at Houston City Hall," Houston Forward Times, October 22, 2014, http://forwardtimesonline.com/2013/index.php/editorial/commentaries/item/1817-reckless-at-houston-city-hall.

5. Valerie Richardson, "Federal Civil Rights Official Calls Houston Pastor Subpoenas 'Abuse of Government Power,'" Washington Times, October 22, 2014, http://www.washingtontimes.com/news/2014/oct/22/federal-civil-rights-official-calls-houston-pastor/.

6. Eric Metaxas, e-mail to Ann Graham Lotz, in Lotz, "Who Will Rise Up Against the Wicked?" Charisma News, October 25, 2014, http://www.charismanews.com/opinion/45889-who-will-rise-up-against-the-wicked.

7. Katherine Driessen and Mike Morris, "Mayor's Decision to Drop Subpoenas Fails to Quell Criticism," *Houston Chronicle*, October 29, 2014, http://www.chron.com/news/houston-texas/houston/article/Mayor-set-to-make-announcement-on-sermon-subpoenas-5855458.php.

8. Linda Hirshman, *Victory: The Triumphant Gay Revolution* (New York: HarperCollins, 2012); see earlier, Mark Thompson and Randy Shilts, eds., *Long Road to Freedom: The Advocate History of the Gay and Lesbian Movement* (New York: St. Martin's Press, 1994). It is easy to have empathy for those who fought so passionately for what they perceived to be their basic human and civil rights without endorsing all their positions.

9. Glenn Greenwald, "Andrew Sullivan's Father Figure," Salon, May 14, 2012, http://www.salon.com/2012/05/14/andrew_sullivans_father_figure/.

10. Mike Morris, "Foes Seize on Mayor's 'Personal' Comment to Fight Ordinance," *Houston Chronicle*, May 27, 2014, http://www.houstonchronicle.com/news/politics/houston/article/Foes-seize-on-mayor-s-personal-comment-to-fight-5505694.php.

11. Ibid.

12. Lawrence D. Jones, "Houston Clergy at Arms over Lesbian Mayor's Orders," *Christian Post*, April 6, 2010, http://www.christianpost.com/news/houston-clergy-at-arms-over-lesbian-mayor-s-orders-44637/.

13. Erik Stanley, "Houston, We Have a Problem," Alliance Defending Freedom, October 13, 2014, http://www.adfmedia.org/News/PRDetail/9349.

14. The entire I Stand Sunday rally video can be found at https://www.youtube.com/watch?v=VFIKrd4gVpA.

15. Kyler Geoffroy, "Right-Wing Freaks Out over Houston's Subpoena of Pastors' Role in City's Equal Rights Ordinance Case," *Towleroad* (blog), October 16, 2014, http://www.towleroad.com/2014/10/right-wing-freaks-out-over-houstons-subpoening-of-pastors-role-in-citys-equal-rights-ordinance-case-.html.

16. Ibid.

17. John Wright, "How Should the LGBT Community Respond to Next Sunday's Anti-Gay Hatefest in Houston?" Lone Star Q, October, 26, 2014, http://www.lonestarq.com/how-should-the-lgbt-community-respond-to-next-sundays-anti-gay-hatefest-in-houston/.

18. "Anti-gay Forces Unite to Oppose Houston Mayor Annise Parker and the 'Radical Agenda' of LGBT Equality," SodaHead, October 26, 2014, http://www.sodahead.com/united-states/anti-gay-forces-unite-to-oppose-houston-mayor-annise-parker-and-the-radical-agenda-of-lgbt-equalit/question-4559321/.

19. Michael Brown, "The Mayor of Atlanta Declares War on Religious Freedom," Charisma News, January 9, 2015, http://www.charismanews.com/opinion/in-the-line-of-fire/47815-the-mayor-of-atlanta-declares-war-on-religious-freedom.

20. Ibid.

21. Ibid.

22. Ibid.

23. "God, Gays and the Atlanta Fire Department," *New York Times*, January, 13, 2015, http://www.nytimes.com/2015/01/13/opinion/god-gays-and-the-atlanta-fire-department.html?_r=3.

24. Todd Starnes, "Christians Rally to Defend Fire Chief Who Wrote 'Anti-Gay' Book," Fox News, January 13, 2015, http://www.foxnews.com/opinion/2015/01/13/christians-rally-to-defend-fire-chief-who-wrote-anti-gay-book/.

25. Michael Brown, "I Hate to Say I Told You So," Townhall.com, April, 7, 2014, http://townhall.com/columnists/michaelbrown/2014/04/07/i-hate-to-say-i-told-you-so-n1819736/page/full.

26. Michael L. Brown, *A Queer Thing Happened to America: And What a Long, Strange Trip It's Been* (Concord, NC: EqualTime Books, 2011), 48–50.

27. Brown, "I Hate to Say I Told You So."

28. Linda Harvey, e-mail to author, October 27, 2014. For Harvey's article on this event in 2009, see http://www.missionamerica.com/articletext.php?artnum=196.

29. Prideworks Conference program, November 16, 2010, http://www.pflagwestchester.org/PrideWorks/2010_Handouts/Program_PW_2010.pdf.

30. Wesley Young, "Gay Couple Files Complaint to Challenge Methodist Marriage Ban," *Winston-Salem Journal*, November 13, 2014, http://www.journalnow.com/news/local/gay-couple-files-complaint-to-challenge-methodist-marriage-ban/article_fa07b47c-6ab8-11e4-a272-cb46ca16935c.html.

31. James Kirchick, "How GLAAD Won the Culture War and Lost Its Reason to Exist," *Atlantic*, May 3, 2013, http://www.theatlantic.com/politics/archive/2013/05/how-glaad-won-the-culture-war-and-lost-its-reason-to-exist/275533/.

32. Thaddeus Baklinski, "Student Banned from Criticizing Gay 'Marriage' in Class at Jesuit College," LifeSite News, November 17, 2014, https://www.lifesitenews.com/news/student-banned-from-criticizing-gay-marriage-in-class-at-jesuit-college, emphasis added.

33. Douglas Wilson, "In Which First Things Does Some Fourth Things," *Blog & Mablog*, November 19, 2014, http://dougwils.com/s7-engaging-the-culture/in-which-first-things-does-some-fourth-things.html.

PRINCIPLE #1: NEVER COMPROMISE YOUR CONVICTIONS

1. Winston S. Churchill, *Never Give In! Winston Churchill's Speeches* (New York: Blumsbury, 2013), 255–56.

2. Elder Don Eastman, "Homosexuality; Not a Sin, Not a Sickness," Los Angeles Universal Fellowship Press, 1990, http://mcchurch.org/download/theology/homosexuality/NotSinNotSick.pdf. For the psychological issues, see note 3; for the theological issues involved, see Michael Brown, *Can You Be Gay and Christian?* (Lake Mary, FL: Charisma Media, 2014.) The most complete academic study remains Robert A. J. Gagnon, *The Bible and Homosexual Practice: Texts and Hermeneutics* (Nashville: Abingdon, 2001).

3. For the real story, see Ronald Bayer, *Homosexuality and American Psychiatry* (Princeton, NJ: Princeton University Press, 1987); Michael L. Brown, *A Queer Thing Happened to America: And What a Long, Strange Trip It's Been* (Concord, NC: EqualTime Books, 2011), 455–92.

4. Dr. R. Albert Mohler Jr., "There Is No 'Third Way'—Southern Baptists Face a Moment of Decision (and So Will You)," AlbertMohler.com, June 2, 2014, http://www.albertmohler.com/2014/06/02/there-is-no-third-way-southern-baptists-face-a-moment-of-decision-and-so-will-you/.

5. Frank Bruni, "Your God and My Dignity," *New York Times*, January 10, 2015, http://www.nytimes.com/2015/01/11/opinion/sunday/frank-bruni-religious-liberty-bigotry-and-gays.html?_r=0. For a good response, see Ramesh Ponnuru, "Frank Bruni vs. Religious Liberty," *The Corner* (blog), January 12, 2015, http://www.nationalreview.com/corner/396231/frank-bruni-vs-religious-liberty-ramesh-ponnuru.

6. Richard Orange, "Gay Danish Couples Win Right to Marry in Church," *Telegraph*, June 7, 2012, http://www.telegraph.co.uk/news/worldnews/europe/denmark/9317447/Gay-Danish-couples-win-right-to-marry-in-church.html.

7. Ian S. Thompson, "The LA Times Agrees—ENDA's Religious Exemption Must Be Narrowed," ACLU blog, May 3, 2013, https://www.aclu.org/blog/lgbt-rights-religion-belief/la-times-agrees-endas-religious-exemption-must-be-narrowed.

8. Dorothy J. Samuels, "An Unholy Religious Exemption," *Taking Note* (blog), July 12, 2013, http://takingnote.blogs.nytimes.com/2013/07/12/an-unholy-religious-exemption/.

9. James Esseks, interview by *Gay USA* with Ann Northrop and Andy Humm, podcast, July 12, 2013, http://www.gayusatv.org/Site/Podcast/Entries/2013/7/12_Gay_USA_with_Ann_Northrop_and_Andy_Humm_photo_by_Bill_Bahlman_1.html.

10. Ibid.

11. Dr. Martin Luther King Jr., "A Proper Sense of Priorities" (speech), Washington, DC, February 6, 1968, http://www.aavw.org/special_features/speeches_speech_king04.html.

12. John M. Becker, "Group of LGBTs, Allies Argues for 'Tolerance' of Homophobia," *The Bilerico Project* (blog), April 23, 2014, http://www.bilerico.com/2014/04/group_of_lgbts_allies_argues_for_tolerance_of_homo.php.

13. Josh Barro tweet, in Andrew Walker and Owen Strachan, "'Stamp Them Out': On Josh Barro and the New Sexual Moralism," *The Corner* (blog), July 24, 2014, http://www.nationalreview.com/corner/383651/stamp-them-out-josh-barro-and-new-sexual-moralism-andrew-walker-owen-strachan.

14. Becker, "Group of LGBTs, Allies Argues for 'Tolerance' of Homophobia." See Robert Oscar Lopez's response ("Stop Crying over Mozilla and Start Fighting Back!") on April 18, 2014, on the *Barbwire* blog, at http://barbwire.com/2014/04/18/stop-crying-mozilla-start-fighting-back/.

15. Andrew Sullivan, "The Hounding of a Heretic," *The Dish* (blog), April 3, 2014, http://dish.andrewsullivan.com/2014/04/03/the-hounding-of-brendan-eich/.

16. Bill Maher, "There Is a Gay Mafia—If You Cross Them, You Do Get Whacked," Real Clear Politics, April 4, 2014, http://www.realclearpolitics.com/video/2014/04/04/bill_maher_there_is_a_gay_mafia_if_you_cross_them_you_do_get_whacked.html.

17. Camille Paglia, *Vamps and Tramps: New Essays* (New York: Vintage, 1994), 73.

18. Bill Muehlenberg, *Dangerous Relations: The Threat of Homosexuality* (Melbourne: CultureWatch Books, 2014), 1–58 (for the entire list of 165 examples); see also the examples cited in Todd Starnes, *God Less America: Real Stories from the Front Lines of the Attack on Traditional Values* (Lake Mary, FL: Frontline, 2014). There are numerous cases cited in Brown, *Queer Thing*, current through the beginning of 2011.

19. Robert Oscar Lopez, "300 Examples You Have to Read to Understand the Term 'Homofascism,'" *Barbwire* (blog), July 7, 2014, http://barbwire.com/2014/07/07/300-examples-read-understand-meant-term-homofascism/. Lopez was raised by his mother and her lesbian partner, then spent a decade actively involved in the gay subculture, ultimately breaking away from homosexuality and becoming an outspoken critic of gay activism. In a subsequent article, Lopez wrote, "Narrowing the list down to 300 was very difficult, because the more our team compiled, the more people came forward with additions upon additions. The whole project turned into something dizzying" (Lopez, "L'Etat, C'est Gay: Taking the New Sexual Fascism Seriously," *American Thinker*, July 10, 2014, http://www.americanthinker.com/2014/07/letat_cest_gay_taking_the_new_sexual_fascism_seriously.html).

20. For strong protests against the bill, see Matt Barber, "Jerry Sandusky Laws: Sick and Twisted," *WND Commentary*, November 30, 2012, http://www.wnd.com/2012/11/jerry-sandusky-laws-sick-and-twisted/; for important facts about ex-gays, see Peter Sprigg, "Truth Matters in Ex-Gay Debate," Family Research Council blog, August 29, 2014, http://www.frcblog.com/2014/08/truth-matters-ex-gay-debate/.

21. Michael Brown, "A California Senator's Attack on Parental Rights," Townhall.com, August 2, 2012, http://townhall.com/columnists/michaelbrown/2012/08/02/a_california_senators_attack_on_parental_rights/page/full.

22. See "Researcher: 74 Percent of Bisexuals Experienced Child Sex Abuse," Americans for Truth about Homosexuality, http://americansfortruth.com/news/researcher-74-percent-of-bisexuals-experienced-child-sex-abuse.html#more-3039.

23. David C. Pruden, "HIV+ Lawmaker Resigns to Head AIDS 'Prevention' Group," *Barbwire*, June 5, 2014, http://barbwire.com/2014/06/05/gay-lawmaker-reveals-hes-infected-hiv-resigns-head-aids-prevention-group/#yFifGTlqWuJYPe0Y.99. Pruden is the executive director for the National Association for Research and Therapy of Homosexuality (NARTH), a professional organization regularly subjected to hate speech for their service to the homosexual community. According to Pruden (and speaking for NARTH), "Simply put, sexual self-determination is the right of any person to determine for themselves their own sexual behavior, identity and direction. . . . Some people with homosexual attractions report being happy and fulfilled engaging in same-sex sex and adopting a gay identity. However, many people with homosexual attractions are primarily identified with their religious convictions or personal life choices and find that their homosexual attractions are not compatible with their personally selected goals. For them, diminishing those attractions and managing their behaviors is a rational and achievable goal." (From a general NARTH e-mail blast dated June 20, 2014.)

24. *Daily Mail* reporter, "The Little Boy Who Started a Sex Change Aged Eight Because He (and His Lesbian Parents) Knew He Always Wanted to Be a Girl," *Daily Mail* (UK), September 30, 2011, http://www.dailymail.co.uk/news/article-2043345/The-California-boy-11-undergoing-hormone-blocking-treatment.html.

25. Kim Petras (in Germany), born Tim Petras, is presently the world's youngest sex-change patient, completing "gender reassignment surgery" at age sixteen, after a number of years of hormone treatments. See *Wikipedia*, s.v. "Kim Petras," http://en.wikipedia.org/wiki/Kim_Petras.

26. Even MSNBC acknowledged this: Adam Serwer, "Efforts to Ban 'Gay Conversion' Therapy Stall in the States," MSNBC, August 8, 2014, http://www.msnbc.com/msnbc/ex-gay-therapy-bans-stall-the-states?cid=sm_m_main_1_20140808_29398496. Ironically, when we tell the gay community that we know former homosexuals, they inevitably tell us that such people are either suppressing their true sexuality or they were never really gay (or were, at most, bisexual). Based on this line of thinking, then, how could gay activists forbid someone to get counseling *just in case* the person wasn't truly gay or else was bisexual?

27. Homosexuals Anonymous and Jason, International Christian Ex-Gay Ministry, "SOCE Bill of Rights," Homosexuals-anonymous.com, July 4, 2014, http://www.homosexuals-anonymous.com/SOCE%20BILL%20OF%20RIGHTS.pdf.

28. Ibid.

29. Ira Kaufman, "NFL Holding Players to Higher Standard," *Tampa Tribune*, July 20, 2014, http://tbo.com/sports/bucs/nfl-holding-players-to-higher-standard-20140720/.

30. Pat Yasinskas and Nick Wagoner, "Dungy: Sam Deserves NFL Chance," *ESPN*, July 23, 2014, http://espn.go.com/nfl/story/_/id/11248177/tony-dungy-clarifies-comments-michael-sam-st-louis-rams.

31. Mike Mazzeo, "Giants Blasted for David Tyree Hire," ESPN New York, July 23, 2014, http://espn.go.com/new-york/nfl/story/_/id/11249783/human-rights-campaign-blasts-new-york-giants-hiring-david-tyree.

32. Dan Graziano, "David Tyree Hire a Bad Move for Giants," ESPN, July 22, 2014, http://espn. go.com/blog/new-york-giants/post/_/id/37199/david-tyree-hire-a-bad-move-for-giants.

33. Is "medieval" now one of the standard words to use? A man named Joe posted this comment to my video reaching out to Christian worship leader (and now declared lesbian) Vicky Beeching: "Michael Brown, you are a smart guy but this video is bigoted and medieval." See Michael Brown, "Dr. Brown Reaches Out to Vicky Beeching," YouTube video, August 19, 2014, https://www.youtube. com/watch?v=aeoO5khx-zw.

34. "Gallaudet's Chief Diversity Officer Signs Anti-Gay Petition," Planet DeafQueer, October 8, 2012, http://planet.deafqueer.com/gallaudets-chief-diversity-officer-signs-anti-gay-petition/.

35. David Hill, "Gallaudet Urged to Reinstate McCaskill," *Washington Times*, October 11, 2012, http://www.washingtontimes.com/news/2012/oct/11/gallaudet-urged-to-reinstate-mccaskill/#ixzz36ZW6cUDt.

36. Arnold Ahlert, "Campus Left Mobilizes Against Diversity Officer," *Frontpage Mag*, October 15, 2012, http://www.frontpagemag.com/2012/arnold-ahlert/diversity-officer-fired-for-gay-marriage-heresy/.

37. Evan Gahr, "Judge Dismisses Diversity Officer's Lawsuit Against Gallaudet University," *Daily Caller*, April 22, 2014, http://dailycaller.com/2014/04/22/judge-dismisses-diversity-officers-lawsuit-against-gallaudet-university/#ixzz36ZYS0NCs.

38. See, for example, "Church Vandalized over Prop 8," CBN News, November 12, 2008, http://www. cbn.com/cbnnews/479857.aspx; and "Prop. 8 passage spawns protests, violence and vandalism," *Christian Examiner*, December 9, 2008, http://www.christianexaminer.com/article/prop.8.passage. spawns.protests.violence.and.vandalism/43390.htm.

39. See Sam Page, "El Coyote Owner Apologizes for Prop. 8 Contribution; Boycott Looms," *Peace Love Lunges* (blog), November 12, 2008, http://www.peacelovelunges.com/topics/luv/el-coyote-owner-expresses-regret-over-prop-8-contribution-but-boycott-looms/.

40. Lisa Derrick from the *Huffington Post*, December 9, 2009, reprinted on the website of Alliance Support, http://www.alliancesupport.org/news/archives/002521.html.

41. Maggie Gallagher, "Marjorie Christofferson's Courage," *The Corner* (blog), December 9, 2008, http://www.nationalreview.com/corner/174578/marjorie-christoffersons-courage/maggie-gallagher.

42. Canada legalized same-sex "marriage" in 2005, making it the fourth country to do so; the first three were the Netherlands (2001), Belgium (2003), and Spain (2005).

43. Lea Singh, "Canada on Verge of Banning Christians from Professional Life," *Frontpage Mag*, May 30, 2014, http://www.frontpagemag.com/2014/lea-singh/canada-on-verge-of-banning-christians-from-professional-life/. This article, written by Harvard Law School graduate Lea Singh, is replete with prescient warnings.

44. Canadian Press, "Lawyers Vote Against Christian Law School: Decision Is the Latest Setback for Trinity Western University," *Maclean's*, June 10, 2014, http://www.macleans.ca/news/canada/b-c-lawyers-vote-against-trinity-western-university-amid-claims-of-gay-discrimination/.

45. Ibid.

46. "Trinity Western Law School: B.C. Advanced Education Minister Revokes Approval," CBC News, http://www.cbc.ca/m/news/canada/british-columbia/trinity-western-law-school-b-c-advanced-education-minister-revokes-approval-1.2870640.

47. Anugrah Kumar, "400,000-Membered American Bar Association Back LGBT Rights in US, Globally," *Christian Post*, August 17, 2014, http://www.christianpost.com/news/400000-membered-american-bar-association-backs-lgbt-rights-in-us-globally-124933/.

48. See Michael Brown, "Gordon College, Don't Sell Your Soul for Secular Accreditation," *Charisma News*, October 3, 2014, http://www.charismanews.com/opinion/in-the-line-of-fire/45631-gordon-college-don-t-sell-your-soul-for-secular-accreditation and http://www.charismanews.com/opinion/in-the-line-of-fire/45716-gordon-college-compassion-yes-compromise-no. For the final, positive outcome, see Billy Hallowell, "Christian College Brought in Scholars, Theologians and Social Scientists to Examine Its Homosexuality Stance — and Here's What They Concluded," *The Blaze*, March 16, 2015, http://www.theblaze.com/stories/2015/03/16/we-are-a-sex-saturated-culture-embattled-christian-college-reveals-whether-it-will-abandon-its-traditional-stance-on-homosexuality/. For caveats and concerns, see Robert A. J. Gagnon, "Gordon College Wins -- And Loses?", May 5, 2015, First Things, http://www.firstthings.com/web-exclusives/2015/05/gordon-college-winsand-loses.

49. Deacon Keith Fournier, "Couple Rejected: Will Christians Be Allowed to Provide Foster Care in England?" *Catholic Online*, March 3, 2011, http://www.catholic.org/news/international/europe/story.php?id=40535.

50. Adrian Warnock, "Does Equality for Homosexuals Trump Religious Freedom? The Case of Eunice and Owen Johns," Adrian Warnock's blog, March 4, 2011, http://www.patheos.com/blogs/adrianwarnock/2011/03/does-equality-for-homosexuals-trump-religious-freedom-the-case-of-eunice-and-owen-johns/#ixzz34rD2Tt1k.

51. Robert Pigott, Analysis, on "Christian Foster Couple Lose 'Homosexuality Views' Case," BBC News, February 28, 2011, http://www.bbc.co.uk/news/uk-england-derbyshire-12598896.

52. The Christian Institute in the UK tracks these violations and releases period reports; see http://www.christian.org.uk/. For a shocking but representative selection, current through early 2011, see Brown, *Queer Thing*, 532–44.

53. Steve Doughty, "I May Have Been Wrong to Condemn Christian B&B Owners for Banning Gay Couple Because People with Religious Beliefs Have Rights Too, Says Top Judge," *Daily Mail*, June 19, 2014, http://www.dailymail.co.uk/news/article-2663037/I-wrong-condemn-Christian-B-amp-B-owners-says-judge.html.

54. Bob Unruh, "Judge Has 'Epiphany' In Ruling Against Christians," *WND*, June 21, 2014, http://www.wnd.com/2014/06/judge-doubts-own-ruling-against-christians/; see also Adrian Smith, "UK court vindicates Christian demoted for opposing gay 'marriage,'" LifeSite, November 23, 2012, http://www.lifesitenews.com/news/uk-court-vindicates-christian-demoted-for-opposing-gay-marriage. Unfortunately, on January 17, 2015, it was reported that an experienced magistrate in England was suspended and sent to equality training after saying behind closed doors to colleagues that an adopted child needed a mom and dad, not gay parents. See Martin Beckford and Jonathan Petre, "Suspended and Sent for 'Equality Training'—Christian Magistrate Who Said: 'Adopted Child Needs Mum and Dad—Not Gay Parents,'" January 17, 2015, http://www.dailymail.co.uk/news/article-2914951/Suspended-sent-equality-training-Christian-magistrate-said-Adopted-child-needs-mum-dad-not-gay-parents.html#ixzz3PDfEKLLR. The judge, Richard Page, is a committed Christian and remarked, "There is tremendous pressure to keep quiet and go along with what is seen to be politically correct. Everyone else seems to be allowed to stand up for their beliefs except for Christians."

55. Robert Oscar Lopez, "Gays Gone Wild: Life in America after the Ball Is Over," *American Thinker*, May 12, 2014, http://www.americanthinker.com/2014/05/gays_gone_wild_life_in_america_after_the_ball_is_over.html; Lopez provided links for each incident cited.

56. In America, see Penny Star, "Bakers on Not Making Lesbians' Wedding Cake: 'It's Never Been about Sexual Orientation, It's about Marriage'," CNS News, September 26, 2014, http://www.

cnsnews.com/news/article/penny-starr/bakers-not-making-lesbians-wedding-cake-its-never-been-about-sexual; in Ireland, see Mark Woods, "Christian bakers will be prosecuted over refusal to make pro-gay marriage cake," *Christian Today*, http://www.christiantoday.com/article/christian.bakers.will.be.prosecuted.over.refusal.to.make.pro.gay.marriage.cake/42664.htm.

57. Todd Starnes, "Baker Forced to Make Gay Wedding Cakes, Undergo Sensitivity Training, after Losing Lawsuit," Fox News, June 3, 2014, http://www.foxnews.com/opinion/2014/06/03/baker-forced-to-make-gay-wedding-cakes-undergo-sensitivity-training-after/?intcmp=latestnews; Colorado civil rights officials likened this baker to a Nazi; see Valerie Richardson, "Cake Maker Who Refused to Bake for Gay Wedding Labeled a 'Nazi' by Colo. Civil Rights Officials," *Washington Times*, January 12, 2015, http://www.washingtontimes.com/news/2015/jan/12/colorado-cake-case-pits-religion-against-tolerance/. Even with rulings coming against him, Phillips continues to hold to his convictions; see CBS4, "Bakery Will Stop Making Wedding Cakes After Losing Discrimination Case," CBS Denver, May 30, 2014, http://denver.cbslocal.com/2014/05/30/bakery-will-stop-making-wedding-cakes-after-losing-discrimination-case/.

58. Todd Starnes, "Baker forced to make gay wedding cakes, undergo sensitivity training, after losing lawsuit," Fox News, June 3, 2014, http://www.foxnews.com/opinion/2014/06/03/baker-forced-to-make-gay-wedding-cakes-undergo-sensitivity-training-after/.

59. Unruh, "Baker Appeals Government Re-Education Order."

60. Austin Ruse, "How Chase Bank and Other Corporations Coerce and Bully Christians," *Crisis Magazine*, July 4, 2014, http://www.crisismagazine.com/2014/chase-bank-corporations-coerce-bully-christians. Note that this was not an anonymous survey; employees were required to provide their employee ID numbers when responding.

61. Robert George, "Brendan Eich Was Only the Beginning . . . ," *Mirror of Justice* (blog), June 29, 2014, http://mirrorofjustice.blogs.com/mirrorofjustice/2014/06/brendan-eich-was-only-the-beginning-.html; see also Austin Ruse, "A second source has confirmed that JP Morgan Chase has asked each of its employees whether they are 'an ally of the LGBT community,' which employees have taken as a veiled threat," Breitbart, July 1, 2014, http://www.breitbart.com/Big-Government/2014/07/01/Chase-Bank-Revealed-as-Bank-Hounding-Employees-about-LGBT-Support.

62. Ruse, "How Chase Bank and Other Corporations Coerce and Bully Christians."

63. Ibid.

64. Ibid.

65. To watch the debate, see Michael Brown, "Dr. Michael Brown vs. Prof. Eric Smaw on Same-Sex 'Marriage': Should It Be Legal?" YouTube, April 22, 2013, https://www.youtube.com/watch?v=kcncyKCi3vk. On January 23, 2015, a judge ruled against a community college that had banned two leaders with Heterosexuals for a Moral Society from distributing literature on campus, since they were allegedly in violation of the school's antidiscrimination laws; see https://www.rutherford.org/files_images/general/01-23-2015_Lela_Memorandum_Opinion-and-Order.pdf. For a very different situation at Notre Dame, see Dominic Lynch, "Notre Dame Denies Official Recognition to Pro-Traditional Marriage Student Group," the College Fix, May 20, 2014, http://www.thecollegefix.com/post/17503/.

66. See Lopez, "300 Examples You Have to Read to Understand the Term 'Homofascism.'"

67. Tish Harrison Warren, "The Wrong Kind of Christian," *Christianity Today*, August 27, 2014, http://www.christianitytoday.com/ct/2014/september/wrong-kind-of-christian-vanderbilt-university.html?share=HEM3rHy3NoDHiyDTDefd4lNjZn9ixdLt&paging=off.

68. For examples of just how absurd things have become, see Michael Brown, "Can a Muslim Lead the Christian Campus Club?" Townhall.com, April 6, 2012, http://townhall.com/columnists/michaelbrown/2012/04/06/can_a_muslim_lead_the_christian_campus_club/page/full.

69. Letter to the U.S. House of Representatives et al., on Jeff Rhoades, "Get Campus Crusade for Christ BANNED from Schools as a Hate Group," Change.org, accessed February 6, 2015, http://www.change.org/p/get-campus-crusade-for-christ-banned-from-schools-as-a-hate-group.

70. Warren, "The Wrong Kind of Christian."

71. Throughout the Bible, believers are warned against deception. Shortly before His crucifixion, Jesus cautioned His followers, "Watch out that no one deceives you" (Matthew 24:4 NIV). Paul frequently wrote to his readers, "Do not be deceived" (e.g., 1 Corinthians 6:9 NIV), while James warned against the dangers of being deceived and of deceiving ourselves (see James 1:16, 22).

72. Soulforce home page, http://www.soulforce.org/.

73. Mel White, *Stranger at the Gate: To Be Gay and Christian in America* (New York: Plume, 1995).

74. Mel White, *Religion Gone Bad: The Hidden Dangers of the Christian Right* (New York: Jeremy P.Tarcher/ Penguin, 2006).

75. Mel White, *Holy Terror: Lies the Christian Right Tells Us to Deny Gay Equality* (New York: Magnus, 2012).

76. Mel White, "Resist Southern Baptist 'Terrorism,'" *The Blog*, June 26, 2012, http://www.huffingtonpost.com/rev-mel-white/southern-baptist-convention-gay-rights_b_1621100.html. The previous two paragraphs were excerpted from *Can You Be Gay and Christian?* 10–11.

77. Warren, "The Wrong Kind of Christian."

78. Frank S. Thielman, *Philippians: The NIV Application Commentary* (Grand Rapids: Zondervan, 2009), 15.

PRINCIPLE #2: TAKE THE HIGHEST MORAL GROUND

1. There are scores of e-mails and comments that are too vulgar and profane to post.

2. It is common to see the FRC and AFA described as "discredited hate groups," as if this had been determined by some kind of actual, objective criteria used by a fair-minded, objective organization. For the SPLC's role in the attempted massacre at FRC headquarters, see Matt Barber, "Bloody Hands: The Southern Poverty Law Center," *WND Commentary*, February 8, 2013, http://www.wnd.com/2013/02/bloody-hands-the-southern-poverty-law-center/.

3. "30 New Activists Heading Up the Radical Right," Southern Poverty Law Center, Summer 2012, http://www.splcenter.org/get-informed/intelligence-report/browse-all-issues/2012/summer/30-to-watch. For my reaction to being placed on the list, see Michael Brown, "Malik Zulu Shabbaz, David Duke, and Me," Townhall.com, May 25, 2012, http://townhall.com/columnists/michaelbrown/2012/05/25/malik_zulu_shabbaz_david_duke_and_me/page/full. See also my August 22, 2012, open letter to SPLC spokesman Mark Potok, on the Charisma News website: http://www.charismanews.com/opinion/34007-an-open-letter-to-splc-spokesman-mark-potok.

4. In light of their recent disgraceful work, criminology professor Mike Adams dubbed them the Intellectual Poverty Law Center; see Adams, "The Intellectual Poverty Law Center," Townhall.com, July 7, 2014, http://townhall.com/columnists/mikeadams/2014/07/07/the-intellectual-poverty-law-center-n1859027/page/full. Adams wrote, "Sadly, the once-great SPLC has abandoned its focus on fighting groups that terrorize the black community. Otherwise, they would be doing something about Planned Parenthood. Instead, the SPLC has turned its efforts towards promoting intellectual terrorism against all opponents of the American Left. Now, virtually everyone who disagrees with SPLC politics is branded a hate group and lumped together with groups like the KKK."

5. He referenced GLAAD's attack on me in their efforts to censor conservative voices on the media; see "GLAAD's Commentator Accountability Project," GLAAD.org, accessed February 6, 2015, http://www.glaad.org/cap.

6. I cited a Townhall.com article exposing GLAAD's hypocrisy; see Michael Brown, "Exposing the Hypocrisy of GLAAD," Townhall.com, March 19, 2012, http://townhall.com/columnists/michaelbrown/2012/03/19/exposing_the_hypocrisy_of_gladd/page/full.

7. SPLC Center, "Michael Brown," Extremist Files, accessed February 6, 2015, http://www.splcenter.org/get-informed/intelligence-files/profiles/michael-brown. Note, however, that as of this same date, my specific page was no longer found on the SPLC website, although I have yet to receive clarification from the SPLC as to whether they have removed me from their extremist list.

8. David Pakman, "HILARIOUS: Fox Has Hate Group 'Clear Up Confusion' on Hobby Lobby Case," YouTube video, 3:30, posted by *Media Matters*, July 2, 2014, https://www.youtube.com/watch?v=r89smDmGJuo; Pakman also complained that the FRC had filed an amicus brief in support of Hobby Lobby, as if this would disqualify Ruse rather than qualify her. Since this broadcast, Pakman has gone even further, comparing conservative, Bible-believing Christians (which equal "right-wing extremist Christians" in his lingo) with ISIS. See Michael Brown, "Debunking the "Conservative Christians = ISIS" Nonsense," YouTube video, 4:22, https://www.youtube.com/watch?v=yvYh8znX8Rc&list=UUbINn3x-intLp88Zrf8acpg. Cf. Bob Unruh, "'Christian-Right' Lumped with ISIS, Boko Haram," WND, October 16, 2014, http://www.wnd.com/2014/10/christian-right-lumped-with-islamic-state-boko-haram/#bopSB4MGWps9ePey.99.

9. "FRC Staff: Cathy Ruse: Senior Fellow—Legal Studies," Family Research Council, accessed February 6, 2015, http://www.frc.org/get.cfm?i=by06k07.

10. See Admin, "Isn't the Southern Poverty Law Center the Real Hate Group?" *Human Events*, July 28, 2011, http://humanevents.com/2011/07/28/isnt-the-southern-poverty-law-center-the-real-hate-group-2/.

11. Austin Ruse, "Study: Southern Poverty Law Center Ignores Liberal Hate," Breitbart, March 10, 2014, http://cdn.breitbart.com/Big-Government/2014/03/09/Southern-Poverty-Law-Center-Ingores-Liberal-Hate.

12. Ibid. See also "The SPLC Exposed—Southern Poverty Law Center—Morris Dees and Hate Crimes," http://www.thesocialcontract.com/answering_our_critics/southern_poverty_law_center_splc_info.html.

13. Tal Kopan, "Floyd Lee Corkins, the Family Research Center shooter, sentenced to 25 years," Politico, September 19, 2013, http://www.politico.com/story/2013/09/frc-shooter-sentenced-to-25-years-97069.html.

14. Mary Katharine Ham, "FRC Shooter: I Targeted Them Because SPLC List Said They Were 'Anti-Gay,'" *Hot Air* (blog), April 24, 2013, http://hotair.com/archives/2013/04/24/frc-shooter-i-targeted-them-because-splc-list-said-they-were-anti-gay/.

15. As noted on the blog *Jihad Watch*, "While the SPLC may have done good work in the 1960s against white racists, in recent years it has become a mere propaganda organ for the Left, tarring any group that dissents from its extreme political agenda as a 'hate group.' Significantly, although it lists hundreds of groups as 'hate groups,' it includes not a single Islamic jihad group on this list" ("Rebuttals: The truth about Robert Spencer: Rebuttals to false charges," accessed February 6, 2015, http://www.jihadwatch.org/rebuttals). For a more devastating critique of the SPLC, see Charlotte Allen's article "King of Fearmongers: Morris Dees and the Southern Poverty Law Center, scaring donors since 1971," in the April 15, 2013, *Weekly Standard*, http://www.weeklystandard.com/articles/king-fearmongers_714573.html.

16. See John Leo, "Jeff Jacoby in the Media: Phobic in the Wrong Places," Pundicity, November 17, 1997, http://www.jeffjacoby.com/784/phobic-in-the-wrong-places. I document this in depth in *A Queer Thing Happened to America* in the chapter titled "Jewish Hitlers, Christian Jihadists, and the Magical Effects of Pushing the 'Hate' Button."

17. Marshall Kirk and Erastes Pill, "The Overhauling of Straight America," Gay Homeland Foundation, November 1987, http://library.gayhomeland.org/0018/EN/EN_Overhauling_Straight.htm.

18. Wayne Besen, "Michael Brown is an Anti-Gay Monster," *Truth Wins Out* (blog), August 31, 2011, http://www.truthwinsout.org/blog/2011/08/18555/.

19. For my mini-debate with Besen on David Pakman's show, see "DEBATE: Anti-Gay Marriage Activist Calls Gay Rights Activist Dangerous," posted August 30, 2012, https://www.youtube.com/watch?v=H8CxBYixXE40.

20. Michael Brown, "When a Gay Jewish Liberal Tries to Redefine Christianity," *Voice of Revolution*, September, 28, 2011, http://www.voiceofrevolution.com/2011/09/28/when-a-gay-jewish-liberal-tries-to-redefine-christianity/.

21. Michael Brown, "The Gay Protest That Encountered the Love of God," *Charisma*, August 28, 2012, http://www.charismanews.com/opinion/34055-the-gay-protest-that-encountered-the-love-of-god. For the audio of the radio show, see http://www.lineoffireradio.com/2012/08/27/update-on-the-gay-protest-at-fire-church-dr-brown-reflects-on-gods-grace-and-answers-your-questions/. For another example of a gay activist thinking that they were full of hate only to encounter "radical love," see http://www.voiceofrevolution.com/2009/07/27/god-has-a-better-way-receives-protest-praise-from-glbt-community/. For the gay activist revision of this very same event years later, in which the facts get turned upside down and truth is called a lie, see http://www.mattcomer.net/807/did-newsweek-let-a-rightwing-hypocrite-and-liar-respond-to-their-bible-commentary/.

22. Matt Comer, "Holy War: 'A Cause Worth Dying For,'" *Q-Notes*, n.d., accessed July 20, 2014, http://goqnotes.com/editorial/editorsnote_012608.html. As of publication, the picture was still running with the article.

23. See Pakman, "HILARIOUS," for one example of many. To give a personal, social media example, note this comment from Mitch C. on October 9, 2014: "You're pathetic and want to make people conform to your beliefs JUST like ISIS. You people are no better than the Muslims" (posted to our YouTube channel, at https://www.youtube.com/watch?v=yvYh8znX8Rc).

24. Among the groups they supported were mainstream organizations such as the Fellowship of Christian Athletes. For the comments of Dan Cathy, then COO of Chick-fil-A, see "Dan Cathy Statements," at *Wikipedia*, s.v., "Chick-fil-A Same-Sex Marriage Controversy," http://en.wikipedia.org/wiki/Chick-fil-A_same-sex_marriage_controversy#Dan_Cathy_statements.

25. See, e.g., Tyler Kingkade, "Chick-Fil-A Voted Out by Elon University Students, Booted from Other Campuses in North Carolina," *Huffington Post*, October 16, 2012, http://www.huffingtonpost.com/2012/10/16/chick-fil-a-elon-university_n_1971376.html.

26. Pete Baklinski, "Canadian City Bans Christian Event Featuring Laura Bush over Chick-fil-A Sponsorship," *Life Site News*, June 26, 2014, http://www.lifesitenews.com/news/canadian-city-bans-christian-event-featuring-laura-bush-over-chick-fil-a-sp.

27. Ezra Levant, "Freedom of Religion for Canadian Students," For Canada, accessed March 31, 2015, http://www.forcanada.ca/freedom_of_religion_for_canadian_students; http://therealbigots.com/nanaimo.php. See also Levant, "Nanaimo Councillors Divide and Censor," *Toronto Sun*, June 23. 2014, accessed March 31, 2015, http://www.torontosun.com/2014/06/23/nanaimo-councillors-divide-and-censor.

28. Unruh, "'Christian-Right' Lumped with ISIS, Boko Haram." And if that weren't bad enough, on September 25, 2014, David Pakman stated on his radio show that he saw no real difference between ISIS and what he called conservative, right-wing extremists (a definition he would use to describe conservative, evangelical Christians). For my video response to these comments, see https://www.youtube.com/watch?v=yvYh8znX8Rc.

29. Originally posted at http://www.godhatesamerica.com/ and posted frequently, in part, online on numerous other sites. See, for example, http://www.kare11.com/news/news_article.aspx?storyid=103703, posted August 1, 2005.

30. Originally posted at http://www.godhatessweden.com/ but since posted on other sites, such as Eric Lottrich's *On Liberty* blog. See his April 2, 2007, posting "God Hates Sweden," http://erikwottrich.blogspot.com/2007/04/god-hates-sweden.html.

31. A Google search on September 1, 2014, yielded more hits for "Fred Phelps" than for "Tony Perkins."

32. Martin Luther King, Jr., "Loving your Enemies," in a reading from *The Class of Nonviolence*, prepared by Colman McCarthy, accessed February 6, 2015, http://www.salsa.net/peace/conv/8weekconv4-2.html.

33. Citing Deuteronomy 32:35.

34. Citing Proverbs 25:21–22; scholars differ on the meaning of "heap burning coals on his head," but it appears to depict bringing someone to a state of contrition and repentance.

35. We must never forget that speaking the truth in love is *not* hate-filled and demeaning, regardless of the constant accusations directed against us for doing so.

36. For the question of whether we can compare the sin of gluttony to the sin of homosexual practice, see Robert A. J. Gagnon, "It's Silly to Compare Homosexual Practice to Gluttony: A Response to Craig Gross's CNN Belief Blog Op-Ed," Robert A. J. Gagnon's website, July 19, 2012, http://www.robgagnon.net/GluttonyComparisonToHomosexualPractice.htm.

PRINCIPLE #3: SEXUAL PURITY TRUMPS SEXUAL ANARCHY

1. See Genesis 1:11–31.

2. Pitirim Sorokin, *The American Sex Revolution* (Boston: Porter Sargent, 1956), 44. Christian activist Louis Sheldon notes that "Sorokin noted in the late 60's that America was committing 'voluntary suicide' through unrestrained sexual indulgence. He observed that as individuals began engaging in pre-marital sex unrelated to marriage, the birth rate would decline and our nation would be slowly depopulated. He predicted an increase in divorce, desertion, and an epidemic of sexual promiscuity resulting in a rise in illegitimate children. His predictions, unfortunately, have come true." See http://www.freerepublic.com/focus/f-news/1402568/posts.

3. This quote and the Coulter quotes that follow are from Ann Coulter, "A Man of Sterling Character," Townhall.com, April 30, 2014, http://townhall.com/columnists/anncoulter/2014/04/30/a-man-of-sterling-character-n1831848.

4. "Lake Co. Boy Runs for Homecoming Queen," wftv.com, October 22, 2014, http://m.wftv.com/news/news/local/lake-co-boy-runs-homecoming-queen/nhp43/, emphasis added. This is becoming more and more common in our children's schools.

5. I'm referring here, of course, to Michael Sam; see my February 11, 2014, article on Townhall.com, titled "5 Questions About the Possibility of an Openly Gay NFL Player," http://townhall.com/columnists/michaelbrown/2014/02/11/5-questions-about-the-possibility-of-an-openly-gay-nfl-player-n1793166.

6. Marshall Kirk and Erastes Pill, "The Overhauling of Straight America," Gay Homeland Library, November 1987, http://library.gayhomeland.org/0018/EN/EN_Overhauling_Straight.htm.

7. Frank Newport and Igor Himelfarb, "In U.S., Record-High Say Gay, Lesbian Relations Morally OK," Gallup, May 20, 2013, http://www.gallup.com/poll/162689/record-high-say-gay-lesbian-relations-morally.aspx; for clear differences in commit levels between cohabiting couples and married couples, see James E. Sheridan, "Marriage Done Right: Are You Sure Cohabitation Gets You What You Think?" *News-Sentinel* (Fort Wayne, IN), January 14, 2015, http://www.news-sentinel.com/apps/pbcs.dll/article?AID=/20150114/LIVING/150119967/1008.

8. Rebecca Riffkin, "New Record Highs in Moral Acceptability," Gallup, May 30, 2014, http://www.gallup.com/poll/170789/new-record-highs-moral-acceptability.aspx.

9. Mark Regnerus, "Tracking Christian Sexual Morality in a Same-Sex Marriage Future," Witherspoon Institute *Public Discourse*, August 11, 2014, http://www.thepublicdiscourse.com/2014/08/13667/. Note also how "Gay and Lesbian Christians" had far lower moral standards than all groups represented with the exception of "Gay and Lesbian non-Christians." For disturbing statistics about porn use in America— another indication of today's sexual anarchy—see "2014 Pornography Survey and Statistics," Proven Men, http://www.provenmen.org/2014PornSurvey/.

10. Mirror.co.uk, "Kim Kardashian Told She Has No Talent during Walters Interview," Mirror Celebrity News, December 16, 2011, http://www.mirror.co.uk/3am/celebrity-news/kim-kardashian-told-she-has-no-talent-281964.

11. Diana Falzone, "Kennedy Summers' Playboy Spread Will Help Her When She's a Doctor, Experts Say," Fox 411, June 6, 2014, http://www.foxnews.com/entertainment/2014/06/06/kennedy-summers-playboy-spread-will-help-her-when-doctor-experts-say/?intcmp=features.

12. The video of a six-year-old boy rapping about women's "booties"— and I don't mean shoes—drew a wave of criticism when it was posted on YouTube (the boy was surrounded by women gyrating in bikinis). Although the director claimed it was a joke before pulling the viral video, there's no doubt that little children emulate these stars, even if they have no clue what the lyrics or motions mean. See Gus Garcia-Roberts, "Director of 6-Year-Old Rapper's Explicit Video Says It's a Joke," *Miami New Times*, July 12, 2012, http://www.miaminewtimes.com/2012-07-12/news/booty-pop-sexually-explicit-6-year-old-rapper-albert-roundtree-jr/full/.

13. Curtis M. Wong, "Beyonce Is 'Selling Sex' to Her Young Audience According to Actress Lily Tomlin," *Huffington Post*, June 10, 2014, http://www.huffingtonpost.com/2014/06/10/lily-tomlin-beyonce-_n_5480301.html?utm_hp_ref=gay-voices.

14. Eric Holmberg, "Pomosexuality: The Real Face of the Sexual Revolution," The Apologetics Group, n.d., accessed February 6, 2015, http://theapologeticsgroup.com/featured/pomosexuality-the-real-face-of-the-sexual-revolution/ .

15. Jessica Bennett, "Polyamory: The Next Sexual Revolution?" *Newsweek*, July 28, 2009, http://www.newsweek.com/polyamory-next-sexual-revolution-82053.

16. Showtime, "Polyamory Season 1: Behind the Scenes," YouTube video, 3:03, July 9, 2012, http://www.youtube.com/watch?v=YE-WYjBPBAY.

17. Steve Nelson, "Polyamory Advocate: Gay Marriage 'Blazing the Marriage Equality Trail,'" *U.S. News & World Report*, June 24, 2013, http://www.usnews.com/news/articles/2013/06/24/polyamorous-advocate-gay-marriage-blazing-the-marriage-equality-trail.

18. Jennifer LeClaire, "Can We Pray the Polyamory Away?" *Charisma News*, June 19, 2014, http://www.charismanews.com/opinion/watchman-on-the-wall/44354-can-we-pray-the-polyamory-away.

19. Fox News, "'Dating Naked,' 'Naked and Afraid' and More Showcase Nude Trend," Fox 411, July 16, 2014, http://www.foxnews.com/entertainment/2014/07/16/naked-dating-naked-and-afraid-and-more-showcase-nude-tv-trend/?intcmp=features.

20. CBS News, "N.Y. State Suggests HIV Tests for 13-Year-Olds, Sex Ed in Elementary School," CBS New York, May 21, 2014, http://newyork.cbslocal.com/2014/05/21/n-y-state-suggests-hiv-tests-for-13-year-olds-sex-ed-in-elementary-school/.

21. Centers for Disease Control and Prevention, "HIV Among Gay and Bisexual Men," CDC website, accessed February 9, 2015, http://www.cdc.gov/hiv/risk/gender/msm/facts/index.html.

22. For recent increases in syphilis, see Centers for Disease Control and Prevention, "Syphilis & MSM (Men Who Have Sex with Men)—CDC Fact Sheet," CDC, accessed February 9, 2015, http://www. cdc.gov/std/Syphilis/STDFact-MSM-Syphilis.htm. It is now estimated that half of all gay men in America will be HIV-positive by the time they reach fifty. For links to various, relevant studies, see Jay Salamone, "What Does 'Gay' Sex Have to Do with Discrimination Anyway?" *Barbwire*, March 20, 2013, http://barbwire.com/2014/03/20/what-does-gay-sex-have-to-do-with-discrimination/.

23. Susan Edelman, "Parent Furor at Bawdy Sex Ed," *New York Post*, October 23, 2011, http://nypost. com/2011/10/23/parent-furor-at-bawdy-sex-ed/.

24. Kirsten Andersen, "Chicago Public Schools to Teach 5th Graders How to 'Increase Sexual Pleasure,'" Life Site News, November 17, 2014, https://www.lifesitenews.com/news/chicago-public-schools-to-teach-5th-graders-how-to-increase-sexual-pleasure.

25. Emily Yahr, "'Scandal' Sex Scene Airs Right after 'It's the Great Pumpkin, Charlie Brown,' 'Making Parents Angry," *Washington Post*, November 3, 2014, http://www.washingtonpost.com/blogs/style-blog/wp/2014/11/03/scandal-sex-scene-airs-right-after-its-the-great-pumpkin-charlie-brown-making-parents-angry/.

26. Proven Men Ministries, "Age Exposed to Porn & Age First Sex," ProvenMen website, accessed February 9, 2015, http://www.provenmen.org/2014pornsurvey/age-exposed-to-porn-age-first-sex/.

27. WCVB, "Condoms for Elementary Students? Yes, Says Mass. Town," WCVB.com, June 24, 2010, http://www.wcvb.com/Condoms-For-Elementary-Students-Yes-Says-Mass-Town/11288760.

28. Michael Brown, "Sex-Ed Classes and the Rape of Our Children's Innocence (Part 2)," Townhall. com, December 2, 2011, http://townhall.com/columnists/michaelbrown/2011/12/02/sexed_classes_and_the_rape_of_our_childrens_innocence_part_2/page/full.

29. Shelby Sebens, "Oregon School District to Offer Condoms to Students Starting in 6th Grade," Yahoo! News, June 4, 2014, http://news.yahoo.com/oregon-school-district-offer-condoms-students-starting-6th-002710449.html;_ylt=AwrBEiSD4o9TdiUAhgzQtDMD.

30. Gabriel Mephibosheth, "X-Rated Sex Ed for Calif. 8th grade; Parents Livid," *Culture News* (blog), June 9, 2014, http://culturecampaign.blogspot.com/2014/06/x-rated-sex-ed-for-calif-8th-grade. html. See also Laurie Higgins, "Sex "Educators" Push the Proverbial Envelope—Again," Illinois Family Institute, June 9, 2014, http://illinoisfamily.org/education/sex-educators-push-the-proverbial-envelope-again/.

31. Tad Cronn, "9th-Grade Curriculum: Bondage, Orgasms and Vibrators," *Political Outcast* (blog), August 8, 2014, http://politicaloutcast.com/2014/08/9th-grade-curriculum-bondage-orgasms-vibrators/#ydyITvvboWUhdDvk.99.

32. The show was called A Shot at Love with Tila Tequila.

33. Larry Tomczak, "Sex, Shock, 'n Sacrilege: Are You Aware How Dirty Comedy Has Become?" Charisma News, June 9, 2014, http://www.charismanews.com/opinion/heres-the-deal/44177-sex-shock-n-sacrilege-are-you-aware-how-dirty-comedy-has-become.

34. Pew Research Forum reported on October 14, 2014, "According to the latest available census data, the percentage of U.S. adults who have never been married has hit a new, all-time high. In 1960, about one in ten adults over the age of 25 fell into that category. By 2012, the number had jumped to one in five." My Fox DC, "Marriage Rates Hit New, All-Time Low," MyFoxDC.com,

October 14, 2014, http://www.myfoxdc.com/story/26779009/marriage-rates-hit-new-all-time-low. For pessimistic, scholarly analyses of the state of marriage in America today, see Andrew J. Cherlin, *Labor's Love Lost* (New York: Russell Sage Foundation, 2014); and Isabel V. Sawhill, *Generation Unbound: Drifting into Sex and Parenthood without Marriage* (Washington, DC: Brookings Institution Press, 2014).

35. Christina Sternbenz, "Marriage Rates Are Near Their Lowest Levels in History—Here's Why," *Business Insider,* May 7, 2014, http://www.businessinsider.com/causes-of-low-marriage-rates-2014-5.

36. Belinda Luscombe, "More Millennial Mothers Are Single Than Married," *Time,* June 17, 2014, http://time.com/2889816/more-millennial-mothers-are-single-than-married/. "As Liza Mundy noted in a May 22, 2013, *Atlantic* article titled 'The Gay Guide to Wedded Bliss,' it is more than a little ironic that gay marriage has emerged as the era's defining civil-rights struggle even as marriage itself seems more endangered every day. Americans are waiting longer to marry: according to the U.S. Census Bureau, the median age of first marriage is 28 for men and 26 for women, up from 23 and 20, respectively, in 1950.   Rates of cohabitation have risen swiftly and sharply, and more people than ever are living single. Most Americans still marry at some point, but many of those marriages end in divorce. . . . All told, this has created an unstable system of what the UCLA sociologist Suzanne Bianchi calls 'partnering and repartnering,' a relentless emotional and domestic churn that sometimes results in people forgoing the institution altogether."

37. Sternbenz, "Marriage Rates Are Near Their Lowest Levels in History."

38. Pew Research Center, "The Decline of Marriage and Rise of New Families," Pew Social Trends, November 18, 2010, http://www.pewsocialtrends.org/2010/11/18/ii-overview/.

39. Janice Shaw Crouse, "The New Twist on Inequality," *American Spectator,* June 19, 2014, http://spectator.org/articles/59684/new-twist-inequality.

40. Rachel Sheffield, "A Majority of Young Adults Are Having Kids Outside Marriage. Why That Hurts Kids' Futures," *Daily Signal,* June 21, 2014, http://dailysignal.com/2014/06/21/majority-young-adults-kids-outside-marriage-hurts-kids-futures/.

41. Benjamin Franklin, "Rules for Matrimonial Happiness," October 8, 1730.

42. Philip Yancey, "The Lost Sex Study," *Christianity Today,* December 12, 1994, http://www.christianitytoday.com/ct/1994/december12/4te080.html.

43. Joseph Daniel Unwin, *Sex and Culture* (London: Oxford University Press; H. Milford, 1934).

44. Yancey, "The Lost Sex Study."

45. J. D. Unwin. "Monogamy as a Condition of Social Energy," *Hibbert Journal* 25 (1927): 662.

46. Yancey, "The Lost Sex Study."

47. According to Lou Sheldon, "[Pitirim] Sorokin's study of decadent cultures convinced him that a healthy society can only survive if strong families exist and sexual activities are restricted to within marriage. Sexual promiscuity leads inevitably to cultural decline and eventual collapse." See Louis Sheldon, "The Destruction of Marriage Precedes the Death of a Culture," *Free Republic,* posted May 13, 2005, http://www.freerepublic.com/focus/f-news/1402568/posts.

48. Jay Michaelson, "Were Christians Right about Gay Marriage All Along?" *Daily Beast,* May 27, 2014, http://www.thedailybeast.com/articles/2014/05/27/did-christians-get-gay-marriage-right.html.

49. Ibid.

50. Daniel F. Case, "America: A Nation in Decline?" Case Studies by Daniel F. Case, accessed February 9, 2015, http://www.case-studies.com/nation-in-decline; for further detail, see "Carl Zimmerman," http://huron2.aaps.k12.mi.us/smitha/HUM/PDF/rome-decline.pdf. For the abridged version of the study, see Carle E. Zimmerman, *Family and Civilization,* ed. James Kurth (Wilmington, DE: ISI Books, 2008); the original edition was published in 1947.

51. Kelly Boggs, "Sexual Anarchy: America's Demise?" Crosswalk.com, July 27, 2009, http://www.crosswalk.com/family/marriage/sexual-anarchy-americas-demise-11606599.html.

52. Bradford Wilcox, "Faith and Family, Better Together? Religion and Family Around the Globe," Institute for Family Studies blog, October 16, 2014, http://family-studies.org/faith-and-family-better-together-religion-and-family-around-the-globe/.

53. For some helpful books on sexual purity, see Steve Gallagher, *At the Altar of Sexual Idolatry* (Dry Ridge, KY: Pure Life Ministries, 2000); Stephen Arterburn and Fred Stoeker, with Mike Yorkey, *Every Man's Battle: Every Man's Guide to Winning the War on Sexual Temptation One Victory at a Time* (Colorado Springs: WaterBrook Press, 2000); Sharon Ethridge, *Every Woman's Battle: Discovering God's Plan for Sexual and Emotional Fulfillment* (Colorado Springs: WaterBrook, 2009).

PRINCIPLE #4: REFUSE TO REDEFINE MARRIAGE

1. For references to same-sex "marriage" in rabbinic writings from the early centuries AD, see chapter 8.

2. John Gray, *Men Are from Mars, Women Are from Venus* (New York: HarperCollins, 1992); this has been reprinted in many editions since.

3. Robert H. Knight, "The Case for Marriage," Concerned Women for America website, September 29, 2003, http://www.cwfa.org/the-case-for-marriage/.

4. Ibid. For important, recent studies on the foundational importance of marriage as being only male-female, see Daniel Heimbach, *Why Not Same-Sex Marriage: A Manual for Defending Marriage Against Radical Deconstruction* (n.p.: Trusted Books, 2014), refuting 101 arguments in favor of same-sex "marriage"; Anthony Esolen, *Defending Marriage: Twelve Arguments for Sanity* (Charlotte: Saint Benedict Press, 2014); Patrick Lee and Robert P. George, *Conjugal Union: What Marriage Is and Why It Matters* (New York: Cambridge Univ. Press, 2014); Sherif Girgis, Ryan T. Anderson, and Robert P. George, *What Is Marriage?: Man and Woman: A Defense* (New York: Encounter Books, 2012); and William B. May, *Getting the Marriage Conversation Right: A Guide for Effective Dialogue* (Steubenville, OH: Emmaus Road, 2012). For earlier studies, through 2010 (including those with opposing views), see Michael L. Brown, *A Queer Thing Happened to America: And What a Long, Strange Trip It's Been* (Concord, NC: EqualTime Books, 2011), 611n63. On a regular basis, Ryan T. Anderson, William E. Simon Fellow at the Heritage Foundation and editor of *Public Discourse*, writes and links relevant articles on the meaning of marriage. Follow him on Twitter at https://twitter.com/ryant_anderson. For reflections on same-sex "marriage" by ex-gay leader Joe Dallas, see "The Gay Marriage Debate: Winning, Losing or Dropping Out? (Part 1)," *Joe Dallas Online* (blog), http://joedallas.com/blog/index.php/2012/06/29/gay-marriage/.

5. Joel Siegel, "Hil Nixes Same-Sex Marriage," *New York Daily News*, January 11, 2000, http://www.nydailynews.com/archives/news/hil-nixes-same-sex-marriage-article-1.864728#ixzz358vYsNM0.

6. Becky Bowers, "President Barack Obama's Shifting Stance on Gay Marriage," PolitiFact.com, May 11, 2012, http://www.politifact.com/truth-o-meter/statements/2012/may/11/barack-obama/president-barack-obamas-shift-gay-marriage/. Of course, it can be argued that he was not being honest in these statements, as I noted in my May 12, 2012, article in Townhall.com, "Equivocating or Evolving, President Obama Is Wrong Either Way": "We know the story well: Barack Obama was for same-sex 'marriage' (1996) before he was against it (2004) before he was for it (2012), although in 2008, he was apparently for it and against it (although mainly against it). Based, however, on his strong support for gay activism during his 'against' years, it seems clear that he was equivocating in his public opposition to same-sex 'marriage'" (http://townhall.com/columnists/michaelbrown/2012/05/12/equivocating_or_evolving_president_obama_is_wrong_either_way/page/full).

7. Peter Hitchens, "So Much for 'Father's Day'—in a Country Where Fatherhood Is Dying Out," Peter Hitchens' blog, June 16, 2013, http://hitchensblog.mailonsunday.co.uk/2013/06/so-much-for-fathers-day-in-a-country-where-fatherhood-is-dying-out.html.

8. Matthew Schmitz, "N.T. Wright on Gay Marriage: Nature and Narrative Point to Complementarity," *First Things* (blog), June 11, 2014, http://www.firstthings.com/blogs/firstthoughts/2014/06/n-t-wrights-argument-against-same-sex-marriage. The article also links to the video from which Wright's comments were transcribed.

9. See Joel Landau, "British Woman Marries Her Dog, Confesses: 'I'm Totally Her B---h'," *New York Daily News*, March 11, 2014, http://www.nydailynews.com/news/world/woman-marries-dog-totally-b-h-article-1.1717772; "Orissa Woman Marries Snake," *Times of India*, June 2, 2006, http://timesofindia.indiatimes.com/india/Orissa-woman-marries-snake/articleshow/1609295. cms; Eric Pfeiffer, "Seattle Woman 'Marries' Building to Protest Its Demolition," *The Sideshow* (blog), January 30, 2012, http://news.yahoo.com/blogs/sideshow/seattle-woman-marries-building-protest-demolition-224250710.html; Rob Quinn, "Man Wants to Marry His Porn-Filled Laptop," *USA Today*, May 7, 2014, http://www.usatoday.com/story/news/nation/2014/05/06/newser-man-wants-to-marry-porn-filled-laptop/8761997/. One man in Japan actually "married" a video game character in 2009! See Kyung Lah, "Tokyo Man Marries Video Game Character," CNN, December 17, 2009, http://www.cnn.com/2009/WORLD/asiapcf/12/16/japan.virtual.wedding/.

10. Michael Brown, "It's an Avalanche, Not a Slippery Slope," Charisma News, July 9, 2013, http://www.charismanews.com/opinion/in-the-line-of-fire/40155-it-s-an-avalanche-not-a-slippery-slope.

11. Shaunte Dunston, "Same-Sex Bridal Magazine Born of Frustration," CNN News, August 12, 2010, http://www.cnn.com/2010/LIVING/08/12/equally.wed/index.html?hpt=C2.

12. Lydia O'Connor, "California Just Got Rid of Its Last Barrier to Same-Sex Marriage," *Huffington Post*, July 8, 2014, http://www.huffingtonpost.com/2014/07/08/california-gay-marriage-language_n_5568029.html.

13. Brown, *Queer Thing*, 563–64.

14. Kevin Gray, "Florida Judge Approves Birth Certificate Listing Three Parents," Reuters, February 7, 2013, http://www.reuters.com/article/2013/02/07/us-usa-florida-adoption-idUSBRE91618L20130207.

15. Tyler McCarthy, "This Baby Is the First in British Columbia to Have 3 Parents Listed on Her Birth Certificate," *Huffington Post*, February 11, 2014, http://www.huffingtonpost.com/2014/02/11/baby-with-3-parents-birth-certificate_n_4767402.html.

16. Cheryl K. Chumley, "California Moves to Let Gay Men Cite Selves as 'Mother' on Birth Records; Lesbians as 'Father,'" *Washington Times*, May 9, 2014, http://www.washingtontimes.com/news/2014/may/9/california-moves-let-gay-men-cites-selves-mother-b/.

17. See the press release from Pacific Justice Institute dated May 15, 2014, at http://www.pacificjustice.org/press-releases/modern-family-birth-certificate-bill-offers-new-options. As noted by Brad Dacus, president of Pacific Justice Institute, "In a season where we have just celebrated Mother's Day and will be celebrating Father's Day next month, it is astounding that lawmakers want to render these concepts meaningless. Playing a labeling game does not change the reality of whether one is a dad or a mom. These types of absurd laws make our state a laughingstock and diminish respect for the law. They also make it clearer than ever that redefining marriage is just the starting point for LGBT activists who want to redefine everything about the family."

18. Michael Koziol, "Gay Groups Angered as Heterosexual Men Marry to Win Rugby Trip," *Sydney Morning Herald*, September 12, 2014, http://www.smh.com.au/world/gay-groups-angered-as-heterosexual-men-marry-to-win-rugby-trip-20140912-10fu3t.html#ixzz3D4Sg1Ovc.

19. Tara Kelly, "Nadine Schweigert, North Dakota Woman, 'Marries Herself,' Opens Up About Self-Marriage," *Huff Post*, May 5, 2014, http://www.huffingtonpost.com/2012/05/25/nadine-schweigert-woman-marries-herself_n_1546024.html; for links to her "date nights" with herself and some of her interview with Anderson Cooper, see Tamara Abraham, "Single Mother-of-Two Reveals Why She Married HERSELF and Even Goes on Date Nights Alone," *Daily Mail*, May 24, 2012, http://www.dailymail.co.uk/femail/article-2149364/Single-mother-reveals-married-HERSELF-goes-date-nights-alone.html.

20. "Taiwanese Woman to Marry Herself," *Telegraph* (UK), October 22, 2010, http://www.telegraph.co.uk/news/worldnews/asia/taiwan/8080685/Taiwanese-woman-to-marry-herself.html; Glen James, "Woman Gets Fed Up with Being Single—and Marries Herself!," *Online Mirror*, October 4, 2014, http://www.mirror.co.uk/news/world-news/woman-gets-fed-up-being-4376646#ixzz3FiJLtBQK.

21. For an excerpt of the program, which is no longer available on the Anderson Cooper website, see Anderson Cooper, "Daytime Exclusive: Woman Marries Herself in Ceremony," YouTube video, 1:27, May 24, 2012, https://www.youtube.com/watch?v=ojZg3e3KSpk.

22. David K. Li, "Married Lesbian 'Throuple' Expecting First Child," *New York Post*, April 23, 2014, http://nypost.com/2014/04/23/married-lesbian-threesome-expecting-first-child/. More recently, three men in Thailand were "married," becoming an overnight internet sensation; see Michael Brown, "If Love Is Love, Why Not Three Men 'Marrying'?" Charisma News, February 24, 2015, http://www.charismanews.com/opinion/in-the-line-of-fire/48454-if-love-is-love-why-not-three-men-marrying.

23. Published in 2009 without any publishing information. Again, I do not doubt the devotion or sincerity of the mothers involved. I'm simply highlighting the absurdity of the book's title, not to mention it denies that a child being with mother and *father* would be the best-case scenario.

24. Even in the many countries in which polygamy has been legal, the fundamental components of marriage remain the same: a man and a woman. Additionally, even in past societies where homosexuality was widely practiced and accepted, the term *marriage* was still reserved for male-female unions, with procreation an essential part of marriage. See, for example, Bruce W. Frier, "Roman Same-Sex Weddings from the Legal Perspective," University of Michigan Online, Winter 2004, http://www.umich.edu/~classics/news/newsletter/winter2004/weddings.html.

25. The information and quotations in this section are from Jim Burroway, "The Tale of the Box Turtle," *Box Turtle Bulletin*, January 9, 2006, http://www.boxturtlebulletin.com/About/AboutUs.htm.

26. See "About This Blog" at http://marriage-equality.blogspot.com/.

27. "British Columbia Court to Rule on Anti-Polygamy Law," BBC News, November 23, 2010, http://www.bbc.co.uk/news/world-us-canada-11817322.

28. Michael Lindenberger/Louisville, "Should Incest Be Legal?" *Time*, April 5, 2007, http://www.time.com/time/nation/article/0,8599,1607322,00.html.

29. Rush Limbaugh, "Stack of Stuff Quick Hits Page," Rush Limbaugh.com, December 14, 2010, http://img.rushlimbaugh.com/home/daily/site_121410/content/01125104.guest.html; see also Robert Stacy McCain, "But They Were *Consenting Adults!*" *The Spectacle* (blog), December 10, 2010, http://spectator.org/blog/24455/they-were-consenting-adults.

30. Jonathan Pearlman, "Australian Judge Says Incest May No Longer Be Taboo," *Telegraph*, July 10, 2014, http://www.telegraph.co.uk/news/worldnews/australiaandthepacific/australia/10958728/Australian-judge-says-incest-may-no-longer-be-a-taboo.html.

31. Julia Marsh, "NY State Blesses 'Incest' Marriage between Uncle, Niece," *New York Post*, October 29, 2014, http://nypost.com/2014/10/29/new-york-state-blesses-incest-marriage-between-uncle-niece/.

32. Thomas Rogers, "Gay Porn's Most Shocking Taboo," *Salon*, May 20, 2010, http://www. salon.com/2010/05/21/twincest/; see also "Brotherly Love," at http://stream.aljazeera.com/ story/201410011930-0024190; and Laurie Higgins, "Slippery Slope; Throuples, Twincest, and Remembering," http://barbwire.com/2014/05/08/throuples-twincest-remembering/.

33. Alexa Tsoulis-Reay, "What It's Like to Date Your Dad," *New York Magazine*, January 15, 2015, http://nymag.com/scienceofus/2015/01/what-its-like-to-date-your-dad.html; see also Matt Barber, "Incest: The next frontier in 'reproductive freedom,'" *WND Commentary*, January 16, 2015, http:// www.wnd.com/2015/01/incest-the-next-frontier-in-reproductive-freedom/.

34. Emily Yoffe, "Brotherly Love: My Twin and I Share an Earth-Shattering Secret That Could Devastate Our Family—Should We Reveal It?" *Slate*, February 16, 2012, http://www.slate.com/ articles/life/dear_prudence/2012/02/incestuous_twin_brothers_wonder_if_they_should_reveal_ their_secret_relationship_.html; Dan Savage, "Those Gay Incest Twins in Prudence This Week," *Slog* (blog), February 17, 2012, http://www.thestranger.com/slog/archives/2012/02/17/those-gay-incest-twins-in-prudence-this-week%26view=comments.

35. Fox News, "'The Notebook' Director Nick Cassavetes Says of Incest: 'Who Gives a Damn?'" Fox 411, September, 10, 2012, http://www.foxnews.com/entertainment/2012/09/10/notebook-director-nick-cassavetes-says-incest-who-gives-damn/?intcmp=features.

36. Dave Itzkoff, "For 'Game of Thrones,' Rising Unease over Rape's Recurring Role," *New York Times*, May 2, 2014, http://www.nytimes.com/2014/05/03/arts/television/for-game-of-thrones-rising-unease-over-rapes-recurring-role.html?_r=0.

37. Brent Bozell, "Step Right Up to MTV's Incest Plot," Townhall.com, July 18, 2014, http://townhall. com/columnists/brentbozell/2014/07/18/step-right-up-to-mtvs-incest-plot-n1863237.

38. Jenny Kutner, "German Committee Says Incest Is a 'Fundamental Right,'" Alternet.com, September 28, 2014, http://www.alternet.org/world/german-committee-says-incest-fundamental-right.

39. Curtis M. Wong, "Should Incest Between Consenting Adult Siblings Be Legalized? Experts Sound off," *Huffington Post*, October 9, 2014, http://www.huffingtonpost.com/2014/10/09/legalization-incestuous-relationships-_n_5959494.html.

40. Katie Dupere, "Falling for Family: Should Consensual Incest Be Legal?" DebateOut.com, December 16, 2014, http://www.debateout.com/falling-for-family-consensual-incest-legal/. This page is no longer available, but a cached copy can be seen at http://webcache.googleusercontent. com/search?q=cache:http://www.debateout.com/falling-for-family-consensual-incest-legal/.

41. Carol, Kuruvilla, "Polygamous Living Is Legal in Utah after Judge Overturns Cohabitation Ban in Favor of 'Sister Wives' Family," *New York Daily News*, August 28, 2014, http://www.nydailynews. com/news/national/polygamous-living-legal-utah-judge-sister-wives-ruling-article-1.1920071.

42. Jillian Kennan, "Legalize Polygamy! No. I Am Not Kidding," Slate, April 15, 2013, http://www. slate.com/articles/double_x/doublex/2013/04/legalize_polygamy_marriage_equality_for_all.html; emphasis in the original.

43. Jessica Bennett, "Polyamory: The Next Sexual Revolution?" *Newsweek*, July 28, 2009, http://www. newsweek.com/polyamory-next-sexual-revolution-82053.

44. See Kuruvilla, "Polygamous Living."

45. Mark Oppenheimer, "Married, with Infidelities," *New York Times*, June 30, 2011, http://www. nytimes.com/2011/07/03/magazine/infidelity-will-keep-us-together.html?_r=1&pagewanted=3.

46. Lisa Haisha, "Is It Time to Change Our Views of Adultery and Marriage?" *Huff Post The Blog*, July 5, 2014, http://www.huffingtonpost.com/lisa-haisha/is-it-time-to-change-our-adultery_b_5242171. html?ncid=txtlnkusaolp00000592.

47. Stanley Kurtz, "Death of Marriage in Scandinavia," Boston.com, March 10, 2004, http://www. boston.com/news/globe/editorial_opinion/oped/articles/2004/03/10/death_of_marriage_in_ scandinavia/.

48. Associated Press, "Woman Marries Dolphin," *The Age*, January 2, 2006, http://www.theage.com. au/news/world/woman-marries-dolphin/2006/01/01/1136050339590.html; Metrowebukmetro, "Man Marries Cat," *Metro*, May 4, 2010, http://metro.co.uk/2010/05/04/man-marries-cat-281021/.

49. Jude Newsome, "13 People Who Married Inanimate Objects," Ranker, accessed February 10, 2015, http://www.ranker.com/list/13-people-who-married-inanimate-objects/jude-newsome.

50. David Millward, "Florida Man Demands Right to Wed Computer," *Telegraph*, May 7, 2014, http:// www.telegraph.co.uk/news/worldnews/northamerica/usa/10814098/marriage-gay-marriage-mac-wedding-computer-Florida-Utah.html.

51. Frank Turek, *Correct, Not Politically Correct: How Same-Sex Marriage Hurts Everyone* (Charlotte: CrossExamined, 2008), 24–25.

52. John Adams to Abigail Adams II: August 13, 1783.

53. For the regrets experienced by a surrogate mother who conceived and carried a child for a gay couple, see http://www.dailymail.co.uk/news/article-2730356/I-felt-like-sold-child-Surrogate-mother-says-regrets-giving-baby-daughter-gay-couple.html.

54. Karen Clark, Norval Glenn, and Elizabeth Marquardt, *My Daddy's Name is Donor: A Pathbreaking New Study of Young Adults Conceived Through Sperm Donation* (Institute for American Values, 2010), in Lisa Belkin, "Are You My Mother? The Changing Norms of Adoption and Donation," *Huff Post*, March 22, 2012, http://www.huffingtonpost.com/lisa-belkin/adoption-egg-sperm-donation_b_1372049.html.

55. Donor Conceived, "Uncertainty Is Killing Me," AnonymousUs.org, February 6, 2012, http:// anonymousus.org/stories/story.php?sid=1482.

56. See, for example, queerspawn.community (http://www.queerspawn.com/), a community website billed as "a new forum for kids of queers."

57. Rebecca Taylor, "In-Vitro Fallout: Donor IVF Teen Says 'I Wish I Had Never Been Born,'" LifeNews.com, June 27, 2014, http://www.lifenews.com/2014/06/27/in-vitro-fallout-donor-ivf-teen-says-i-had-never-been-born/. According to the story, "She was adopted as a 'leftover' IVF embryo. Gracie keenly feels the loss of her genetic roots, but the law in the UK prevents her from ever knowing who her biological parents are."

58. "One Man Impregnated 30 Lesbians, Sparking Incest Fears," *Courier Mail*, October 8, 2008, http://www.couriermail.com.au/news/one-man-impregnated-30-lesbians-sparking-incest-fears/ story-e6freon6-1111117703946.

59. Thaddeus Baklinski, "'Sibling Incest Should Be Legal,' Says Danish Professor of Criminal Justice Ethics," Life Site News, October 17, 2014, https://www.lifesitenews.com/news/sibling-incest-should-be-legal-says-danish-professor-of-criminal-justice-et.

60. http://mcguffeyreaders.com/1828dictionary.htm; http://www.merriam-webster.com/dictionary/ marriage, accessed February 10, 2015. On June 19, 2014, the Presbyterian Church (U.S.A.) "approved a recommendation to change language in the Book of Order to indicate that 'marriage involves a unique commitment between two people, traditionally a man and a woman.'" For their official statement, see Presbyterian Church USA, "PC(USA) leaders issue pastoral letter to the church on Assembly's marriage actions," PCUSA.org, June 19, 2014, http://www.pcusa.org/ news/2014/6/19/pcusa-leaders-issue-pastoral-letter-church-assembl/.

61. See the studies referenced in note 4, and compare the works of Unwin and Zimmerman cited in chapter 3.

62. Robert H. Knight, "The Case for Marriage," Marriage Resources for Clergy, accessed February 10, 2015, http://www.marriageresourcesforclergy.com/site/Articles/articles021.htm.

63. Andrew Sullivan, *Virtually Normal*, repr. ed. (n.p.: Vintage, 1996), 185.

64. Knight, "The Case for Marriage."

65. Ibid.

66. Gavin Off, "NC Magistrates Resign over Gay Marriage Rulings," *Charlotte Observer*, October 25, 2014, http://www.charlotteobserver.com/2014/10/25/5266424/nc-magistrates-resign-over-gay. html#.VMBscCvF-DA. More recently, the battle over marriage escalated in Alabama when the Supreme Court of that state ordered their magistrates *not* to perform same-sex "wedding" ceremonies after the vote of the people was overturned by an activist judge; see Kyle Whitmire, "Alabama Supreme Court orders halt to same-sex marriages," AL.com, March 3, 2015, http://www. al.com/news/index.ssf/2015/03/alabama_supreme_court_orders_h.html.

67. Judith Levine, "Stop the Wedding! Why Gay Marriage Isn't Radical Enough," *Village Voice*, July 22, 2003, in Knight, "The Case for Marriage." Said Knight, "Levine declines to mention that the 1972 Gay Rights Platform also called for abolishing age of consent laws. This is a curious omission since Levine herself has written in favor of lowering the age of consent to 12 for sex between children and adults in her book *Harmful to Minors: The Perils of Protecting Children from Sex* (p. 88)." For further background to the assault on marriage, see Paul Kengor, Ph.D., *Takedown: From Communists to Progressives, How the Left Has Sabotaged Family and Marriage* (Washington, DC: WND Books, 2015). Kengor is a law professor at Grove City College.

68. See John Corvino, "Homosexuality and the PIB Argument," JohnCorvino.com, April 2005, http://johncorvino.com/wp/academic/Corvino-PIB.pdf.

69. Alexis de Tocqueville, *Democracy in America*, ed. Isaac Kramnick; trans. Gerald Bevan (New York: Penguin Classics, 2003), 340–41.

PRINCIPLE #5: CELEBRATE GENDER DISTINCTIONS

1. Even from an entirely anthropological, nonfaith point of view, the human race had its origins in a male-female couple (or in multiple such couples). For a popular report, see Tia Ghose, "Genetic 'Adam' and 'Eve' Uncovered," Live Science, August 1, 2013, http://www.livescience.com/38613-genetic-adam-and-eve-uncovered.html.

2. Todd Starnes, "'Gender Inclusive' School District Says Drop 'Boys and Girls,' Call Kids 'Purple Penguins,'" Fox News, October 9, 2014, http://www.foxnews.com/opinion/2014/10/09/gender-inclusive-school-district-says-drop-boys-and-girls-call-kids-purple/?intcmp=latestnews.

3. Christin Scarlett Milloy, "Don't Let the Doctor Do This to Your Newborn," *Outward* (blog), June 26, 2014, http://www.slate.com/blogs/outward/2014/06/26/infant_gender_assignment_unnecessary_and_potentially_harmful.html.

4. For some of the history, see Sunnivie Brydum, "Will Trans Folk Become an ENDA Bargaining Chip?" Advocate.com, November 8, 2013, http://www.advocate.com/politics/transgender/2013/11/08/will-trans-folk-become-enda-bargaining-chip?page=full.

5. See, for example, "Univ. of Chicago Students Offended by Gay Activist's 'Transphobic Slur,'" http://illinoisreview.typepad.com/illinoisreview/2014/06/university-of-chicago-students-offended-by-gay-rights-activists-use-of-transphobic-slur.html (and what of his anti-Christian slurs?).

6. It is transcribed in full at http://www.npr.org/templates/story/story.php?storyId=202729367. All quotations from the show in this chapter are found here.

7.   For comparisons in the psychopathy of gender dysphoria (until recently, also referred to as *Gender Identity Disorder*, or GID, a term that has been largely dropped because of trans-activist pressure) and body identity integrity disorder, or BIID, see Michael L. Brown, *A Queer Thing Happened to America: And What a Long, Strange Trip It's Been* (Concord, NC: EqualTime Books, 2011), 582–84.

8.   Gender Equity Resource Center, "Definition of Terms," accessed February 11, 2015, http://geneq. berkeley.edu/lgbt_resources_definiton_of_terms#sexual_minority, emphasis added.

9.   Joseph Brean, "Vancouver School Board's Genderless pronouns—xe, xem, xyr—not likely to stick, if history is any indication," *National Post*, June 17, 2014, http://news.nationalpost.com/2014/06/17/ vancouver-school-boards-genderless-pronouns-not-likely-to-stick-if-history-is-any-indication/.

10.   Stephen Petrow, October 27, 2014, "Gender-Neutral Pronouns: When 'They' Doesn't Identify as Either Male or Female," *Washington Post*, October 27, 2014, http://www.washingtonpost. com/lifestyle/style/gender-neutral-pronouns-when-they-doesnt-identify-as-either-male-or-female/2014/10/27/41965f5e-5ac0-11e4-b812-38518ae74c67_story.html.

11.   "Transgender Couple Who BOTH Changed Sex Prepare to Explain to Their Two Children How Their Father Gave Birth While Their Mom Provided the Sperm," *Daily Mail*, August 11, 2014, http://www.dailymail.co.uk/news/article-2721891/Transgender-couple-prepare-telling-children-father-actually-mother-vice-versa.html#ixzz3A8kHlAGo.

12.   Matthew Day, "Swedish Toy Catalogue Goes Gender Neutral," *Telegraph*, November 26, 2012, http://www.telegraph.co.uk/news/worldnews/europe/sweden/9703127/Swedish-toy-catalogue-goes-gender-neutral.html.

13.   The quotes that follow are from Nathalie Rothschild, "Sweden's New Gender-Neutral Pronoun: *Hen*," *Doublex* (blog), April 11, 2012, http://www.slate.com/articles/double_x/doublex/2012/04/ hen_sweden_s_new_gender_neutral_pronoun_causes_controversy_.html. In March, 2015, the gender neutral pronoun was introduced in the official Swedish dictionary; see "Sweden adds gender-neutral pronoun to dictionary," *The Guardian*, March 24, 2015, http://www.theguardian. com/world/2015/mar/24/sweden-adds-gender-neutral-pronoun-to-dictionary.

14.   "Dad Wears Skirt in Solidarity with His 5-Year-Old Son," *Huff Post*, Parents, August 29, 2012, http://www.huffingtonpost.com/2012/08/29/nils-pickert-german-dad_n_1840290.html.

15.   Neetzan Zimmerman, "Father of the Year Helps Dress-Wearing Son Feel Comfortable By Putting on a Skirt Himself," *Gawker*, August 28, 2012, http://gawker.com/5938676/father-of-the-year-helps-dress+wearing-son-feel-comfortable-by-putting-on-a-skirt-himself.

16.   Ben Shapiro, "Children's Network Launches Transsexual Superhero Show," Breitbart, May 28, 2013, http://www.breitbart.com/Big-Hollywood/2013/05/28/Children-network-transsexual-superhero.

17.   Penny Starr, "Girl Scouts Allow 7-Year-Old Boy to Join Because He is 'Living Life as a Girl,'" cnsnews.com, October 27, 2011, http://www.cnsnews.com/news/article/girl-scouts-allow-7-year-old-boy-join-because-he-living-life-girl.

18.   Rich Ferraro, "Facebook Introduces Custom Gender Field to Allow Users to More Accurately Reflect Who They Are," GLAAD, February 13, 2014, http://www.glaad.org/blog/facebook-introduces-custom-gender-field-allow-users-more-accurately-reflect-who-they-are. One year later, the list had expanded to fifty-eight terms, but still this was not enough, prompting Facebook to add a "Fill in the blank" option. See Martha Mendoza, "Facebook Adds New Gender Option for Users: Fill in the Blank," AP News, February 26, 2015, http://abcnews.go.com/Health/wireStory/ facebook-adds-gender-option-users-fill-blank-29245549.

19.   *It's Pronounced Metrosexual* (blog), accessed February 11, 2015, http://itspronouncedmetrosexual. com/2013/01/a-comprehensive-list-of-lgbtq-term-definitions/#sthash.LzOXk61z.dpuf.

20.   "Lesbian Professor Urges Deconstruction of Gender," October 9, 2007, http://www.narth.org/ docs/deconstruction.html.

21. Performer bio in the program description for "Girl Talk: A Trans Y Cis Woman Dialogue," on the Health Community Arts Program page, accessed February 11, 2015, http://www.queerculturalcenter.org/Pages/HealthyC/girlTalk.html.

22. "Girl Talk 2011—Tobi Hill-Meyer," YouTube video, 14:51, posted by HandbasketMedia, May 14, 2011, https://www.youtube.com/watch?v=cQu_2hOannU.

23. Nick Duffy, "La Roux: I Don't Feel Man or Woman, Gay or Straight," Pink News, May 27, 2014, http://www.pinknews.co.uk/2014/05/27/la-roux-i-dont-feel-man-or-woman-gay-or-straight/.

24. Mark Steyn, *America Alone: The End of the World as We Know It* (Washington, DC: Regnery, 2006), xvi–xvii.

25. For an individual illustration of this, gay activist Harry Knox, once a prominent leader in the HRC (Human Rights Campaign), whom I debated in 2008 (see "Can you be Gay and Christian? Michael Brown vs. Harry Knox," posted January 17, 2014, by ThomisticTheist, https://www.youtube.com/watch?v=ZGPaYc0jSDk), left the HRC to become the president and chief executive officer of the Religious Coalition for Reproductive Choice.

26. To be sure, the "conservative" wing of gay activism has carried the movement in recent years, with its emphasis on marriage and family, but this hardly reflects the history of the movement, and it is not reflective of large parts of gay society, since the great majority still choose not to "marry" even given the opportunity.

27. For larger, related issues, see "How Schools Are Pushing Transgenderism to Children. More Radical and Aggressive Than Ever," Mass Resistance, June 6, 2014, http://www.massresistance.org/docs/gen2/14b/GLSEN-Conference-040514/transgender-agenda/index.html.

28. Alyssa Newcomb, "Transgender Student in Women's Locker Room Raises Uproar," *Nation* (blog), November 3, 2012, http://abcnews.go.com/blogs/headlines/2012/11/transgender-student-in-womens-locker-room-raises-uproar/.

29. "Colleen Brenna Francis" profile, posted on the blog *Pretendbians* by user "blargh" on October 7, 2012, http://pretendbians.com/2012/10/07/colleen-brenna-francis/.

30. Associated Press, "Calif. Law Lets Schoolkids Choose Restrooms, Sports Based on Their Gender IDs," *New York Daily News*, July 3, 2013, http://www.nydailynews.com/news/national/new-calif-law-win-transgender-students-article-1.1389901#ixzz327X2U0oF.

31. "Information on GLSEN's Ally Week," True Tolerance website, accessed February 11, 2015, http://www.truetolerance.org/2011/information-on-glsens-ally-week-october/.

32. "Be an Ally to Transgender and Gender-Nonconforming Students," accessed February 11, 2015, http://glsen.org/sites/default/files/AllyWeek_transGNC.pdf.

33. http://conchitawurst.com/about/biography/; https://www.facebook.com/ConchitaWurst (likes)

34. James St. James, "NSFW: Carmen Carrera's Super-Shocking, Super-Gorgeous Life Ball Poster by David LaChapelle,"*The Wow Report*, accessed February 11, 2015, http://worldofwonder.net/nsfw-carmen-carreras-super-shocking-super-gorgeous-life-ball-poster-david-lachapelle/.

35. I am not saying this is an example of "multiple personality disorder" (which some psychologists reject) or schizophrenia, nor am I attempting to "diagnose" Tom. I am simply pointing out that this is hardly something to celebrate. I am simply pointing out that this is an aberrant mind-set, and certainly not something to applaud.

36. *Wikipedia*, s.v. "Chelsea Manning," accessed February 11, 2015, http://en.wikipedia.org/wiki/Chelsea_Manning.

37. MilitaryCorruption.com, accessed February 11, 2015, http://militarycorruption.com/manning.htm; Ed Pilkington, "Bradley Manning: I Was Bullied in the Military for Being Gay," *Guardian*, July 3, 2011, http://www.theguardian.com/world/2011/jul/04/wikileaks-bradley-manning-bullying.

38. "Chelsea Manning Named Marshal of Gay Pride Parade," *Here & Now* radio show website, April 15, 2014, http://hereandnow.wbur.org/2014/04/15/manning-pride-parade.

39. Ultimately, the diagnosis of "gender dysphoria" is based totally on the patient's perception since, outside of cases where there are clear biological issues, there are no fixed, external tests for the condition.

40. Grace Macaskill, "'I Was a Boy . . . Then a Girl . . . Now I Want to Be a Boy Again': Agony of Teen Who Is Britain's Youngest Sex-Swap Patient," *Mirror*, October 28, 2012, http://www.mirror. co.uk/news/uk-news/britains-youngest-sex-swap-patient-wants-1403321#ixzz327kpxu00. See also http://www.politicalforum.com/political-opinions-beliefs/291459-transgender-man-has-surgery-but-later-changes-his-mind.html. In a similar story from 2014, it was reported that "a British transsexual who had a $15,000 sex change in 2007 now deems living as a female to be too 'exhausting,' and wants British taxpayers to pay roughly $22,000 to undo the original procedure." See Douglas Ernst, "U.K. transsexual expects taxpayers to fund reverse sex change: 'No one should deny me,'" *Washington Times*, October 4, 2014, http://www.washingtontimes.com/news/2014/ oct/4/uk-transsexual-expects-taxpayers-to-fund-reverse-s/#ixzz3GNZvSDGb.

41. For a sympathetic story, see Steve Friess, "Mike Penner, Christine Daniels: A Tragic Love Story," *LA Weekly*, August 19, 2010, http://www.laweekly.com/2010-08-19/news/mike-penner-christine-daniels-a-tragic-love-story/.

42. See, for example, the article by Dr. Paul McHugh in the *Wall Street Journal*, http://www.wsj.com/ articles/paul-mchugh-transgender-surgery-isnt-the-solution-1402615120, and note the strong responses to his piece, e.g., Cristan Williams's "World's Experts Condemn the McHugh Hoax," *The TransAdvocate*, July 4, 2014, http://www.transadvocate.com/worlds-experts-condemn-the-mchugh-hoax_n_13924.htm.

43. "Don Ennis Who Changed to Dawn Stacey Ennis Sacked by ABC News," News.com, June 18, 2014, http://www.news.com.au/entertainment/tv/don-ennis-who-changed-to-dawn-stacey-ennis-sacked-by-abc-news/story-e6frfmyi-1226958949813.

44. Don Kaplan, "ABC Producer Who Changed Gender 3 Times Was Fired in May for 'Performance-Related Issues,'" *New York Daily News*, June 17, 2014, http://www.nydailynews.com/news/national/ abc-fires-exec-changed-gender-3-times-article-1.1832330#ixzz352vKQHou.

45. *Time* magazine's cover story for May 29, 2014, was titled "Orange [referring to transgender] Is the New Black," http://time.com/132769/transgender-orange-is-the-new-black-laverne-cox-interview/; and in January, 2015, Amazon's TV show *Transparent* was named "Best TV Series, Musical or Comedy" at the Golden Globes while *Entertainment Weekly* voted it the number one show in 2014. Attorney General Holder has also declared transgender identity a civil right; see J. Christian Adams, "Holder Decrees Crossdressing Protected Under Federal Law," PJ Media, December 19, 2014, http://pjmedia.com/jchristianadams/2014/12/19/holder-decrees-crossdressing-protected-under-federal-law/.

46. Stella Morabito, "Trouble in Transtopia: Murmurs of Sex Change Regret," *The Federalist* (blog), November 11, 2014, http://thefederalist.com/2014/11/11/trouble-in-transtopia-murmurs-of-sex-change-regret/?utm_source=The+Federalist+List&utm_campaign=23d0544c79-RSS_ DAILY_EMAIL_CAMPAIGN&utm_medium=email&utm_term=0_cfcb868ceb-23d0544c79-83773797. Reflecting on her sex-change surgery, Verhelst said, "I was ready to celebrate my new birth. But when I looked in the mirror, I was disgusted with myself. My new breasts did not match my expectations and my new penis had symptoms of rejection. I do not want to be . . . a monster." See Michael Brown, "What the Sex Change Industry Doesn't Tell You," CharismaNews, October 4, 2013, http://www.charismanews.com/opinion/in-the-line-of-fire/41250-what-the-sex-change-industry-doesn-t-tell-you.

47. Damien Gayle, "Mother of Belgian Transsexual Who Chose to Die by Euthanasia after Botched Sex-Change Operation Says 'Her Death Doesn't Bother Me,'" *Daily Mail*, October 2, 2013, http://www.dailymail.co.uk/news/article-2441468/Mother-Belgian-transsexual-chose-die-says-death-doesnt-bother-me.html.

48. Morabito, "Trouble in Transtopia."

49. Erick Erickson, "Tolerate or Be Stamped Out," Townhall.com, August 7, 2014, http://townhall.com/columnists/erickerickson/2014/08/07/tolerate-or-be-stamped-out-n1875995.

50. As reported June 5, 2014, "People born in New York State will no longer have to provide proof of sex-reassignment surgery to change gender markers." The requirement still stands for those born in New York City. See Tony Merevick, "New York State Makes It Easier for Transgender People to Change Their Birth Certificates," BuzzFeed, June 6, 2014, http://www.buzzfeed.com/tonymerevick/new-york-state-makes-it-easier-for-transgender-people-to-cha.

51. "Transgender Californians Celebrate Streamlined Name & Gender Changes," Transgender Law Center website, accessed February 12, 2015, http://transgenderlawcenter.org/archives/10611.

52. According to a story posted May 18, 2014, "With children rejecting the birth gender at younger ages and the transgender rights movement gaining momentum, schools in districts large and small, conservative and liberal, are working to help transitioning youth fit in without a fuss." Lisa Leff, "Schools Work to Help Transgender Students Fit In."

53. Dan Tracer, "12-Year-Old Transgender Boy Granted Historic New Birth Certificate," *Queerty*, June 17, 2014, http://www.queerty.com/12-year-old-transgender-boy-granted-historic-new-birth-certificate-20140617.

54. See *Wikipedia*, s.v. "species dysphoria," http://en.wikipedia.org/wiki/Species_dysphoria. See also Daniel Greenfield, "Forget Transgender, Get Ready for Transpecies," *FrontPage Mag*, March 2, 2013, http://www.frontpagemag.com/2013/dgreenfield/forget-transgender-get-ready-for-transpecies/. For an academic study seeking to distinguish between "gender identity disorder" and "species disorder," see Fiona Probyn-Rapsey, "Furries and the Limits of Species Identity Disorder: A Response to Gerbasi et al," *Society & Animals* 19 (2011): 294–301; https://www.academia.edu/2903078/Furries_and_limits_of_species_identity_disorder.

55. LogoTV website, accessed February 12, 2015, http://www.logotv.com/video/what-i-think-im-an-animal/1706138/playlist.jhtml. See also Michael Brown, "The Girl Who Thought She Was a Werewolf Vampire," Townhall.com, October 3, 2011, http://townhall.com/columnists/michaelbrown/2011/10/03/the_girl_who_thought_she_was_a_werewolf_vampire.

56. "What?! I think I'm an animal (Part 2)," YouTube video, 15:24, posted by Breanne Abercrombie, April 24, 2013, https://www.youtube.com/watch?v=ubPjv90jHPk. The individual who published this on YouTube explained, "My name is Alpha Blue-Eye. I'm a blue and white arctic wolf."

57. "Introduction: What Is a Therianthrope?" Therian-Guide.com, accessed February 12, 2015, http://therian-guide.com/?page=Introduction.

58. I recognize that many children raised in single-parent homes grow up to be exemplary human beings. Even so, I know very few people who would argue that a single-parent home represents the ideal setting for a child to be raised.

59. The bulk of the preceding four paragraphs were borrowed from Brown, *Queer Thing*, 592–93. After this chapter was completed, the suicide of seventeen-year-old Joshua Alcorn, who went by the name "Leelah" among his friends, energized the transgender movement, since he blamed his Christian parents' lack of acceptance of his female identity for his suicide. For my article on this tragic and painful issue, see "Did Christian Parents Drive Their Child to Suicide?" CharismaNews, December 21, 2014, http://www.charismanews.com/opinion/in-the-line-of-fire/46616-did-christian-parents-drive-their-child-to-suicide.

PRINCIPLE #6: KEEP PROPAGATING THE TRUTH UNTIL THE LIES ARE DISPELLED

1. Robert Reilly, interview by Michael Brown, *Line of Fire* radio program, June 11, 2014, http://www. lineoffireradio.com/2014/06/11/two-cutting-edge-interviews-on-critical-social-issues/; see further Robert R. Reilly, *Making Gay Okay: How Rationalizing Homosexual Behavior Is Changing Everything* (San Francisco: Ignatius, 2014). Reilly's book raises many important questions for consideration.

2. See "Khruschev—We Will Bury You," YouTube, 4:38, posted by Ryan Pouson, April 18, 2013, https://www.youtube.com/watch?v=Mm0yQg1hS_w; apparently the words were mistranslated, and according to one report, cited in this video, his real claim was that communism would outlast capitalism.

3. See my article, "From Mao to Gucci," http://townhall.com/columnists/michaelbrown/2013/11/29/from-mao-to-gucci-n1754100/page/full

4. And communism was oppressively violent, leaving as many as 100 million dead in its train; see Jean-Louis Panné, Andrzej Paczkowsk, et al., *The Black Book of Communism: Crimes, Terror, Repression* (Cambridge, MA: Harvard Univ. Press, 2014).

5. Marshall Kirk and Hunter Madsen, *After the Ball: How America Will Conquer Its Fear and Hatred of Gays in the 90's* (New York: Penguin, 1989), 153. In the words of Camille Paglia, *Vamps & Tramps*, 74, "The 10 percent figure, servilely repeated by the media, was pure propaganda, and it made me, as a scholar, despise gay activists for their unscrupulous disregard for the truth."

6. See Michael L. Brown, *A Queer Thing Happened to America: And What a Long, Strange Trip It's Been* (Concord, NC: EqualTime Books, 2011), 625n19, for relevant studies on Kinsey and for the recognition by major gay activist organizations that the homosexual population of America was less than 3 percent. Remarkably, Channel 4 in England has mandated that 6 percent of its employees must be gay or lesbian by 2020, with serious penalties for executives who fail to implement this, allegedly based on the percentage of gays and lesbians in the population. See Nick Duffy, "Channel 4: Six percent of employees must be LGBT," PinkNews, January 12, 2015, http://www.pinknews.co.uk/2015/01/12/channel-4-six-percent-of-employees-must-be-lgbt/.

7. See Brown, *Queer Thing*, 163, for one example of many.

8. Sandhya Somashekhar, "Health Survey Gives Government Its First Large-Scale Data on Gay, Bisexual Population," *Washington Post*, July 14, 2014, http://www.washingtonpost.com/national/health-science/health-survey-gives-government-its-first-large-scale-data-on-gay-bisexual-population/2014/07/14/2db9f4b0-092f-11e4-bbf1-cc51275e7f8f_story.html. The article notes, "The overwhelming majority of adults, 96.6 percent, labeled themselves as straight in the 2013 survey. An additional 1.1 percent declined to answer, responded 'I don't know the answer' or said they were 'something else.'" So, even if every single person in that additional 1.1 percent were gay, that would still mean that one in thirty-three Americans was gay and bisexual.

9. Joseph Patrick McCormick, "New UK Stats Find 1.6% of Adults Identify as Gay, Lesbian or Bisexual," PinkNews, October 7, 2014, http://www.pinknews.co.uk/2014/10/07/new-uk-stats-find-1-6-of-adults-identify-as-gay-lesbian-or-bisexual/.

10. Lymari Morales, "U.S. Adults Estimate That 25% of Americans Are Gay or Lesbian," Gallup, May 27, 2011, http://www.gallup.com/poll/147824/adults-estimate-americans-gay-lesbian.aspx.

11. According to a report in *USA Today*, "David Mariner, executive director of the Washington, D.C., Center for the LGBT Community, said he believes the gay percentage in the CDC study might be low. He said differences can come from how questions are asked, as well as the ages of participants. Mariner noted that in another CDC study that focused on youth in the Washington area, 15.3% of high school respondents identified as gay, lesbian or bisexual. He said young people can be more comfortable with their sexuality and more likely to report being gay, lesbian or bisexual."

Kim Painter, "Just over 2% Tell CDC They Are Gay, Lesbian, Bisexual," July 15, 2015, http://www.usatoday.com/story/news/nation/2014/07/15/gay-lesbian-bisexual-cdc-survey/12671717/. In reality, this figure points to young people being more unsure about their sexuality due to typical adolescent questions about sexual development; the media's pro-gay bombardment and its effects on young people in particular; societal encouragement, even in school sex-ed curricula, for young people to explore homosexuality and bisexuality. What is striking is that, based on previous studies, if these same young people were interviewed ten years later, the percentage of those identifying as gay, lesbian, or bisexual would have dropped dramatically. See Margaret Rosario et al., "Sexual Identity Development among Gay, Lesbian, and Bisexual Youths: Consistency and Change over Time," *Journal of Sex Research* 43, no. 1 (2006): 46–58; online at http://www.ncbi.nlm.nih.gov/pmc/articles/PMC3215279/.

12. Remember that questions about the number of bisexuals living in America were not included in this poll, which makes the results all the more striking.

13. Morales, "U.S. Adults Estimate That 25% of Americans Are Gay or Lesbian," emphasis added.

14. Meredith Blake, "GLAAD: A&E, History, TNT 'Failing' in Terms of LGBT Representation," *LA Times*, October 2, 2014, http://www.latimes.com/entertainment/tv/showtracker/la-et-st-glaad-report-ae-history-tnt-fail-lgbt-representation-20141002-story.html.

15. Quoted in Austin Ruse, "Slate: Conservatives Offended by New, Tiny Gay Numbers from CDC," Breitbart, August 5, 2014, http://www.breitbart.com/Big-Journalism/2014/08/05/Slate-Stikes-Back-at-the-New-and-Tiny-Gay-Numbers.

16. The only exception to this would be if you lived in a neighborhood populated largely by gays (for which, see note 23).

17. Kirk and Madsen, *After the Ball*, 149.

18. Marshall Kirk and Erastes Pill, "The Overhauling of Straight America," Gay Homeland Library, November 1987, http://library.gayhomeland.org/0018/EN/EN_Overhauling_Straight.htm; note that Erastes Pill was a pseudonym for Madsen.

19. Shankar Vedantam, "Shift in Gay Marriage Support Mirrors a Changing America," NPR, March 25, 2013, http://www.npr.org/2013/03/25/174989702/shift-in-gay-marriage-support-mirrors-a-changing-america.

20. Paul Hitlin, Mark Jurkowitz, and Amy Mitchell, "News Coverage Conveys Strong Momentum for Same-Sex Marriage," Pew Research Center, June 17, 2013, http://www.journalism.org/2013/06/17/news-coverage-conveys-strong-momentum/ (emphasis added).

21. See Brown, *Queer Thing*, 153–95; the exception to this paradigm would, of course, be faith-based movies and TV.

22. David Ehrenstein, in Larry Gross and James P. Woods, *The Columbia Reader on Lesbians & Gay Men in Media, Society, and Politics* (New York: Columbia Univ. Press, 1999), 336. Those familiar with TV sitcoms would immediately think of highly acclaimed shows like *Modern Family*, *Glee*, and *Ugly Betty*, just to name a few.

23. Stevie St. John, "Lesbians Make a Life in Gay-Dominated West Hollywood," *WeHoville*, December 18, 2013, http://www.wehoville.com/2013/12/18/lesbians-make-life-gay-dominated-west-hollywood/.

24. For example, see Thaddeus Baklinski, "2011 List of TV Networks Which Most Promote Homosexuality," August 4, 2011, http://www.lifesitenews.com/news/2011-list-of-tv-networks-which-most-promote-homosexuality; and GLAAD's *2014 Studio Responsibility Index*, http://www.glaad.org/sri/2014.

25. James Kirchick, "How GLAAD Won the Culture War and Lost Its Reason to Exist," *Atlantic*, May 2013, http://www.theatlantic.com/politics/archive/2013/05/how-glaad-won-the-culture-war-and-lost-its-reason-to-exist/275533/.

26. David and Jason Benham with Scott Lamb, *Whatever the Cost* (Nashville: W Publishing Group, 2015).

27. The Benham Brothers are now listed among many others whom RightWingWatch.com tracks and seeks to expose (naturally, I'm on their list too, and I often give them shout-outs on my radio show, not taking their "tracking" too seriously); see "David Benham," Right Wing Watch, http://www.rightwingwatch.org/category/people/david-benham. For a typical report on their firing, see the Deadline Team, "HGTV Pulls New Home-Flipping Series after Report Emerges Identifying Its Stars as Anti-Gay Activists," *Deadline*, May 7, 2014, http://www.deadline.com/2014/05/hgtv-pulls-new-home-flipping-series-after-report-emerges-identifying-its-stars-as-anti-gay-activists/. For a critique, see Kirsten Powers, "Liberals' Dark Ages," *USA Today*, May 15, 2014, http://www.usatoday.com/story/opinion/2014/05/14/liberal-thought-police-lagarde-hgtv-benham-free-speech-column/9098133/.

28. Media Research Center, "Media Bias Basics," MRC.org, accessed February 12, 2015, http://archive.mrc.org/biasbasics/biasbasics.asp. For the book itself, see S. Robert Lichter, Stanley Rothman, and Linda S. Lichter, *The Media Elite: America's New Power Brokers* (n.p.: Hastings House, 1990).

29. Bill Muehlenberg wrote, "Truth always hurts—especially to those who hate the truth. And one of the main groups which hates truth, distorts truth, and runs from truth, is the militant homosexual lobby. Indeed, the entire homosexualist movement is based on a mountain of lies: I was born that way, change is not possible, my lifestyle will not impact anyone else, etc." See Muehlenberg, "Truth-Telling and Homosexuality," *CultureWatch*, December 11, 2014, http://billmuehlenberg.com/2014/11/12/truth-telling-and-homosexuality-2/.

30. Jack Nichols, The Gay Agenda: Talking Back to the Fundamentalists (New York: Prometheus, 1996).

31. For ongoing documentation, see http://americansfortruth.com/.

32. From the video posted on the Towleroad website on June 25, 2009, http://www.towleroad.com/2009/06/camille-paglia-gay-activists-childish-for-demanding-rights.html. For the record, many of the LGBT comments responding to this video were quite critical of Paglia's statements; see the accompanying article by Andy Towle.

33. Kirk and Madsen, *After the Ball*, 330.

34. The actor who related this to me is a personal friend who preferred to remain anonymous. His comment is reminiscent of the painful words of Andrew Sullivan, who, after learning he had contracted HIV, confessed that he didn't know from whom he had been infected, since he had slept with so many men: "Too many, God knows. Too many for meaning and dignity to be given to every one; too many for love to be present at each; too many for sex to be very often more than a temporary but powerful release from debilitating fear and loneliness." Cited by Al Mohler in "Gay Culture and the Riddle of Andrew Sullivan," on AlbertMohler.com, October 27, 2005, http://www.albertmohler.com/2005/10/27/gay-culture-and-the-riddle-of-andrew-sullivan/.

35. Austin Ruse, "State Dept. Honors Advocate of Destruction of Marriage," Breitbart, June 23, 2014, http://www.breitbart.com/Big-Government/2014/06/23/State-Dept-Honoree-Calls-for-Destruction-of-Marriage/. Here is Gessen's description of her own family: "We have three kids and five parents . . . more or less, and I don't see why they shouldn't have five parents legally." Her own brother is the father of her second wife's daughter (ibid.).

36. Dan Savage, "Why Monogamy Is Ridiculous," an interview by Max Miller, October 18, 2010, transcript available on the *Big Think* blog, at http://bigthink.com/videos/why-monogamy-is-ridiculous.

37. See, for example, Andrew Gilligan, "'Paedophilia Is Natural and Normal for Males,'" *Telegraph* (UK), July 5, 2014, http://www.telegraph.co.uk/comment/10948796/Paedophilia-is-natural-and-normal-for-males.html. Gilligan reports that at summer conferences in the UK, university academics claimed that "paedophilic interest is natural and normal for human males. At least a sizeable minority of normal males would like to have sex with children. . . . Normal males are aroused by children." For more, sickening documentation, see Bill Muehlenberg, "Promoting Paedophilia," *CultureWatch*, August 7, 2014, http://billmuehlenberg.com/2014/07/08/promoting-paedophilia/. See Brown, *Queer Thing*, 226–71, where I parallel the arguments used by pederast activists with the arguments used by gay activists. See further Les Kinsolving, "Baltimore Conference: Normalize Pedophilia," *WND Commentary*, http://www.wnd.com/2011/08/339113/, for reporting on a 2011 academic conference on pedophilia in America. For the increasingly common argument that pedophilia is innate and immutable, see CBS Atlanta, "Study: Pedophiles' Brains 'Abnormally Tuned' To Find Young Children Attractive," CBS Atlanta, May 25, 2014, CBS Atlanta, http://atlanta.cbslocal.com/2014/05/25/study-pedophiles-brains-abnormally-tuned-to-find-young-children-attractive/.

38. Randy Shilts, The Mayor of Castro Street: The Life and Times of Harvey Milk (New York: St. Martin's Press, 1982), 6.

39. Michelangelo Signorile, "Tom Daley Is 20 Years Younger Than Dustin Lance Black . . . So What?" *Huff Post Gay Voices*, December 6, 2013, http://www.huffingtonpost.com/michelangelo-signorile/tom-daley-is-20-years-younger-than-dustin-lance-black-so-what_b_4397666.html. Signorile explains some of the sociological reasons for this tendency, as well as renounces "the ugliest lie about gay men out there," namely, that "gay men are more likely to sexually abuse underage teens." For a scientific study that indicates that Signorile's statement is incorrect, see Ryan C. W. Hall, MD, and Richard C. W. Hall, MD, PA, "A Profile of Pedophilia: Definition, Characteristics of Offenders, Recidivism, Treatment Outcomes, and Forensic Issues," available at http://www.abusewatch.net/pedophiles.pdf.

40. Nigel Jaquiss, "Terry Bean Arrested on Charges of Sex Abuse of a Minor," *Williamette Week*, November 19, 2014, http://www.wweek.com/portland/blog-32476-terry_bean_arrested_on_charges_of_sex_abuse_of_a_minor.html; Chris Doyle, an ex-gay counselor and cofounder and president of Voice for the Voiceless, said this when he read of the news of Bean's arrest: "It is outrageous and tragic that the Founder of the largest gay activist organization in the world is molesting boys, while at the same time their leadership is pushing for laws across the United States to keep those same boys out of the counseling office to heal trauma at the hands of homosexual pedophiles." See "Ex-Gays Call on Human Rights Campaign to Fund Reparative Therapy for HRC's Alleged Pedophile Founder and His Child Victim," *BarbWire*, November 21, 2014, http://barbwire.com/2014/11/21/ex-gays-call-human-rights-campaign-fund-reparative-therapy-hrcs-alleged-pedophile-founder-child-victim/.

41. See Michael Brown, "Ted Haggard, Larry Brinkin, and Glaring Media Bias," Townhall.com, July 9, 2012, http://townhall.com/columnists/michaelbrown/2012/07/09/ted_haggard_larry_brinkin_and_glaring_media_bias/page/full.

42. Matt Barber, "How Not Surprising: Top 'Gay' Charged with Raping Boy," *WND Commentary*, November 21, 2014, http://www.wnd.com/2014/11/how-not-surprising-top-gay-charged-with-raping-boy/.

43. See "Are Same-Sex Unions the Same as Heterosexual Married Unions?" *Winter Knight* (blog), June 24, 2014, http://winteryknight.wordpress.com/2014/06/24/are-same-sex-unions-the-same-as-heterosexual-married-unions/.

44. Luis Pabon, "Why I No Longer Want to Be Gay," *Thought Catalog* (blog), November 17, 2014, http://thoughtcatalog.com/luis-pabon/2014/11/why-i-no-longer-want-to-be-gay/; as expected, many commenters took Pabon to task for what they felt was a misleading description.

45. James E. Phelan, Neil Whitehead, and Philip M. Sutton, "What Research Shows: NARTH's Response to the APA Claims on Homosexuality" (a report of the Scientific Advisory Committee of the National Association for Research and Therapy of Homosexuality), *Journal of Human Sexuality* 1 (2009), 93. See http://www.narth.com/docs/journalsummary.html.

46. See note 11.

47. Press Association, "Gay Sex 'Linked to Drink and Drugs,'" *Gazette & Herald* (UK), July 31, 2014, http://www.gazetteandherald.co.uk/news/national/news/11380817.Gay_sex__linked_to_drink_and_drugs_/.

48. Monty Moncrieff, "Comment: Why Is Drug Use Higher in the Gay Community?" PinkNews, July 29, 2014, http://www.pinknews.co.uk/2014/07/29/comment-why-is-drug-use-higher-in-the-gay-community/.

49. Ben Johnson, "Relationship Problems, Not Family Rejection, Leading Cause of Higher Gay Suicides: Study," LifeSite News, May 30, 2014, http://www.lifesitenews.com/news/homosexuals-more-likely-to-commit-suicide-due-to-problems-with-gay-lovers-t; for the actual study, see http://onlinelibrary.wiley.com/enhanced/doi/10.1111/appy.12128/.

50. Michael Brown, "Sex Change Regret," CharismaNews, June 19, 2014, http://www.charismanews.com/opinion/in-the-line-of-fire/44353-sex-change-regret-don-ennis.

51. According to a recent study, the average age when those who identify as gay today first felt they were different was twelve; the average age at which they became convinced they were gay was seventeen. It is obviously a matter of projection for them to now say they were born that way. That is quite a jump! See Pew Research Center, "A Survey of LGBT Americans," June 13, 2013, http://www.pewsocialtrends.org/2013/06/13/a-survey-of-lgbt-americans/. For the average age of people coming out gay, see Ellen Friedrichs, "What Is the Average Age to Come Out?" About.com, accessed February 12, 2015, http://gayteens.about.com/od/quesitons/f/What-Is-The-Average-Age-To-Come-Out.htm.

52. American Psychological Association, "Answers to Your Questions for a Better Understanding of Sexual Orientation & Homosexuality," p. 2, APA.org, accessed February 12, 2015, http://www.apa.org/topics/lgbt/orientation.pdf.

53. Sexual Orientation & Homosexuality, American Psychological Association website, accessed February 12, 2015, http://www.apa.org/topics/lgbt/orientation.aspx.

54. "Royal College of Psychiatrists' Statement on Sexual Orientation: Position Statement PS02/2014: April 2014," p. 2, http://www.rcpsych.ac.uk/pdf/PS02_2014.pdf. For a significant essay on this development, see Blake Adams, "Is Biological Determinism on its Way Out?" *Juicy Ecumenism* (blog), June 12, 2014, http://juicyecumenism.com/2014/06/12/is-biological-determinism-on-its-way-out-or-why-choice-is-taboo-in-lgbtq-circles/.

55. Sherry Wolf, "Interview with John D'Emilio; LGBT liberation: Build a broad movement," *International Socialist Review*, no. 65 (May–June 2009), http://isreview.org/issue/65/lgbt-liberation-build-broad-movement.

56. Karen Booth, "Do Homosexuals Change?" *Good News Magazine*, May 23, 2014, http://karenbooth.goodnewsmag.org/do-homosexuals-change/; http://www.layman.org/homosexuals-change/.

57. See "Lisa Diamond on Sexual Fluidity of Men and Women," YouTube video, 44:26, posted by Cornell University, December 16, 2013, https://www.youtube.com/watch?feature=player_embedded&v=m2rTHDOuUBw. For an important historical reflection, see David Benkof, "Nobody Is 'Born That Way,' Gay Historians Say," *Daily Caller*, March 19, 2013, http://dailycaller.com/2014/03/19/nobody-is-born-that-way-gay-historians-say/.

58. Andrew Belonsky, "When Bill de Blasio's Wife Was a Lesbian," *Out* magazine, September 3, 2013, http://www.out.com/news-opinion/2013/09/03/when-bill-de-blasios-wife-was-lesbian; for Camille Paglia's salient comments on the *Dennis Prager Show*, see "Camille Paglia Talks Gender Politics with Dennis Prager," YouTube video, 23:38, posted by "Papa Giorgio," January 10, 2014, https://www.youtube.com/watch?v=2xXThqohiZo; Paglia, a lesbian, notes that there is "absolutely not a shred of evidence" that anyone is born gay.

59. Rebby Kern, "I'm Going Back to Bi: Confessions of a Former Lesbian," *Advocate*, June 26, 2014, http://www.advocate.com/commentary/2014/06/26/op-ed-im-going-back-bi-confessions-former-lesbian.

60. Camille Paglia, *Vamps and Tramps: New Essays* (New York: Vintage, 1994), 70. Remarkably, when a school chaplain in Tasmania, Australia, reposted a Facebook comment saying that "homosexuality is not normal" and "no-one is born gay," there was an outcry against him, causing him to issue a public apology: "I've made a mistake and learnt from it. I'm deeply sorry for any offence I've caused. I was very careless in posting that image for discussion. I will work with my employers to ensure there is no repeat." Despite this apology, he was still fired – and the organization he worked for was Christian! For more on this, see http://billmuehlenberg.com/2014/08/05/when-the-pink-mafia-are-in-control/ and http://billmuehlenberg.com/2014/08/08/christian-persecution-in-australia/.

61. Paglia, *Vamps and Tramps*, 77.

62. Adams, "Is Biological Determinism on its Way Out?"

63. Stephen Jimenez, The Book of Matt: Hidden Truths about the Murder of Matthew Shepard, Kindle ed. (Hanover, NH: Steerforth, 2013).

64. Julie Bindel, "The Truth Behind America's Most Famous Gay-Hate Murder," *Guardian*, October 26, 2014, http://www.theguardian.com/world/2014/oct/26/the-truth-behind-americas-most-famous-gay-hate-murder-matthew-shepard.

65. This is all carefully documented in Jimenez, *The Book of Matt*.

66. Ibid., loc. 2116.

67. "*Out* Exclusives: Power 50," *Out*, accessed February 13, 2015, http://www.out.com/out-exclusives/power-50.

68. "Love, War—and Gay Marriage," Breitbart, March 19, 2009, http://bighollywood.breitbart.com/cwinecoff/2009/03/19/love-war-and-gay-marriage/. No longer accessible.

69. Christopher Doyle, "Transgendered 'Woman' Lies about Therapy 'Torture'," *WND Opinion*, March 21, 2013, http://www.wnd.com/2013/03/transgendered-woman-lies-about-therapy-torture/. It appears that gays being sent to "True Directions" camp may be something of an urban gay myth. An e-mail I received from a man struggling with his own homosexual desires read, "I don't know why but it never occurred to me that many of these stories of barbaric gay to straight therapy might be fabrications. In particular one I have heard about several times is a camp called True Directions in Ohio."

70. For the SPLC's lawsuit against JONAH (Jews Offering New Alternatives for Healing), alleging counseling malpractice, see Gina Miller, "SPLC's Baseless Attack on JONAH Is Evil Assault on Freedom," RenewAmerica, February 16, 2014, http://www.renewamerica.com/columns/miller/140216.

PRINCIPLE #7: FACTOR IN THE GOD FACTOR

1.   See James Edwin Orr Jr., *The Fervent Prayer: The Worldwide Impact of the Great Awakening of 1858* (Chicago: Moody Press, 1974). The revival began in 1857, and by 1858 it had spread across America and into other nations.

2.   Mary Stewart Relfe, *The Cure of All Ills* (n.p.: League of Prayer: 1988), 49.

3.   See, for example, Joseph Tracy, *The Great Awakening: A History of the Revival of Religion in the time of Edwards and Whitefield* (Boston: Charles Tappan, 1845; repr., n.p.: Counted Faithful, 2014); and Daniel Walker Howe, *What Hath God Wrought: The Transformation of America, 1815–1848* (New York: Oxford Univ. Press, 2007). For the relationship between spiritual awakenings and the abolition movement, see Eric Metaxas, *Amazing Grace* (New York: Harper Collins, 2009). For inspirational reflections on the role of revival in American history, see Michael L. Brown, *The End of the American Gospel Enterprise*, 2nd ed. (Shippensburg, PA: Destiny Image, 1993).

4.   Austin Ruse, "Pew Poll: GOP Youth Supports Gay Marriage," Breitbart, March 11, 2014, http://www.breitbart.com/Big-Government/2014/03/11/Poll-Shows-GOP-Youth-Supports-Gay-Marriage.

5.   Sheryl Gay Stolberg, "Republicans Sign Brief in Support of Gay Marriage," *New York Times*, February 25, 2013, http://www.nytimes.com/2013/02/26/us/politics/prominent-republicans-sign-brief-in-support-of-gay-marriage.html?pagewanted%3Dall&_r=0.

6.   David Von Drehle, "Gay Marriage Already Won," *Time*, April 8, 2013, cover, http://content.time.com/time/covers/0,16641,20130408,00.html.

7.   Sarah Posner, "A Decade Later, Same-Sex Marriage Tide Has Almost Completely Turned," Aljazerra America, May 17, 2014, http://america.aljazeera.com/articles/2014/5/17/gay-marriage-10.html.

8.   Jim Hinch, "Evangelicals Are Changing Their Minds on Gay Marriage and the Bible Isn't Getting in Their Way," *Politico*, July 7, 2014, http://www.politico.com/magazine/story/2014/07/evangelicals-gay-marriage-108608.html#ixzz38iEl3yLP. It should be noted that Hinch's article is far from unbiased, even with some (presumably unintentional) misrepresentation (see, for example his mischaracterization of Rick Warren's activities, as Warren remains actively involved behind the scenes in his stand against redefining marriage).

9.   Wayne Besen, "Gay Marriage Might Cause the GOP to Divorce the Religious Right," Truth Wins Out, February 26, 2013, http://www.truthwinsout.org/pressrelease/2013/02/33494/.

10. Gene Robinson, God Believes in Love: Straight Talk about Gay Marriage (New York: Vintage, 2012).

11. See, for example, the statement of Rev. Gary Hall, "Gary Hall Says Homophobia Is a Sin: National Cathedral Dean Speaks Out During LGTB Weekend of Honor," *Huffington Post*, October 7, 2013, http://www.huffingtonpost.com/2013/10/07/gary-hall-national-cathedral-homobia-is-a-sin_n_4057614.html.

12. Abortion clinics continue to close at a rapid rate; see Neil Stevens, "Abortion Clinics Are Closing. Slowly, We're Winning," *RedState* (blog), January 22, 2015, http://www.redstate.com/2015/01/22/abortion-clinics-closing-slowly-winning/. The situation in Texas was recently deemed "urgent" by pro-abortion activists as thirteen abortion clinics closed "overnight"; see Laura Bassett, "Situation In Texas Is 'Urgent' After 13 Abortion Clinics Close Overnight," *HuffPost*, October 3, 2014, http://www.huffingtonpost.com/2014/10/03/texas-abortion-clinics_n_5927698.html.

13. Ruse, "Pew Poll.

14. Nina Martin, "This Alabama Judge Has Figured Out How to Dismantle Roe v. Wade," *New Republic*, October 10, 2014, http://www.newrepublic.com/article/119766/tom-parker-alabama-judge-dismantling-roe-v-wade. Note that Martin is not pro-life.

15. Alan Suderman and David Espo, "House Majority Leader Cantor Defeated in Primary," Yahoo! News, June 11, 2014.

16. Ron Fournier, "Elites Beware: Eric Cantor's Defeat May Signal a Populist Revolution," *National Journal*, June 11, 2014, http://www.nationaljournal.com/politics/elites-beware-eric-cantor-s-defeat-may-signal-a-populist-revolution-20140611.

17. David G. Myers, "Wanting More in an Age of Plenty," *Christianity Today*, April 24, 2000, http://www.christianitytoday.com/ct/2000/april24/6.94.html.

18. The Eskridge quotes that follow are from Larry Eskridge, *God's Forever Family: The Jesus People Movement in America* (New York: Oxford Univ. Press, 2013), 11.

19. Mark Engler and Paul Engler, "How to Duplicate the Sweeping Victory of Same-Sex Marriage," *In These Times*, July 14, 2014, http://inthesetimes.com/article/16956/same-sex_marriage_spurs_the_movement.

20. Aliyah Frumin, "Timeline: Bill Clinton's Evolution on Gay Rights," NBC News, March 8, 2013, http://www.nbcnews.com/id/51104832/t/timeline-bill-clintons-evolution-gay-rights/.

21. Michael Brown, "Equivocating or Evolving, President Obama Is Wrong Either Way," Townhall.com, May 12, 2012, http://townhall.com/columnists/michaelbrown/2012/05/12/equivocating_or_evolving_president_obama_is_wrong_either_way/page/full.

22. For more on Obama's views on homosexuality, see Tracy Baim, *Obama and the Gays: A Political Marriage* (Chicago: Prairie Avenue Productions, 2010).

23. Josh Nathan-Kazis, "Orthodox Population Grows Faster Than First Figures in Pew #JewishAmerica Study," *Jewish Daily Forward*, November 12, 2013, http://forward.com/articles/187429/orthodox-population-grows-faster-than-first-figure/?p=all.

24. Philip Jenkins, "The World's Fastest Growing Religion (Either Christianity or Islam, Depending on Location)," *Real Clear Religion*, November 13, 2012, http://www.realclearreligion.org/articles/2012/11/13/the_worlds_fastest_growing_religion.html.

25. For detailed documentation, browse the World Christian Database at http://www.worldchristiandatabase.org/wcd/.

26. Alister McGrath, The Twilight of Atheism: The Rise and Fall of Disbelief in the Modern World (New York: Doubleday, 2006); see also his later book, Why God Won't Go Away: Is the New Atheism Running on Empty? (Nashville: Thomas Nelson, 2011).

27. Albert Mohler, "Looking Back: TIME Asks, "Is God Dead?" AlbertMohler.com, September 21, 2009, http://www.albertmohler.com/2009/09/21/looking-back-time-asks-is-god-dead/.

28. See Eskridge, *God's Forever Family*, for relevant examples.

29. "The Alternative Jesus: Psychedelic Christ," *Time*, June 21, 1971, http://content.time.com/time/magazine/article/0,9171,905202,00.html.

30. Jeff Jacoby, "Marriage and the 'Wrong Side of History,'" Townhall.com, June 18, 2014, http://townhall.com/columnists/jeffjacoby/2014/06/18/marriage-and-the-wrong-side-of-history-n1853054/page/full.

31. "Wesley to Wilberforce," *Chrisitianity Today*, January 1, 1983, http://www.christianitytoday.com/ch/1983/issue2/229.html; for more on Wilberforce, see Metaxas, *Amazing Grace*. The source here translated "Athanasius contra mundum," which was in the original.

32. Donald S. Whitney, "Revival Was the Church's Only Hope," EvanWiggs.com, accessed February 12, 2015, http://www.evanwiggs.com/revival/prepare/onlyhope.html.

33. Ibid.

34. See note 3 for books about revival and cultural change. For one study among many on the Cane Ridge revival at the turn of the nineteenth century, see Paul K. Conkin, *Cane Ridge: America's Pentecost* (Madison, WI: Univ. of Wisconsin Press, 1990). For talk about a Third Great Awakening, see Paul Strand, "Capturing America's Heart: A Third Awakening?" CBN News, July 3, 2014, http://www.cbn.com/cbnnews/us/2014/May/Casting-a-Gospel-Net-Across-the-Nations-Heart/.

PRINCIPLE #8: BE DETERMINED TO WRITE THE LAST CHAPTER OF THE BOOK

1. Elaine Showalter, *Sexual Anarchy: Gender and Culture at the Fin de Siècle* (New York: Viking, 1990), 3.

2. A more literal translation reads, "What has been is what will be, and what has been done is what will be done, and there is nothing new under the sun. Is there a thing of which it is said, 'See, this is new'? It has been already in the ages before us" (ESV).

3. For relevant citations, see Preston Sprinkle, "Review of Matthew Vines, God & the Gay Christian, Part 2," Eternity Bible College's *Theology for Real Life* faculty blog, April 23, 2014, http://facultyblog. eternitybiblecollege.com/2014/04/review-of-matthew-vines-god-and-the-gay-/ship/.

4. Anthony C. Thiselton, The First Epistle to the Corinthians: A Commentary on the Greek Text (New International Commentary on the Greek New Testament) (Grand Rapids: Eerdmans, 2000), 452.

5. Amy Orr-Ewing, Is the Bible Intolerant? Sexist? Oppressive? Homophobic? Outdated? Irrelevant? (Downers Grove, IL: InterVarsity, 2005), 118–19.

6. Sifra *Acharei Mot, parashah* 9:8, in Gail Labovitz, "Same-Sex Marriage," Feminist Sexual Ethics /

7. Genesis Rabbah 26:5, in ibid.; see also the parallel in Leviticus Rabbah 23:9 (p. 2).

8. Hullin 92b (the whole relevant discussion begins at 92a), in ibid, p. 3.

9. Interestingly, graduates from our ministry school who worked among the Fayu tribes in Papua, Indonesia, reported to me that these tribal peoples, who were not discovered until after World War II, and who, for all practical purposes, lived in almost Stone Age conditions, had their own story of a massive flood that wiped out the population. For more on the Fayus, see Sabine Kuegler, *Child of the Jungle: The True Story of a Girl Caught Between Two Worlds* (New York: Warner Books, 2007).

10. Labovitz, "Same-Sex Marriage," 4.

11. See Billy Hallowell, "Are the End Times Upon Us? Author Says 'Unrestrained Immorality' Mirrors 'Pandemic Godlessness' Seen in the Bible," *The Blaze*, May 2, 2014, http://www.theblaze.com/ stories/2014/05/02/are-the-end-times-upon-us-author-says-unrestrained-immorality-mirrors- pandemic-godlessness-seen-in-the-bible/, referring to Jeff Kinley, *As It Was in the Days of Noah: Warnings from Bible Prophecy about the Coming Global Storm* (Eugene, OR: Harvest House, 2014).

12. Even if Jesus is not coming in our lifetimes, it's still important to be sure you are in right relationship with God today. None of us have a guarantee on tomorrow.

13. Of course, there are Jews who commit these practices too, but the Jews who have endured as a people have not.

14. Tom Strode, "Young Evangelicals Defy Sexual Liberalism," Baptist Press, July 9, 2014, http:// www.bpnews.net/42941/young-evangelicals-defy-sexual-liberalism. Note that Professor Regnerus came under serious professional attack after publishing his research indicating that children raised in same-sex households did not fare as well as children raised with a mother and father. For background, see Peter Sprigg, "What You Need to Know about the Mark Regnerus Study of Homosexual Parents," Family Research Council blog, September 7, 2012, http://www.frcblog. com/2012/09/what-you-need-to-know-about-the-mark-regnerus-study-of-homosexual-parents/;

and Peter LaBarbera, "U. of Texas Dismisses Homosexual Extremist Scott Rose's Misconduct Complaint against Prof. Mark Regenerus, Author of 'Gay Parenting' Study," Americans for Truth about Homosexuality, August 31, 2012, http://americansfortruth.com/2012/08/31/u-of-texas-dismisses-homosexual-extremist-scott-roses-misconduct-complaint-against-prof-mark-regenerus-gay-parenting-study/.

15. Strode, "Young Evangelicals Defy Sexual Liberalism."

16. Ibid.

17. John Lomperis, "Young United Methodists Reject Gay Marriage," *Juicy Ecumenism* (blog), July 23, 2014, http://juicyecumenism.com/2014/07/23/young-united-methodists-reject-gay-marriage/.

18. http://www.gallup.com/poll/1576/abortion.aspx.

19. Marshall Kirk and Hunter Madsen, After the Ball: How America Will Conquer Its Fear and Hatred of Gays in the 90's (New York: Penguin, 1989), xv.

20. See, conveniently, "Homosexual Agenda Platforms from 1972–2000 [plus other resources]," originally published at http://www.afa.net/homosexual_agenda/agenda.asp but since removed and posted, instead, by "Polycarp" on *Free Republic*, May 8, 2003, http://www.freerepublic.com/focus/f-news/908140/posts.

21. Carl Wittman, "Refugees from Amerika: Gay Manifesto" (1970), *History Is a Weapon* (blog), accessed February 13, 2015, http://www.historyisaweapon.com/defcon1/wittmanmanifesto.html.

22. There are even gay theologians who claim that Paul was warning about conservative Christians who, by listening to demonic deception, would forbid others to marry! What Paul was talking about, of course, was a false asceticism that claimed that for a man to be truly spiritual, he could not marry a woman. Talk about turning the Bible on its head! See 1 Timothy 4:1–3 for Paul's words; for a gay activist turning things upside down, see "The Bed Keeper: A Biblical Case for Gay Marriage: Chapter 2: God Sanctioned Gay Marriage," Brian Bowen Ministries website, accessed February 13, 2015, http://brianbowenministries.com/2-god-sanctioned-gay-marriage.html.

23. Dale Carpenter, "Fourth Circuit strikes down Virginia ban on same-sex marriage," *The Volokh Conspiracy* (blog), July 27, 2014, http://www.washingtonpost.com/news/volokh-conspiracy/wp/2014/07/28/fourth-circuit-strikes-down-virginia-ban-on-same-sex-marriage.

24. Phil Reese, "HRC Store Vandalized; Radical Queer Group Claims Responsibility," *Washington Blade*, June 29, 2011, http://www.washingtonblade.com/2011/06/29/hrc-store-vandalized-radical-queer-group-claims-responsibility/#sthash.RV2X8FWQ.dpuf. They especially protested the multiplied millions in income received by the HRC and the high salaries paid to its leaders, with ostensibly meager results. I have left out the most vulgar parts of their statement.

25. Ryan Janek Wolowski, "HRC Human Rights Campaign Building Vandalized on the day of the National Equality March," October 11, 2009, https://www.flickr.com/photos/ryanisland/4480625191/.

26. One gay journalist told me privately that two factors contributed to the taming of the movement; first, many of the gay male pioneers died of AIDS; second, lesbians took a more prominent leadership role.

27. This loss is real whether it is recognized or not; for one woman's story, with relevant resources, see the book description for Dawn Stefanowicz's *Out from Under*, http://www.dawnstefanowicz.org/index.html.

28. The other possible variant to this is that with the triumph of gay activism, the only thing that will remain for them to do is silence completely people of faith who oppose their agenda.

29. This was communicated to me privately by their leadership upon my request.

30. See my October 19, 2011, article "The Death of a Gay Activist Pioneer," on the death of activist Frank Kameny, at Townhall, com, http://townhall.com/columnists/michaelbrown/2011/10/19/the_death_of_a_gay_activist_pioneer/page/full.

31. To be clear, in 1 Corinthians 6:9–10, Paul listed men who practice homosexuality (the combined meaning of two Greek words) in the category of the unrighteous, along with the sexually immoral, idolaters, adulterers, thieves, the greedy, drunkards, revilers, and swindlers (esv). But he was not branding people as wicked simply because they are romantically and sexually attracted to the same sex.

32. Again to be clear, in 2 Thessalonians 1:5–10, Paul teaches that when Jesus returns there will be fiery judgment for all who refuse to obey God and believe the Gospel. Again, no specific group is being singled out.

33. Colin Smith, "Jonathan Edwards' Powerful Example of Leaving a Godly Legacy," *Unlocking the Bible* (blog), June 4, 2012, https://www.unlockingthebible.org/jonathan-edwards-leaving-a-godly-legacy/.

34. A. E. Winship, *Jukes-Edwards: A Study in Education and Heredity* (Harrisburg, PA: R. L. Myers, 1900); note that "Jukes" was a pseudonym. Although the social theories espoused by Winship will be disputed in some circles, the evidence he marshaled is compelling.

35. Smith, "Jonathan Edwards' Powerful Example of Leaving a Godly Legacy."

36. Note Franklin Graham's comments about the contemporary culture of death in Michael W. Chapman, "Franklin Graham: America's 'Culture of Death' Stems From a 'Sinful, Godless Worldview That Rejects Christ,'" cnsnews.com, January 12, 2015, http://cnsnews.com/blog/michael-w-chapman/franklin-graham-americas-culture-death-stems-sinful-godless-worldview-rejects.

37. For a collection of his most relevant works on revival, see *The Revival Writings of Jonathan Edwards: Account of the Revival of Religion, A Faithful Narrative, Distinguishing Marks of a Work of the Spirit of God, Thoughts Concerning the Present Revival* (Amazon Digital Services, 2012).

38. "The Return of the Spirit," *Christian History*, no. 23, 24, cited in Donald S. Whitney, "Revival Was the Church's Only Hope," EvanWiggs.com, accessed February 12, 2015, http://www.evanwiggs.com/revival/prepare/onlyhope.html.

39. Peter Hitchens, "So Much for 'Father's Day'—in a Country Where Fatherhood Is Dying Out," Peter Hitchens's Blog, June 16, 2013, http://hitchensblog.mailonsunday.co.uk/2013/06/so-much-for-fathers-day-in-a-country-where-fatherhood-is-dying-out.html. For further statistics, note that "in 1964 a full 93 percent of children born in the United States were born to married parents." Now less than 59 percent of all children born in American can boast the same. See PPD Staff, "Father's Day 2014 Poll: Importance Diminished, But Role Remains Paramount," *People's Pundit Daily*, June 15, 2014, http://www.peoplespunditdaily.com/2014/06/15/polls/fathers-day-2014-poll-importance-diminished-role-remains-paramount/.

40. Ben Johnson, "'THE WRONG SIDE OF HISTORY' 2.0," *BarbWire*, October 2, 2014, http://barbwire.com/2014/10/02/wrong-side-history-2-0/#SFf0s1tcuV5swE7X.99.

41. Ibid.

42. Andrew Walker, "A Church in Exile: Hillsong Shifts on Homosexuality," *First Things* (blog), October 17, 2014, http://www.firstthings.com/blogs/firstthoughts/2014/10/a-church-in-exile.

43. To be absolutely clear, I am not suggesting for a moment that gay activists want to kill us as Haman wanted to kill the Jews. Absolutely not. I *am* suggesting that they want to silence us and cause our opposition to stop.

44. For similar language from Mike Huckabee, see Matt Barber, "Mike Huckabee at Marriage March: 'We Will Not Bow Our Knees to Nebuchadnezzar!,'" *Freedom Outpost*, June 22, 2014, http://freedomoutpost.com/2014/06/mike-huckabee-marriage-march-will-bow-knees-nebuchadnezzar/. It is interesting that Bill O'Reilly, coming from another angle entirely, believes that traditional America will make a comeback; see "Why Traditional America Is Poised to Come Back," Fox News, December 18, 2014 http://video.foxnews.com/v/3951591969001/why-traditional-america-is-poised-to-come-back/?#sp=show-clips.

INDEX